P9-DFO-734

AngularJS: Up And Running

Shyam Seshadri and Brad Green

Beijing · Cambridge · Farnham · Köln · Sebastopol · Tokyo

AngularJS: Up And Running

by Shyam Seshadri and Brad Green

Copyright © 2014 Shyam Seshadri and Brad Green. All rights reserved.

Printed in the United States of America.

Published by O'Reilly Media, Inc., 1005 Gravenstein Highway North, Sebastopol, CA 95472.

O'Reilly books may be purchased for educational, business, or sales promotional use. Online editions are also available for most titles (*http://safaribooksonline.com*). For more information, contact our corporate/institutional sales department: 800-998-9938 or *corporate@oreilly.com*.

Editors: Simon St. Laurent and Brian MacDonald	**Indexer:** Judy McConville
Production Editor: Kara Ebrahim	**Cover Designer:** Ellie Volckhausen
Copyeditor: Gillian McGarvey	**Interior Designer:** David Futato
Proofreader: Kim Cofer	**Illustrator:** Rebecca Demarest

September 2014:   First Edition

Revision History for the First Edition:

2014-09-05:   First release

See *http://oreilly.com/catalog/errata.csp?isbn=9781491901946* for release details.

Nutshell Handbook, the Nutshell Handbook logo, and the O'Reilly logo are registered trademarks of O'Reilly Media, Inc. *AngularJS: Up and Running*, the image of a thornback cowfish, and related trade dress are trademarks of O'Reilly Media, Inc.

Many of the designations used by manufacturers and sellers to distinguish their products are claimed as trademarks. Where those designations appear in this book, and O'Reilly Media, Inc. was aware of a trademark claim, the designations have been printed in caps or initial caps.

While every precaution has been taken in the preparation of this book, the publisher and authors assume no responsibility for errors or omissions, or for damages resulting from the use of the information contained herein.

ISBN: 978-1-491-90194-6

[LSI]

Table of Contents

Introduction

I remember the very first time I was introduced to AngularJS. It was called Angular, and it was an open source library built as a hobby by one of my fellow engineers, Misko. At that point, we had spent months struggling to develop Google Feedback (the project we were developing) in an efficient and maintainable manner. We had written over 18,000 lines of code, a lot of which were untested, and were frustrated with our inability to continue adding features quickly. Misko Hevery, the engineer I mentioned, made a bold statement that he could reproduce everything we had developed in the past six months within two weeks. I should mention that we were all Java engineers at that point, with a complete lack of JavaScript knowledge.

After what we expected to be an entertaining two weeks of watching Misko struggle, scramble, and fail, it wasn't done. But one more week later, he had replicated what took us six months. What had been an 18,000-line codebase had dropped to a mere 1,500 lines, and almost every single piece of functionality was modular, reusable, and testable. Misko was on to something!

Brad Green, this book's coauthor, saw the beginning of something amazing there, and decided with Misko to build a team around the core idea of making it simple to build web applications. Google Feedback, which I was leading, became the first project to ship with AngularJS, and really helped us understand what was important from a web developer's perspective in a JavaScript framework.

What started as a side project quickly took off into one of the leading JavaScript frameworks (or meta-framework, as I call it) on the Web. There are a lot of reasons why AngularJS is awesome, and a super community of helpful developers and contributors is just one of them. The more recent releases have all incorporated features from the open source community around AngularJS. Thousands of developers rely on AngularJS daily, and thousands more start using it every month. And each developer makes AngularJS better through his or her experience.

I am excited to present this book, and look forward to learning from your experiences.

Who Should Read This Book

This book is for anyone who is looking to get started with AngularJS, whether as a side project, as an additional tool, or for their main work. It is expected that readers are comfortable with JavaScript before starting this book, but a basic knowledge of Java-Script should be sufficient to learn AngularJS. The book will cover everything from getting started with AngularJS, to advanced concepts like directives. We will take it step by step, so relax and have fun learning with us.

Why We Wrote This Book

When we wrote the first book on AngularJS, there was no easy way to learn it. The documentation was (and still is to some extent) confusing. With this book, the aim is to present a step-by-step guide on getting started with AngularJS. AngularJS is layered, with some very simple and powerful concepts, and some advanced and hard-to-get features. This book aims to walk developers through each of these in an organized, step-wise fashion, adding complexity bit by bit.

At the end of the book, you should be able to quickly get started with an AngularJS project, and really understand how to develop large, maintainable, and performant applications.

A Word on Web Application Development Today

JavaScript has come a long way from being just a scripting language (or hack, as it was affectionately called) that was only used to do minor validations to becoming a full-fledged programming language. jQuery did a lot of ground work in ensuring browser compatibility and giving a solid, stable API to work across all browsers and interact with the DOM. As applications grew in complexity and size, jQuery, which is a DOM ma-nipulation layer, became insufficient by itself to provide a solid, modular, testable, and easily understandable framework for developing applications. Each jQuery project would look completely different from another.

AngularJS (and quite a lot of other MVC frameworks for JavaScript) tackles this very problem of providing a layer on top of jQuery, and on top of the DOM, to think in terms of application structure and maintainability, while reducing the amount of boilerplate code you would end up writing. The best part about using a framework in a consistent manner is that a new developer coming in has a sense of the structure, the layout, and how to develop right off the bat. We want a framework where we can spend time wor-rying about our look and feel, and our core functionality, without having to worry about the boilerplate and cruft.

Some of the concepts that are currently at the center of web application development and thus also at the core of AngularJS are:

- Data-driven programming, where the aim is to manipulate the model, and let the framework do the heavy lifting and UI rendering.

- Declarative programming, which entails declaring your intent when you are performing an action, instead of imperative programming, where the actual work is performed in a separate file/function and not where the effect is needed.

- Modularity and separation of concerns, which is the ability to separate your application into smaller, reusable functional pieces, each responsible for one and only one thing.

- Testability, so that we can ensure that what we as developers write actually does what it is supposed to.

- And much more.

With the help of frameworks like AngularJS, we can focus on developing amazing New Age web applications with immense complexity in a manageable and maintainable fashion.

Navigating This Book

This book aims to walk a developer through each part of AngularJS, step by step. Each chapter that introduces a new concept will be immediately followed by a chapter on how we can unit test it. The book is roughly organized as follows:

- Chapter 1, *Introducing AngularJS*, is an introduction to AngularJS as well as the concepts behind it. It also covers what it takes to start writing an AngularJS application.

- Chapter 2, *Basic AngularJS Directives and Controllers*, starts introducing some built-in AngularJS directives, and the concept of controllers.

- Chapter 3, *Unit Testing in AngularJS*, digs into unit testing AngularJS projects with Karma and Jasmine.

- Chapter 4, *Forms, Inputs, and Services*, covers forms and how best to leverage AngularJS when working with them.

- Chapter 5, *All About AngularJS Services*, introduces the concept of AngularJS services, some common built-in AngularJS services, and how to create your own.

- Chapter 6, *Server Communication Using $http*, involves server communication in AngularJS using $http and advanced $http concepts like interceptors and transformers.

- Chapter 7, *Unit Testing Services and XHRs*, then digs into unit testing of services and mocking server requests using $httpBackend.

- Chapter 8, *Working with Filters*, and Chapter 9, *Unit Testing Filters*, introduce AngularJS filters as well as how to unit test them.

- Chapter 10, *Routing Using ngRoute*, covers routing in an SPA using the optional ngRoute module.

- Chapter 11, *Directives*, introduces some basic concepts of directives and how to create them.

- Chapter 12, *Unit Testing Directives*, covers unit testing of directives.

- Chapter 13, *Advanced Directives*, involves advanced directive creation concepts like compile, transclusion, controllers, and require. It also provides some examples of third-party widget integration as a directive.

- Chapter 14, *End-to-End Testing*, covers end-to-end testing of an AngularJS application using Protractor and WebDriver.

- Chapter 15, *Guidelines and Best Practices*, brings everything together into best practices, guidelines, and useful tools.

The entire code repository is hosted on GitHub, so if you don't want to type in the code examples from this book, or want to ensure that you are looking at the latest and greatest code examples, do visit the repository and grab the contents (*http://bit.ly/1pNdTQg*).

If you're like us, you don't read books from front to back. If you're really like us, you usually don't read the Introduction at all. However, on the off chance that you will see this in time, here are a few suggestions:

- You can skip Chapter 1 if you have already worked on AngularJS in the past.

- Chapter 2 digs into ng-repeat and all the various ways you can use and optimize it.

- Chapters 3, 7, 9, and 12 cover unit testing of controllers, services, filters, and directives, so if you want to know more about those, jump to those chapters directly.

- Chapter 14 is where you want to jump to in case you are interested in end-to-end testing using Protractor.

- Chapters 11 and 13 are essential if you really want to understand directives and leverage the power that it provides.

- If you want to look at a full-fledged AngularJS application that uses routing, authorization, and more, check out the last example in Chapter 10.

This book uses AngularJS version 1.2.19 for all its code examples, and Karma version 0.12.16 for the unit tests.

Online Resources

The following resources are a great starting point for any AngularJS developer, and should be always available at your fingertips:

- The Official AngularJS API Documentation (*http://docs.angularjs.org/api*)
- The Official AngularJS Developer Guide (*https://docs.angularjs.org/guide/*)
- The AngularJS PhoneCat Tutorial App (*https://docs.angularjs.org/tutorial*)
- ngModules: A list of all known open source AngularJS modules (*http://ngmodules.org*)
- Egghead.io: Great AngularJS video tutorials (*http://egghead.io*)

Conventions Used in This Book

The following typographical conventions are used in this book:

Italic
: Indicates new terms, URLs, email addresses, filenames, and file extensions.

`Constant width`
: Used for program listings, as well as within paragraphs to refer to program elements such as variable or function names, databases, data types, environment variables, statements, and keywords.

`Constant width bold`
: Shows commands or other text that should be typed literally by the user.

`Constant width italic`
: Shows text that should be replaced with user-supplied values or by values determined by context.

 This element signifies a tip or suggestion.

 This element signifies a general note.

This element indicates a warning or caution.

Using Code Examples

Supplemental material (code examples, exercises, etc.) is available for download at *https://github.com/shyamseshadri/angularjs-up-and-running*.

This book is here to help you get your job done. In general, if example code is offered with this book, you may use it in your programs and documentation. You do not need to contact us for permission unless you're reproducing a significant portion of the code. For example, writing a program that uses several chunks of code from this book does not require permission. Selling or distributing a CD-ROM of examples from O'Reilly books does require permission. Answering a question by citing this book and quoting example code does not require permission. Incorporating a significant amount of example code from this book into your product's documentation does require permission.

We appreciate, but do not require, attribution. An attribution usually includes the title, author, publisher, and ISBN. For example: "*AngularJS: Up and Running* by Shyam Seshadri and Brad Green (O'Reilly). Copyright 2014 Shyam Seshadri and Brad Green, 978-1-491-90194-6."

If you feel your use of code examples falls outside fair use or the permission given above, feel free to contact us at *permissions@oreilly.com*.

Safari® Books Online

Safari Books Online is an on-demand digital library that delivers expert content in both book and video form from the world's leading authors in technology and business.

Technology professionals, software developers, web designers, and business and creative professionals use Safari Books Online as their primary resource for research, problem solving, learning, and certification training.

Safari Books Online offers a range of plans and pricing for enterprise, government, education, and individuals.

Members have access to thousands of books, training videos, and prepublication manuscripts in one fully searchable database from publishers like O'Reilly Media, Prentice Hall Professional, Addison-Wesley Professional, Microsoft Press, Sams, Que, Peachpit Press, Focal Press, Cisco Press, John Wiley & Sons, Syngress, Morgan Kaufmann, IBM Redbooks, Packt, Adobe Press, FT Press, Apress, Manning, New Riders, McGraw-Hill,

Jones & Bartlett, Course Technology, and hundreds more. For more information about Safari Books Online, please visit us online.

How to Contact Us

Please address comments and questions concerning this book to the publisher:

O'Reilly Media, Inc.
1005 Gravenstein Highway North
Sebastopol, CA 95472
800-998-9938 (in the United States or Canada)
707-829-0515 (international or local)
707-829-0104 (fax)

We have a web page for this book, where we list errata, examples, and any additional information. You can access this page at *http://bit.ly/angularjs-up*.

To comment or ask technical questions about this book, send email to *bookques tions@oreilly.com*.

For more information about our books, courses, conferences, and news, see our website at *http://www.oreilly.com*.

Find us on Facebook: *http://facebook.com/oreilly*

Follow us on Twitter: *http://twitter.com/oreillymedia*

Watch us on YouTube: *http://www.youtube.com/oreillymedia*

Acknowledgments

I'd like to thank Misko Hevery, Igor Minar, and the entire AngularJS team for building AngularJS, and for continuing to make it more awesome with every release (and thinking of hilarious release names such as curdling-stare, insomnia-induction, and tofu-animation, to name a few). I'd also like to thank my untiring reviewers, Brad Green, Brian Holt, Ross Dederer, and Jesse Palmer, who willingly waded through pages and pages multiple times and never missed a single detail. You guys are amazing.

I'd also like to thank my team at Fundoo Solutions (Abhiroop Patel, Pavan Jartarghar, Suryakant Sharma, and Amol Kedari) who helped me test all the code examples and give me feedback on the order in which I introduced content.

Finally, I don't think this book would have happened without my mom, dad, and grand-mom, who ensured that I was well-fed, caffeinated at the right times, and motivated to sit and write for long stretches. And this book would definitely not have finished on time without the support of my loving wife, Sanchita, who was a great sport and didn't complain while I typed away at this book during our wedding and honeymoon!

And finally, thank you to the amazing AngularJS community for all their contributions, feedback, and support, and for teaching us how to use and make it better.

CHAPTER 1

Introducing AngularJS

The Internet has come a long way since its inception. Consumption-oriented, non-interactive websites started moving toward something users interacted with. Users could respond, fill in details, and eventually access all their mail on websites. Concurrent usage, offline support, and so many other things became basic features, and the size and scope of client-side applications has kept on accelerating and increasing.

As applications have gotten bigger, better, and faster, so has the complexity a developer has to manage. A pure JavaScript/jQuery solution would not always have the right structure to ensure a rapid speed of development or long-term maintainability. Projects became heavily dependent on having a great software engineer to set up the initial framework. Even then, modularity, testability, and separation of concerns may not make it into a project. Testing and reliability were often pushed to the backburner in such cases.

AngularJS (*http://www.angularjs.org*) was started to fill this basic need. Could we provide a standard structure and meta-framework within which web applications could be developed reliably and quickly? Could the same software engineering concepts like testable code, separation of concerns, MVC (Model-View-Controller) (or rather, MVVM), and so on be applied to JavaScript applications? Could we have the best of both worlds—the succinctness of JavaScript and the pleasure of rapid, maintainable development? We think so, but we'll let you be the final judge as we walk through AngularJS throughout the rest of this book.

By the end of this chapter, we will build a basic AngularJS "hello world" example to get a sense of some common concepts and philosophies behind AngularJS. We will also see how to bootstrap and convert any HTML into an AngularJS application, and see how to use common data-binding techniques in AngularJS.

Introducing AngularJS

AngularJS is a superheroic JavaScript MVC framework for the Web. We call it super-heroic because AngularJS does so much for us that we only have to focus on our core application and let AngularJS take care of everything else. It allows us to apply standard, tried-and-tested software engineering practices traditionally used on the server side in client-side programming to accelerate frontend development. It provides a consistent scalable structure that makes it a breeze to develop large, complex applications as part of a team.

And the best part? It's all done in pure JavaScript and HTML. No need to learn another new programming or templating language (though you do have to understand the MVC and MVVM paradigms of developing applications, which we briefly cover in this book). And how does it fulfill all these crazy and wonderful, seemingly impossible-to-satisfy promises?

The AngularJS philosophy is driven by a few key tenets that drive everything from how to structure your application, to how your applications should be hooked together, to how to test your application and integrate your code with other libraries. But before we get into each of these, let's take a look at why we should even care in the first place.

What Is MVC (Model-View-Controller)?

The core concept behind the AngularJS framework is the MVC architectural pattern. The Model-View-Controller pattern (or MVVM, which stands for Model-View-ViewModel, which is quite similar) evolved as a way to separate logical units and concerns when developing large applications. It gives developers a starting point in deciding how and where to split responsibilities. The MVC architectural pattern divides an application into three distinct, modular parts:

- The *model* is the driving force of the application. This is generally the data behind the application, usually fetched from the server. Any UI with data that the user sees is derived from the model, or a subset of the model.

- The *view* is the UI that the user sees and interacts with. It is dynamic, and generated based on the current model of the application.

- The *controller* is the business logic and presentation layer, which peforms actions such as fetching data, and makes decisions such as how to present the model, which parts of it to display, etc.

Because the controller is responsible for basically deciding which parts of the model to display in the view, depending on the implementation, it can also be thought of as a *viewmodel*, or a *presenter*.

At its core, though, each of these patterns splits responsibilities in the application into separate subunits, which offers the following benefits:

- Each unit is responsible for one and only one thing. The model is the data, the view is the UI, and the controller is the business logic. Figuring out where the new code we are working on belongs, as well as finding prior code, is easy because of this single responsibility principle.

- Each unit is as independent from the others as possible. This makes the code much more modular and reusable, as well as easy to maintain.

AngularJS Benefits

We are going to make some claims in this section, which we will expand on in the following section when we dive into how AngularJS makes all this possible:

- AngularJS is a Single Page Application (SPA) meta-framework. With client-side templating and heavy use of JavaScript, creating and maintaining an application can get tedious and onerous. AngularJS removes the cruft and does the heavy lifting, so that we can focus solely on the application core.

- An AngularJS application will require fewer lines of code to complete a task than a pure JavaScript solution using jQuery would. When compared to other frameworks, you will still find yourself writing less boilerplate, and cleaner code, as it moves your logic into reusable components and out of your view.

- Most of the code you write in an AngularJS application is going to be focused on business logic or your core application functionality, and not unnecessary routine cruft code. This is a result of AngularJS taking care of all the boilerplate that you would otherwise normally write, as well as the MVC architecture pattern.

- AngularJS's declarative nature makes it easier to write and understand applications. It is easy to understand an application's intent just by looking at the HTML and the controllers. In a sense, AngularJS allows you to create HTMLX (instead of relying on HTML5 or waiting for HTML6, etc.), which is a subset of HTML that fits your needs and requirements.

- AngularJS applications can be styled using CSS and HTML independent of their business logic and functionality. That is, it is completely possible to change the entire layout and design of an application without touching a single line of JavaScript.

- AngularJS application templates are written in pure HTML, so designers will find it easier to work with and style them.

- It is ridiculously simple to unit test AngularJS applications, which also makes the application stable and easier to maintain over a longer period of time. Got new features? Need to make changes to existing logic? All of it is a breeze with that rock-solid bed of tests underneath.

- We don't need to let go of those jQueryUI or BootStrap components that we love and adore. AngularJS plays nicely with third-party component libraries and gives us hooks to integrate them as we see fit.

The AngularJS Philosophy

There are five core beliefs to which AngularJS subscribes that enable developers to rapidly create large, complex applications with ease:

Data-driven (via data-binding)

In a traditional server-side application, we create the user interface by merging HTML with our local data. Of course, this means that whenever we need to change part of the UI, the server has to send the entire HTML and data to the client yet again, even if the client already has most of the HTML.

With client-side Single Page Applications (SPAs), we have an advantage. We only have to send from the server to the client the data that has changed. But the client-side code still has to update the UI as per the new data. This results in boilerplate that might look something like the following (if we were using jQuery). First, let's look at some very simple HTML:

```
Hello  <span id="name"></span>
```

The JavaScript that makes this work might look something like this:

```
var updateNameInUI = function(name) {
    $('#name').text(name);
};

// Lots of code here...
// On initial data load
updateNameInUI(user.name);

// Then when the data changes somehow
updateNameInUI(updatedName);
```

The preceding code defines a updateNameInUI function, which takes in the name of the user, and then finds the UI element and updates its innerText. Of course, we would have to be sure to call this function whenever the name value changes, like the initial load, and maybe when the user logs out and logs back in, or if he edits his name. And this is just one field. Now imagine dozens of such lines across your entire codebase. These kinds of operations are very common in a CRUD (Create-Retrieve-Update-Delete) model like this.

Now, on the other hand, the AngularJS approach is driven by the model backing it. AngularJS's core feature—one that can save thousands of lines of boilerplate code —is its data-binding (both one-way and two-way). We don't have to waste time funneling data back and forth between the UI and the JavaScript in an AngularJS application. We just bind to the data in our HTML and AngularJS takes care of getting its value into the UI. Not only that, but it also takes care of updating the UI whenever the data changes.

The exact same functionality in an AngularJS application would look something like this:

```
Hello <span>{{name}}</span>
```

Now, in the JavaScript, all that we need to do is set the value of the name variable. AngularJS will take care of figuring out that it has changed and update the UI automatically.

This is one-way data-binding, where we take data coming from the server (or any other source), and update the Document Object Model (DOM). But what about the reverse? The traditional way when working with forms—where we need to get the data from the user, run some processing, and then send it to the server—would look something like the following. The HTML first might look like this:

```
<form name="myForm" onsubmit="submitData()">
  <input type="text" id="nameField"/>
  <input type="text" id="emailField"/>
</form>
```

The JavaScript that makes this work might look like this:

```
// Set data in the form
function setUserDetails(userDetails) {
    $('#nameField').value(userDetails.name);
    $('#emailField').value(userDetails.email);
}

function getUserDetails() {
    return {
        name: $('#nameField').value(),
        email: $('#emailField').value()
    };
}

var submitData = function() {
  // Assuming there is a function which makes XHR request
  // Make POST request with JSON data
  makeXhrRequest('http://my/url', getUserDetails());
};
```

In addition to the layout and templating, we have to manage the data flow between our business logic and controller code to the UI and back. Any time the data changes, we need to update the UI, and whenever the user submits or we need to run validation, we need to call the getUserDetails() function and then do our actual core logic on the data.

AngularJS provides two-way data-binding, which allows us to skip writing this boilerplate code as well. The two-way data-binding ensures that our controller and the UI share the same model, so that updates to one (either from the UI or in our code) update the other automatically. So, the same functionality as before in AngularJS might have the HTML as follows:

```
<form name="myForm" ng-submit="ctrl.submitData()">
  <input type="text" ng-model="user.name"/>
  <input type="text" ng-model="user.email"/>
</form>
```

Each input tag in the HTML is bound to an AngularJS model declared by the ng-model attribute (called directives in AngularJS). When the form is submitted, AngularJS hooks on by triggering a function in the controller called submitData. The JavaScript for this might look like:

```
// Inside my controller code
this.submitData = function() {
    // Make Server POST request with JSON object
    $http.post('http://my/url', this.user);
};
```

AngularJS takes care of the two-way data-binding, which entails getting the latest values from the UI and updating the name and email in the user object automatically. It also ensures that any changes made to the name or email values in the user object are reflected in the DOM automatically.

Because of data-binding, in an AngularJS application, you can focus on your core business logic and functionality and let AngularJS do the heavy lifting of updating the UI. It also means that it requires a shift in our mindset to develop an AngularJS application. Need to update the UI? Change the model and let AngularJS update the UI.

Declarative

A single-page web application (also known as an AJAX application) is made up of multiple separate HTML snippets and data stitched together via JavaScript. But more often than not, we end up having HTML templates that have no indication of what they turn into. For example, consider HTML like the following:

```
<ul class="nav nav-tabs">
  <li>Home</li>
  <li class="selected">Profile</li>
</ul>

<div class="tab1">
```

```
    Some content here
</div>
<div class="tab2">
    <input id="startDate" type="text"/>
</div>
```

Now, if you are used to certain HTML constructs or are familiar with jQuery or similar frameworks, you might be able to divine that the preceding HTML reflects a set of tabs, and that the second tab has an input field that needs to become a datepicker. But none of that is actually mentioned in the HTML. It is only because there is some JS and CSS in your codebase that has the task of converting these li elements into tabs, and the input field into a datepicker.

This is essentially the *imperative paradigm*, where we tell the application exactly how to do each and every action. We tell it to find the element with class nav-tabs and make it a tab component, then to select the first tab by default. We accomplish this entirely in our JavaScript code and not where the actual HTML needs to change. The HTML does not reflect any of this logic.

AngularJS instead promotes a *declarative paradigm*, where you declare right in your HTML what it is you are trying to accomplish. This is done through something that AngularJS calls *directives*. Directives basically extend the vocabulary of HTML to teach it new tricks. We let AngularJS figure out how to accomplish what we want it to do, whether it is creating tabs or datepickers. The ideal way to write the previous code in AngularJS would be something like the following:

```
<tabs>
  <tab title="Home">Some content here</tab>
  <tab title="Profile">
    <input type="text"
           datepicker
           ng-model="startDate"/>
  </tab>
</tabs>
```

The AngularJS-based HTML uses <tab> tags, which tells AngularJS to figure out how to render the tabs component, and declares that the <input> is a datepick er that is bound to an AngularJS model variable called startDate.

There are a few advantages to this approach:

- It's declarative, so just by looking at the HTML we can immediately figure out that there are two tabs, one of which has a datepicker inside of it.

- The business logic of selecting the current tab, unselecting the other tabs, and hiding and showing the correct content is all encapsulated inside the tab directive.

- Similarly, any developer who wants a datepicker does not have to know whether we are using jQueryUI, BootStrap, or something else underneath. It separates out the usage from the implementation so there is a clear separation of concerns.

- Because the entire functionality is encapsulated and contained in one place, we can make changes in one central place and have it affect all usages, instead of finding and replacing each API call manually.

Separate your concerns

AngularJS adopts a Model-View-Controller (MVC)-like pattern for structuring any application. If you think about it, there are three parts to your application.

There is the actual data that you want to display to the user, or get the user to enter through your application. This is the model in an AngularJS project, which is mostly pure data, and represented using JSON objects.

Then there is the user interface or the final rendered HTML that the user sees and interacts with, which displays the data to the user. This is the view.

Finally, there is the actual business logic and the code that fetches the data, decides which part of the model to show to the user, how to handle validation, and so on —core logic specific to your application. This is the controller for an AngularJS application.

We think MVC or an MVC-like approach is neat for a few solid reasons:

- There is a clear separation of concerns between the various parts of your application. Need some business logic? Use the controller. Need to render something differently? Go to the view.

- Your team and collaborators will have an instant leg up on understanding your codebase because there is a set structure and pattern.

- Need to redesign your UI for any reason? No need to change any JavaScript code. Need to change how something is validated? No need to touch your HTML. You can work on independent parts of the codebase without spilling over into another.

- AngularJS is not completely MVC; the controller will never have a direct reference to the view. This is great because it keeps the controller independent of the view, and also allows us to easily test the controller without needing to instantiate a DOM.

Because of all of these reasons, MVC allows you develop and scale your application in a way that is easy to maintain, extend, and test.

Dependency Injection

AngularJS is the one of the few JavaScript frameworks with a full-fledged Dependency Injection system built in. Dependency Injection (discussed in Chapter 5) is the concept of asking for the dependencies of a particular controller or service, instead of instantiating them inline via the `new` operator or calling a function explicitly (for example, `DatabaseFactory.getInstance()`). Some other part of your code becomes responsible (in this case, the *injector*) for figuring out how to create those dependencies and provide them when asked for.

This is helpful because:

- The controller, service, or function asking for the dependency does not need to know how to construct its dependencies, and traverse further up the chain, however long it might be.

- It's explicit, so we immediately know what we need before we can start working with our piece of code.

- It makes for super easy testing because we can replace heavy dependencies with nicer mocks for testing. So instead of passing an `HttpService` that talks to the real server, we pass in a `MockHttpService` that talks to a server created in memory.

  Dependency Injection in AngularJS is used across all of its parts, from controllers and services to modules and tests. It allows you to easily write modular, reusable code so that you can use it cleanly and simply as needed.

Extensible

We already mentioned directives in the previous section when we talked about AngularJS's declarative nature. Directives are AngularJS's way of teaching the browser and HTML new tricks, from handling clicks and conditionals to creating new structure and styling.

But that is just the built-in set of directives. AngularJS exposes the same API that it uses internally to create these directives so that anyone can extend existing directives or create their own. We can develop robust and complex directives that integrate with third-party libraries like jQueryUI and BootStrap, to name a few, to create a language that is specific to our needs. We'll see how to create our own directives in Chapter 11.

The bottom line is that AngularJS has a great core set of directives for us to get started, and an API that allows us to do everything AngularJS does and more. Our imagination is really the only limit for creating declarative, reusable components.

Test first, test again, keep testing

A lot of the benefits that we mentioned previously actually stem from the singular focus on testing and testability that AngularJS has. Every bit and piece of AngularJS is designed to be testable, from its controllers, services, and directives to its views and routes.

Between Dependency Injection and the controller being independent of references to the view, the JS code that we write in an AngularJS application can easily be tested. Because we get the same Dependency Injection system in our tests as in our production code, we can easily instantiate any service without worrying about its dependencies. All of this is run through our beautiful, insanely fast test runner, Karma (*http://karma-runner.github.io/*).

Of course, to ensure that our application actually works end to end, we also have Protractor (*https://github.com/angular/protractor*), which is a WebDriver-based end-to-end scenario runner designed from the ground up to be AngularJS-aware. This means that we will not have to write any random waits and watches in our end-to-end test, like waiting for an element to show or waiting for five seconds after a click for the server to respond. Protractor is able to hook into AngularJS and figure out when to proceed with the test, leaving us with a suite of solid, deterministic end-to-end tests.

We will start using Karma, and talk about how to set it up and get started in Chapter 3, and Protractor in Chapter 14. So there really is no excuse for your AngularJS application not to be completely tested. Go ahead, you and your teammates will thank yourself for it.

Now that you have had a brief overview of what makes AngularJS great, let's see how to get started with writing your own AngularJS applications.

Starting Out with AngularJS

Starting an AngularJS application has never been easier, but even before we jump into that, let's take a moment to answer a few simple questions to help you decide whether or not AngularJS is the right framework for you.

What Backend Do I Need?

One of the first questions we usually get is regarding the kind of a backend one would need to be able to write an AngularJS application. The very short answer is: there are no such requirements.

AngularJS has no set requirements on what kind of a backend it needs to work as a Single-Page Application. You are free to use Java, Python, Ruby, C#, or any other language you feel comfortable with. The only thing you do need is a way of communicating back and forth with your server. Ideally, this would be via XHR (XML HTTP requests) or sockets.

If your server has REST or API endpoints that provide JSON values, then it makes your life as a frontend developer even easier. But even if your server doesn't return JSON, that doesn't mean you should abandon AngularJS. It's pretty easy to teach AngularJS to talk with an XML server, or any other format for that matter.

Does My Entire Application Need to Be an AngularJS App?

In a word, no. AngularJS has a concept (technically, a directive, but we'll get to that in the next section) called ng-app. This allows you to annotate any existing HTML element with the tag (and not just the main <html> or <body> tag). This tells AngularJS that it is only allowed to work on, control, and modify that particular section of the HTML.

This makes it pretty simple to start with a small section of an existing application and then grow the part that AngularJS controls over time gradually.

A Basic AngularJS Application

Finally, with all that out of the way, let's get to some code. We'll start with the most basic of AngularJS applications, which just imports the AngularJS library and proves that AngularJS is bootstrapped and working:

```
<!-- File: chapter1/basic-angularjs-app.html -->
<!DOCTYPE html>
<html ng-app>

<body>
  <h1>Hello {{1 + 2}}</h1>

<script
  src="https://ajax.googleapis.com/ajax/libs/angularjs/1.2.19/angular.js">
</script>
</body>

</html>
```

Examples in This Book

All the examples in this book are hosted at its GitHub repository (*https://github.com/shyamseshadri/angularjs-up-and-running*). The latest updated and correct version will always be available there in case you run into any issues when running the example from the book. Each example will also give the filename so that you can find it in the GitHub repository. Each chapter has its own folder to make it easier to find examples from the book.

There are two parts to starting an AngularJS application:

Loading the AngularJS source code

We have included the unminified version directly from the Google Hosted Libraries, but you could also have your own local version that you serve. The Google CDN (*https://developers.google.com/speed/libraries/devguide*) hosts all the latest versions of AngularJS that you can directly reference it from, or download it from the AngularJS website (*http://www.angularjs.org*).

Bootstrapping AngularJS

This is done through the `ng-app` directive. This is the first and most important directive that AngularJS has, which denotes the section of HTML that AngularJS controls. Putting it on the `<html>` tag tells AngularJS to control the entire HTML application. We could also put it on the `<body>` or any other element on the page. Any element that is a child of that will be handled with AngularJS and be annotated with directives, and anything outside would not be processed.

Finally, we have our first taste of AngularJS one-way data-binding. We have put the expressions "1+2" within double curly braces. The double curly is an AngularJS syntax to denote either one-way data-binding or AngularJS expressions. If it refers to a variable, it keeps the UI up to date with changes in the value. If it is an expression, AngularJS evaluates it and keeps the UI up to date if the value of the expression changes.

If for any reason AngularJS had not bootstrapped correctly, we would have seen {{1 + 2}} in the UI, but if there are no errors, we should see Figure 1-1 in our browser.

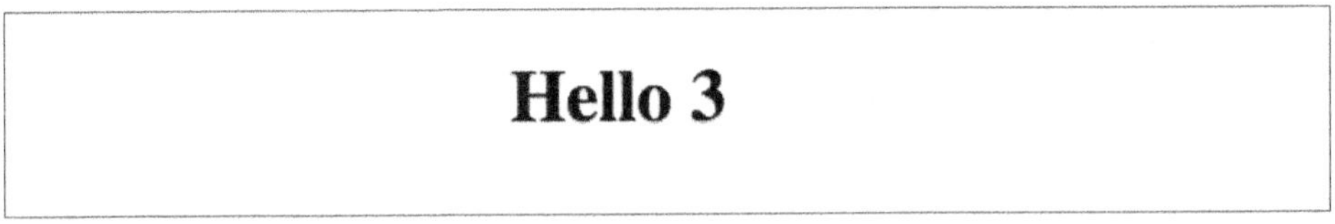

Hello 3

Figure 1-1. Screenshot of a basic AngularJS application

AngularJS Hello World

Now that we've seen how to create an AngularJS application, let's build the traditional "hello world" application. For this, we will have an input field that allows users to type in their name. Then, as the user types, we will update the UI with the latest value from the text box. Sound complicated? Let's see how it would look:

```
<!-- File: chapter1/angularjs-hello-world.html -->
<!DOCTYPE html>
<html>

<body ng-app>
  <input type="text"
         ng-model="name"
         placeholder="Enter your name">
```

```
    <h1>Hello <span ng-bind="name"></span></h1>
<script
  src="https://ajax.googleapis.com/ajax/libs/angularjs/1.2.19/angular.js">
</script>
</body>

</html>
```

We have added two new things from the last example, and kept two things:

- The AngularJS source code is still the same. The ng-app directive has moved to the <body> tag.

- We have an input tag, with a directive called ng-model on it. The ng-model directive is used with input fields whenever we want the user to enter any data and get access to the value in JavaScript. Here, we tell AngularJS to store the value that the user types into this field in a variable called name.

- We also have another directive called ng-bind. ng-bind and the double-curly notation are interchangeable, so instead of <span ng-bind="name"></span>, we could have written {{ name }}. Both accomplish the same thing, which is putting the value of the variable name inside the tag, and keeping it up to date if it changes.

The end result is captured in Figure 1-2.

Figure 1-2. AngularJS "hello world" example screenshot

Conclusion

We wrote two very simple AngularJS applications. The first demonstrated how to create a very simple AngularJS application, and the second showcased the power of AngularJS two-way data-binding. The best part was that we were able to do that without writing a single line of JavaScript. The same application in pure JavaScript would require us to create listeners and jQuery DOM manipulators. We were able to do away with all of that.

We also went over the basic philosophies of AngularJS and some of its benefits and how it differs from existing solutions. In the next chapter, we become familiar with some of the most common pieces of AngularJS, such as common directives, working with controllers, and using services.

CHAPTER 2

Basic AngularJS Directives and Controllers

We saw in Chapter 1 how to create a very simple and trivial AngularJS application, which was basically the "hello world" of the AngularJS world. In this chapter, we will expand on that example.

We explore AngularJS modules and controllers, and create our very own controllers. Then we use these controllers to load data or state into our application, and manipulate the HTML to perform common tasks such as displaying an array of items in the UI, hiding and showing elements conditionally, styling HTML elements based on certain conditions, and more.

AngularJS Modules

The very first thing we want to introduce is the concept of *modules*. Modules are AngularJS's way of packaging relevant code under a single name. For someone coming from a Java background, a simple analogy is to think of modules as packages.

An AngularJS module has two parts to it:

- A module can define its own controllers, services, factories, and directives. These are functions and code that can be accessed throughout the module.
- The module can also depend on other modules as *dependencies*, which are defined when the module is instantiated. What this means is that AngularJS will go and find the module with that particular name, and ensure that any functions, controllers, services, etc. defined in that module are made available to all the code defined in this module.

In addition to being a container for related JavaScript, the module is also what AngularJS uses to bootstrap an application. What that means is that we can tell AngularJS what module to load as the main entry point for the application by passing the module name to the ng-app directive.

Let's clear this up with the help of a few examples.

This is how we define a module named notesApp:

```
angular.module('notesApp', []);
```

The *first argument* to the module function in AngularJS is the *name of the module*. Here, we define a module named notesApp. The *second argument* is an *array of module names* that this module depends on. Do note the empty square brackets we pass as the second argument to the function. This tells AngularJS to create a new module with the name notesApp, with no dependencies.

This is how we define a module named notesApp, which depends on two other modules: notesApp.ui, which defines our UI widgets, and thirdCompany.fusioncharts, which is a third-party library for charts:

```
angular.module('notesApp',
    ['notesApp.ui', 'thirdCompany.fusioncharts']);
```

If we want to load an existing module that has already been defined in some other file, we use the the angular.module function with just the first argument, as follows:

```
angular.module('notesApp');
```

This line of code tells AngularJS to find an *existing* module named notesApp, and to make it available to use, add, or modify in the current file. This is how we refer to the same module across multiple files and add code to it.

There are two common mistakes to watch out for:

- Trying to define a module, but forgetting to pass in the second argument. This would cause AngularJS to try to look up a module instead of defining one, and we would get an error ("No module found").
- Trying to load a module from another file to modify, but the file that defines the module has not been loaded first. Make sure the file that defines the module is loaded first in your HTML before you try to use it.

Now that the module has been defined, how do we use it? We can of course add our functionality to it, and modularize our codebase into distinct sections. But more importantly, we can tell AngularJS to use these modules to bootstrap our application. The ng-app directive takes an *optional argument*, which is the *name of the module to load* during bootstrapping.

Let's take a look at a complete example to make sense of this:

```
<!-- File: chapter2/module-example.html -->
<html ng-app="notesApp">
<head><title>Hello AngularJS</title></head>
<body>
  Hello {{1 + 1}}nd time AngularJS

<script
  src="https://ajax.googleapis.com/ajax/libs/angularjs/1.2.19/angular.js">
</script>
<script type="text/javascript">
  angular.module('notesApp', []);
</script>
</body>
</html>
```

This example defines a module (note the empty array as the second argument), and then lets AngularJS bootstrap the module through the ng-app directive.

Creating Our First Controller

We saw how to create modules, but what do we do with them? So far, they have just been empty modules.

Let's now take a look at controllers. Controllers in AngularJS are our workhorse, the JavaScript functions that perform or trigger the majority of our UI-oriented work. Some of the common responsibilities of a controller in an AngularJS application include:

- Fetching the right data from the server for the current UI

- Deciding which parts of that data to show to the user

- Presentation logic, such as how to display elements, which parts of the UI to show, how to style them, etc.

- User interactions, such as what happens when a user clicks something or how a text input should be validated

An AngularJS controller is almost always directly linked to a view or HTML. We will never have a controller that is not used in the UI (that kind of business logic goes into services). It acts as the gateway between our model, which is the data that drives our application, and the view, which is what the user sees and interacts with.

So let's take a look at how we could go about creating a controller for our notesApp module:

```
<!-- File: chapter2/creating-controller.html -->
<html ng-app="notesApp">
<head><title>Hello AngularJS</title></head>
<body ng-controller="MainCtrl">
  Hello {{1 + 1}}nd time AngularJS
```

```
<script
  src="https://ajax.googleapis.com/ajax/libs/angularjs/1.2.19/angular.js">
</script>
<script type="text/javascript">
  angular.module('notesApp', [])
    .controller('MainCtrl', [function() {
      // Controller-specific code goes here
      console.log('MainCtrl has been created');
    }]);
</script>
</body>
</html>
```

We define a controller using the `controller` function that is exposed on an AngularJS module. The `controller` function takes the name of the controller as the first argument, which in the previous example is creatively named `MainCtrl`. The second argument is the actual controller definition, of what it does and how it does it.

But there is a slight twist here, which is the array notation. Notice that we have defined our `controller` definition function inside an array. That is, the first argument to the controller function on the module is the name of the controller (`MainCtrl`), and the second argument is an array. The array holds all the dependencies for the controller as string variables, and the last argument in the array is the actual controller function. In this case, because we have no dependencies, the function is the only argument in the array. The function then houses all the controller-specific code.

We also introduce a new directive, `ng-controller`. This is used to tell AngularJS to go instantiate an instance of the controller with the given name, and attach it to the DOM element. In this case, it would load `MainCtrl`, which would end up printing the `console.log()` statement.

Dependency Injection Syntax and AngularJS

The notation that we have used is one of the two ways in which we can declare AngularJS controllers (or services, directives, or filters). The style we have used (and will use for the remainder of the book), which is also the recommended way, is *safe-style of Dependency Injection*, or declaration. We could also use:

```
angular.module('notesApp', [])
    .controller('MainCtrl', function() {
    });
```

and it would work similarly, but it might cause problems when we have a build step that minifies our code. We will delve into this more when we introduce Dependency Injection in Chapter 5.

Now, for our first AngularJS application with a controller, we are going to move the "hello world" message from the HTML to the controller, and get and display it from the controller. Let's see how this would look:

```html
<!-- File: chapter2/hello-controller.html -->
<html ng-app="notesApp">
<head><title>Notes App</title></head>
<body ng-controller="MainCtrl as ctrl">
  {{ctrl.helloMsg}} AngularJS.
  <br/>
  {{ctrl.goodbyeMsg}} AngularJS

<script
  src="https://ajax.googleapis.com/ajax/libs/angularjs/1.2.19/angular.js">
</script>
<script type="text/javascript">
  angular.module('notesApp', [])
    .controller('MainCtrl', [function() {
        this.helloMsg = 'Hello ';
        var goodbyeMsg = 'Goodbye ';
  }]);
</script>
</body>
</html>
```

If we run this application, our UI should look something like Figure 2-1.

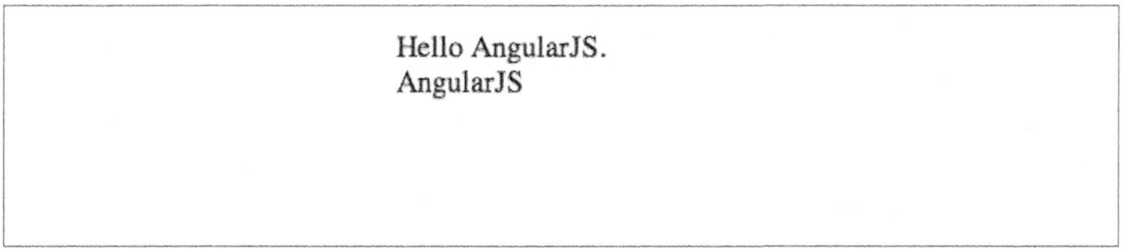

Hello AngularJS.
AngularJS

Figure 2-1. "Hello world" controller example screenshot

Yes, we only see "Hello AngularJS." The "Goodbye" message is not printed in the UI. Let's dig into the example to see if we can clarify what is happening:

- We defined our notesApp module as we saw before.

- We created a controller called MainCtrl using the controller function on the module.

- We defined the variable helloMsg on the controller's instance (using the this keyword), and the variable goodbyeMsg as a local inner variable in the controller's instance (using the var keyword).

- We used this controller in the UI through the use of another directive: ng-controller. This directive allows us to associate an instance of a controller with a UI element (in this case, the body tag).

- We also gave this particular instance of the MainCtrl a name when we used ng-controller. Here, we called it ctrl. This is known as the controllerAs syntax in AngularJS, where we can give each instance of the controller a name to recognize its usage in the HTML.

- We then referred to the helloMsg and goodbyeMsg variables from the controller in the HTML using the double-curly notation.

By now, it should be obvious that variables that were defined on the this keyword in the controller are accessible from the HTML, but local, inner variables are not.

Furthermore, any variable defined on the controller instance (on *this* in the controller, as opposed to declaring variables with the *var* keyword like *goodbyeMsg*) can be accessed and displayed to the user via the HTML. This is basically how we funnel and expose data from our controller and business logic to the UI.

Getting Data to the HTML
Changing ctrl.goodbyeMsg to goodbyeMsg in the HTML will not help either. We will not get the value of the goodbyeMsg variable from the controller to the UI without declaring it on the controller instance using the this keyword.

Anything that the user needs to see, or the HTML needs to use, needs to be defined on this. Anything that the HTML does not directly access should not be put on this, but should rather be saved as local variables in the controller's scope, similar to goodbyeMsg.

$scope Versus controllerAs Syntax

If you used AngularJS prior to 1.2, you might have expected the $scope variable to be injected into the controller, and the variables helloMsg and goodbyeMsg to be set on it. In AngularJS 1.2 and later, there is a new syntax, the controllerAs syntax, which allows us to define the variables on the controller instance using the this keyword, and refer to them through the controller from the HTML.

The advantage of this over the earlier syntax is that it makes it explicit in the HTML which variable or function is provided by which controller and which instance of the controller. So with a complicated, nested UI, you don't need to play a game of "Where's Waldo?" to find your variables in your codebase. It becomes immediately obvious because the controller instance is present in the HTML.

Let's take a look at one more example before we delve into how AngularJS works and accomplishes this:

```html
<!-- File: chapter2/controller-click-message.html -->
<html ng-app="notesApp">
<head><title>Notes App</title></head>
<body ng-controller="MainCtrl as ctrl">
  {{ctrl.message}} AngularJS.

  <button ng-click="ctrl.changeMessage()">
    Change Message
  </button>
<script
  src="https://ajax.googleapis.com/ajax/libs/angularjs/1.2.19/angular.js">
</script>
<script type="text/javascript">
  angular.module('notesApp', [])
    .controller('MainCtrl', [function() {
      var self = this;
      self.message= 'Hello ';
      self.changeMessage = function() {
        self.message = 'Goodbye';
      };
  }]);
</script>
</body>
</html>
```

What has changed here?

- We now have only one binding, which is in the `ctrl.message` variable.
- There is a button with the label "Change Message." There is a built-in directive on it, `ng-click`, to which we pass a function as an argument. The `ng-click` directive evaluates any expression passed to it when the button is clicked. In this case, we tell AngularJS to trigger the controller's `changeMessage()` function.
- The `changeMessage()` function in the controller sets the value of message to "Goodbye."
- Also, as good practice, we avoid referring to the `this` keyword inside the controller, preferring to use a proxy `self` variable, which points to `this`. The following note has more information on why this is recommended.

What we will see in play is that the app starts with "Hello AngularJS," but the moment we click the button, the text changes to "Goodbye AngularJS." This is the true power of data-binding in AngularJS. Here are a few things of note from the example:

- The controller we wrote has no direct access to the view or any of the DOM elements that it needs to update. It is pure JavaScript.

- When the user clicked the button and `changeMessage` was triggered, we did not have to tell the UI to update. It happened automatically.
- The HTML connects parts of the DOM to controllers, functions, and variables, and not the other way around.

This is one of the core principles of AngularJS at play here. An AngularJS application is a data-driven app. We routinely say "The model is the truth" in an AngularJS application. What this means is that our whole aim in an AngularJS application should be to manipulate and modify the model (pure JavaScript), and let AngularJS do the heavy lifting of updating the UI accordingly.

Before we talk about how AngularJS accomplishes this, let's take a look at one more example that will help clarify things.

this in JavaScript

People used to languages like Java have trouble getting their heads around the `this` keyword in JavaScript. One of the insane and crazy (and downright cool) things about JavaScript is that the `this` keyword inside a function can be overridden by whoever calls the function. Thus, the `this` outside and inside a function can refer to two completely different objects or scopes.

Thus, it is generally better to assign the `this` reference inside a controller to a proxy variable, and always refer to the instance through this proxy (`self`, for example) to be assured that the instance we are referring to is the correct one.

If you want to read more about this, as well as understand a bit more about the craziness that can be JavaScript, do check out Kyle Simpson's *You Don't Know JS: this & Object Prototypes* (O'Reilly, 2014).

Working with and Displaying Arrays

We have seen how to create a controller, and how to get data from the controller into the HTML. But we worked with very simplistic string messages. Let's now take a look at how we would work with a collection of data; for example:

```
<!-- File: chapter2/ng-repeat-example-1.html -->
<html ng-app="notesApp">
<head><title>Notes App</title></head>
<body ng-controller="MainCtrl as ctrl">

  <div ng-repeat="note in ctrl.notes">
    <span class="label"> {{note.label}}</span>
    <span class="status" ng-bind="note.done"></span>
  </div>
```

```
<script
  src="https://ajax.googleapis.com/ajax/libs/angularjs/1.2.19/angular.js">
</script>
<script type="text/javascript">
  angular.module('notesApp', [])
    .controller('MainCtrl', [function() {
      var self = this;
      self.notes = [
        {id: 1, label: 'First Note', done: false},
        {id: 2, label: 'Second Note', done: false},
        {id: 3, label: 'Done Note', done: true},
        {id: 4, label: 'Last Note', done: false}
      ];
    }]);
  </script>
</body>
</html>
```

We introduced a few new concepts in this example. Before we delve into those, Figure 2-2 shows how the HTML and JS would look when we run it.

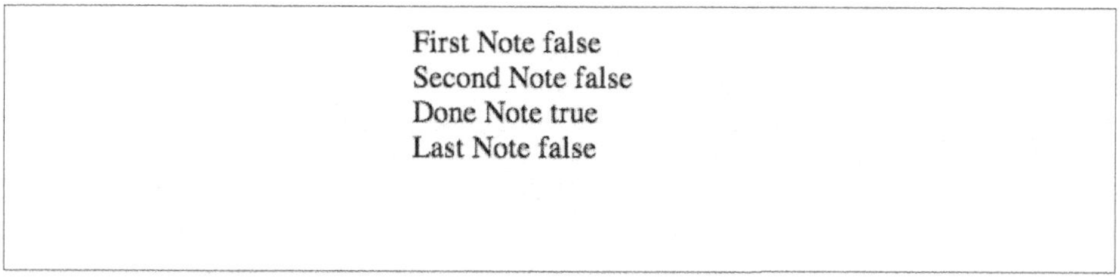

First Note false
Second Note false
Done Note true
Last Note false

Figure 2-2. ng-repeat example screenshot

First things first, we removed the `message` variable and introduced an array of JSON objects in our `MainCtrl`. We exposed this on the controller instance with the name `notes`.

In our HTML, we used a directive called `ng-repeat`. `ng-repeat` is one of the most versatile and heavily used directives of AngularJS, because it allows us to iterate over an array or over the keys and values of an object and display them in the HTML.

When we use the `ng-repeat` directive, the contents of the element on which the directive is applied is considered the *template* of the `ng-repeat`. AngularJS picks up this template, makes a copy of it, and then applies it for each instance of the `ng-repeat`. In the previous case, the `label` and `status` span elements were repeated four times, once for each item in the `notes` array.

The ng-repeat is basically the same as a for each loop in any programming language, so the syntax is similar:

```
ng-repeat="eachVar in arrayVar"
```

We'll cover more details about ng-repeat in the following section.

The next point of interest is the template that we used for the ng-repeat. Inside the context of the ng-repeat, we now have a new variable, note, which is not present in our controller. This is created by ng-repeat, and each instance of the ng-repeat has its own version and value of note, obtained from each item of the array.

The final thing to note is that we used the double-curly notation to print the note's label, but used a directive called ng-bind for the note's done field. There is no functional difference between the two; both take the value from the controller and display it in the UI. Both of them also keep it data-bound and up to date, so if the value underneath changes, the UI will change automatically. We can use them interchangeably, because the expression between the double curly braces will directly drop into the ng-bind.

Using ng-bind Versus Double Curlies

The advantage ng-bind has over the double-curly notation is that it takes AngularJS time to bootstrap and execute before it can find and replace all the double curly braces from the HTML. That means, for a portion of a second while the browser starts, you might see flashing double curly braces in the UI before AngularJS has the chance to kick in and replace them. This is only for the very first page load, and not on views loaded after the first load. You will not have that issue with ng-bind. You can also get around that issue with the ng-cloak directive.

Waiting for AngularJS to Load

AngularJS has a directive called *ng-cloak*, which is a mechanism to hide sections of the page while AngularJS bootstraps and finishes loading. ng-cloak uses the following CSS rules, which are automatically included when you load *angular.js* or *angular.min.js*:

```
[ng\:cloak], [ng-cloak], [data-ng-cloak], [x-ng-cloak],
    .ng-cloak, .x-ng-cloak {
  display: none !important;
}
```

After this, any section or element that needs to be hidden in your HTML needs to have class="ng-cloak" added to it. This applies the preceding CSS and hides the element by default. After AngularJS finishes loading, it goes through your HTML and removes ng-cloak from all these elements, thus ensuring that your UI is shown after AngularJS has finished bootstrapping.

You can apply ng-cloak on the body tag, but it is often better to add it on smaller sections so that your application can load progressively instead of all at once.

Do note that the ng-cloak styling is loaded as part of the *angular.js* source code. So if you load your AngularJS library at the very end of your HTML (as you should), the style will not be applied to the HTML until AngularJS has finished loading. Thus it is often a good idea to include the preceding CSS as part of your own CSS to ensure it is loaded upfront before your HTML starts displaying.

With this example in place, let's dig in and understand how AngularJS is working behind the scenes:

1. The HTML is loaded. This triggers requests for all the scripts that are a part of it.

2. After the entire document has been loaded, AngularJS kicks in and looks for the ng-app directive.

3. When it finds the ng-app directive, it looks for and loads the module that is specified and attaches it to the element.

4. AngularJS then traverses the children DOM elements of the root element with the ng-app and starts looking for directives and bind statements.

5. Each time it hits an ng-controller or an ng-repeat directive, it creates what we call a *scope* in AngularJS. A scope is the context for that element. The scope dictates what each DOM element has access to in terms of functions, variables, and the like.

6. AngularJS then adds watchers and listeners on the variables that the HTML accesses, and keeps track of the current value of each of them. When that value changes, AngularJS updates the UI immediately.

7. Instead of polling or some other mechanism to check if the data has changed, AngularJS optimizes and checks for updates to the UI only on certain events, which can cause a change in the data or the model underneath. Examples of such events include XHR or server calls, page loads, and user interactions like click or type.

In our previous example with the ng-repeat, we have a template that shows the note's label and status. That template accesses a variable called note, which is created in our for each loop that is the ng-repeat. Now, if each template accessed the same context, each instance would show the same text. But to ensure that each template instance of the ng-repeat shows its own value, each ng-repeat also gets its own scope with a variable called note defined in it, which is specific to it.

Also note that while the ng-repeat instances each get their own scope, they still have access to the parent scope. If there were a function in our controller that we wanted to access within the ng-repeat, we could still do that.

In summation, AngularJS creates scopes or context for various elements in the DOM to ensure that there is no global state and each element accesses only what is relevant to it. These scopes have a parent-child relation by default, which allows children scopes to access functions and controllers from a parent scope.

More Directives

Let's now build on our example, and add more functionality to our ongoing application:

```
<!-- File: chapter2/more-directives.html -->
<html ng-app="notesApp">
<head>
  <title>Notes App</title>
  <style>
    .done {
      background-color: green;
    }
    .pending {
      background-color: red;
    }
  </style>
</head>

<body ng-controller="MainCtrl as ctrl">

  <div ng-repeat="note in ctrl.notes"
       ng-class="ctrl.getNoteClass(note.done)">
      <span class="label"> {{note.label}}</span>
      <span class="assignee"
            ng-show="note.assignee"
            ng-bind="note.assignee">
      </span>
  </div>

<script
  src="https://ajax.googleapis.com/ajax/libs/angularjs/1.2.19/angular.js">
</script>
<script type="text/javascript">
  angular.module('notesApp', []).controller('MainCtrl', [
    function() {
      var self = this;
      self.notes = [
        {label: 'First Note', done: false, assignee: 'Shyam'},
        {label: 'Second Note', done: false},
        {label: 'Done Note', done: true},
        {label: 'Last Note', done: false, assignee: 'Brad'}
      ];

      self.getNoteClass = function(status) {
        return {
            done: status,
```

```
                pending: !status
            };
        };
    }]);
    </script>
    </body>
    </html>
```

We added two more directives in this example. Let's take a look at what they are and what they do:

ng-show

> There are two directives in AngularJS that deal with hiding and showing HTML elements: ng-show and ng-hide. They inspect a variable and, depending on the truthiness of its value, show or hide elements in the UI, respectively. In this case, we say show the assignee span if note.assignee is true. AngularJS treats true, nonempty strings, nonzero numbers, and nonnull JS objects as truthy. So in this case, we get to see the assignee span if the note has an assignee.

ng-class

> The ng-class directive is used to selectively apply and remove CSS classes from elements. There are multiple ways of using ng-class, and we will talk about what we feel is the most declarative and cleanest option. The ng-class directive can take strings or objects as values. If it is a string, it simply applies the CSS classes directly. If it is an object (which we are returning from the function in the controller), AngularJS takes a look at each key of the object, and depending on whether the value for that key is true or false, applies or removes the CSS class.

In this case, the CSS class done gets added and pending gets removed if note.done is true, and done gets removed and pending gets added if note.done is false.

Notice also that ng-bind, ng-show, and most of these directives can directly refer to a variable on the controller or call a function to get the value, as we did with the ng-class. We can pass variables and arguments to the function as normal by directly referring to the variable. No need for the double-curly syntax.

Working with ng-repeat

The ng-repeat directive is one of the most versatile directives in AngularJS, and can be used for a whole variety of situations and requirements. We saw how we can use it to repeat an array in the previous examples. In this section, we will explore some of the other options we have when using the ng-repeat directive.

ng-repeat Over an Object

Just like we used the ng-repeat directive to show an array of elements in the HTML, we can also use it to show all the keys and values of an object:

```html
<!-- File: chapter2/ng-repeat-object.html -->
<html ng-app="notesApp">
<head><title>Notes App</title></head>
<body ng-controller="MainCtrl as ctrl">

  <div ng-repeat="(author, note) in ctrl.notes">
    <span class="label"> {{note.label}}</span>
    <span class="author" ng-bind="author"></span>
  </div>

<script
  src="https://ajax.googleapis.com/ajax/libs/angularjs/1.2.19/angular.js">
</script>
<script type="text/javascript">
  angular.module('notesApp', [])
    .controller('MainCtrl', [function() {
      var self = this;
      self.notes = {
        shyam: {
          id: 1,
          label: 'First Note',
          done: false
        },
        Misko: {
          id: 3,
          label: 'Finished Third Note',
          done: true
        },
        brad: {
          id: 2,
          label: 'Second Note',
          done: false
        }
      };
    }]);
  </script>
</body>
</html>
```

In this example, we have intentionally capitalized Misko while leaving brad and shyam lowercase. When we use the ng-repeat directive over an object instead of an array, the keys of the object will be sorted in a case-sensitive, alphabetic order. That is, uppercase first, and then sorted by alphabet. So in this case, the items would be shown in the HTML in the following order: Misko, brad, shyam.

The ng-repeat directive takes an argument in the form `variable in arrayExpression` or `(key, value) in objectExpression`. When used with an array, the items will be in the order in which they exist in the array.

Helper Variables in ng-repeat

The ng-repeat directive also exposes some variables within the context of the HTML template that gets repeated, which allows us to gain some insight into the current element:

```
<!-- File: chapter2/ng-repeat-helper-variables.html -->
<html ng-app="notesApp">
<head><title>Notes App</title></head>
<body ng-controller="MainCtrl as ctrl">

  <div ng-repeat="note in ctrl.notes">
    <div>First Element: {{$first}}</div>
    <div>Middle Element: {{$middle}}</div>
    <div>Last Element: {{$last}}</div>
    <div>Index of Element: {{$index}}</div>
    <div>At Even Position: {{$even}}</div>
    <div>At Odd Position: {{$odd}}</div>

    <span class="label"> {{note.label}}</span>
    <span class="status" ng-bind="note.done"></span>
    <br/><br/>
  </div>

<script
  src="https://ajax.googleapis.com/ajax/libs/angularjs/1.2.19/angular.js">
</script>
<script type="text/javascript">
  angular.module('notesApp', [])
    .controller('MainCtrl', [function() {
      var self = this;
      self.notes = [
        {id: 1, label: 'First Note', done: false},
        {id: 2, label: 'Second Note', done: false},
        {id: 3, label: 'Done Note', done: true},
        {id: 4, label: 'Last Note', done: false}
      ];
    }]);
</script>
</body>
</html>
```

In this example, we use the same array that we did in the example with the ng-repeat over the array of items. The only difference is that we now display more state about the item being repeated in the HTML. For each item, we display which index the item is in, and whether it is the first, middle, last, odd, or even item.

Each of the $ prefixed variables we use within the context of the ng-repeat are provided by AngularJS, and refer to the state of the repeater for that particular element. They include:

- $first, $middle, and $last are Boolean values that tell us whether that particular element is the first, between the first and last, or the last element in the array or object.

- $index gives us the index or position of the item in the array.

- $odd and $even tell us if the item is in an index that is odd or even (we could use this for conditional styling of elements, or other conditions we might have in our application).

Do note that in the case of an ng-repeat over an object, all of these list items exist and are still applicable, but the index of the item may or may not correspond to the order in which we declare the keys in the object. This is because of the way AngularJS ng-repeat sorts the keys of the object alphabetically, as we saw in the "ng-repeat Over an Object" on page 28.

Track by ID

By default, ng-repeat creates a new DOM element for each value in the array or object that we iterate over. But to optimize performance, it caches or reuses DOM elements if the objects are exactly the same, according to the hash of the object (calculated by AngularJS).

In some cases, we might want AngularJS to reuse the same DOM element, even if the object instance does not hash to the same value. That is, if we have objects coming from a database and we do not care about the exact object properties, we want AngularJS to treat two objects with the same ID as identical for the purpose of the repeat. For this purpose, AngularJS allows us to provide a tracking expression when specifying our ng-repeat:

```html
<!-- File: chapter2/ng-repeat-track-by-id.html -->
<html ng-app="notesApp">
<body ng-controller="MainCtrl as ctrl">

  <button ng-click="ctrl.changeNotes()">Change Notes</button>
  <br/>
  DOM Elements change every time someone clicks
  <div ng-repeat="note in ctrl.notes1">
    {{note.$$hashKey}}
    <span class="label"> {{note.label}}</span>
    <span class="author" ng-bind="note.done"></span>
  </div>

  <br/>
```

```
DOM Elements are reused every time someone clicks
<div ng-repeat="note in ctrl.notes2 track by note.id">
  {{note.$$hashKey}}
  <span class="label"> {{note.label}}</span>
  <span class="author" ng-bind="note.done"></span>
</div>

<script
  src="https://ajax.googleapis.com/ajax/libs/angularjs/1.2.19/angular.js">
</script>
<script type="text/javascript">
  angular.module('notesApp', [])
    .controller('MainCtrl', [function() {
      var self = this;
      var notes = [
        {
          id: 1,
          label: 'First Note',
          done: false,
          someRandom: 31431
        },
        {
          id: 2,
          label: 'Second Note',
          done: false
        },
        {
          id: 3,
          label: 'Finished Third Note',
          done: true
        }
      ];
      self.notes1 = angular.copy(notes);
      self.notes2 = angular.copy(notes);
      self.changeNotes = function() {
        notes = [
          {
            id: 1,
            label: 'Changed Note',
            done: false,
            someRandom: 4242
          },
          {
            id: 2,
            label: 'Second Note',
            done: false
          },
          {
            id: 3,
            label: 'Finished Third Note',
            done: true
          }
```

```
        ];
        self.notes1 = angular.copy(notes);
        self.notes2 = angular.copy(notes);
    };
  }]);
</script>
</body>

</html>
```

Here we have two arrays, notes1 and notes2, which are identical in all respects. Both of them are shown in the UI using the ng-repeat directive. The difference is that one uses the plain vanilla ng-repeat (ng-repeat="note in ctrl.notes1") and the other uses the track by ID version (ng-repeat="note in ctrl.notes2 track by note.id").

We also included an ng-click, which we used before. This allows us to trigger a function in our controller whenever someone clicks that element. In this case, we call change Notes() on our controller. The function changes the notes arrays to a new array.

Now we can see that the hashKeys and the DOM elements in the first ng-repeat are getting changed every time we click a button. In the second ng-repeat, there is no $ $hashKey that AngularJS needs to generate, because we tell it what the unique identifier is for each element. So the DOM elements are reused based on the ID of the object.

 Do not use any variables that start with $$ in your application. An-gularJS uses them to denote private variables that it uses for its own purposes, and does not guarantee their presence or continued work-ing across different versions of AngularJS. If you find yourself reach-ing out to a $$ variable, stop! You need to rethink your approach.

We would use the track-by expression to optimize DOM manipulation in our appli-cation. This would generally be on the IDs of objects returned from our databases, to ensure AngularJS reuses DOM elements even if we fetch the data multiple times from the server.

ng-repeat Across Multiple HTML Elements

An uncommon requirement, but something that still pops up every now and then, is the ability to repeat multiple sibling HTML elements that may not be in a single con-tainer element. For example, think of the case where we need to repeat two table rows (<tr>) for each item in our array, maybe one as a header row and one as a child row.

For these kinds of situations, AngularJS provides the ability to mark where our ng-repeat starts and tell which HTML element is considered part of the ng-repeat. It does so through the use of ng-repeat-start and ng-repeat-end directives:

```
<!-- File: chapter2/ng-repeat-across-elements.html -->
<html ng-app="notesApp">
<body ng-controller="MainCtrl as ctrl">

  <table>
    <tr ng-repeat-start="note in ctrl.notes">
      <td>{{note.label}}</td>
    </tr>
    <tr ng-repeat-end>
      <td>Done: {{note.done}}</td>
    </tr>
  </table>


<script
  src="https://ajax.googleapis.com/ajax/libs/angularjs/1.2.19/angular.js">
</script>
<script type="text/javascript">
  angular.module('notesApp', [])
    .controller('MainCtrl', [function() {
      var self = this;
      self.notes = [
        {id: 1, label: 'First Note', done: false},
        {id: 2, label: 'Second Note', done: false},
        {id: 3, label: 'Finished Third Note', done: true}
      ];
    }]);
</script>
</body>

</html>
```

In this example, we are creating a table to display the list of notes. For each note, we want a row where we display the label of the note, followed by a second table row where we display the status of the note. This could very well contain the author information, when it was created, and so on. Because we can't have a wrapper element around the `tr` table row element, we can use the `ng-repeat-start` and `ng-repeat-end` directives.

We mark the first `tr` as where our `ng-repeat` starts, and use our traditional `ng-repeat` expression as the argument. We then define our template, which contains the first element with the label, and then move on to the second table row element. We mark this element as where our repeater ends by using the `ng-repeat-end` directive.

AngularJS will then ensure that it creates both `tr` elements for each element in the array we are repeating.

Conclusion

We covered the very basic features of AngularJS, and introduced some commonly used directives like `ng-repeat` and `ng-click`. We used these to show arrays and objects in the UI, as well as to handle user interactions and style applications conditionally. We also saw how to create controllers, and how to get data from our controllers into our views. Finally, we did a deep dive into the `ng-repeat` to see what it is and how we could use it in a variety of situations.

As we mentioned earlier, AngularJS has a huge focus on unit testing. To this end, each and every part of AngularJS is easy to unit test. In the next chapter, we will see how we might write some simple unit tests for the controllers we have written so far. We will cover how unit testing is done in AngularJS, how to set up Karma (which is used to run unit tests in AngularJS), and how we can instantiate controllers and set our expectations on their behavior.

CHAPTER 3

Unit Testing in AngularJS

In Chapter 2, we looked at starting a very basic AngularJS application. We saw some commonly used AngularJS directives, and then looked at using controllers to add behavior and functionality to our application.

JavaScript does not have all the niceties of a strongly typed language like type safety and a compiler. That puts the onus on us developers to ensure that what we write actually works as intended, and continues to run as intended well into the future. Unit tests provide a way to write expectations about how code should behave, and running them in an automated way ensures that behaviors don't change unexpectedly.

Because AngularJS and testing are so well integrated, we introduce a small chapter on testing after each major concept to show how each concept can be unit tested independently, and in isolation. We also dive into Karma (*http://karma-runner.github.io/*), the unit test runner for AngularJS, and Jasmine, the test framework. Finally, we bring all these pieces together to write our first AngularJS unit test.

Unit Testing: What and Why?

Unit testing is the concept of taking a single function or part of our code, and writing assertions and tests to ensure that it works as intended. While very common on the server side, we often find the habit of writing unit tests amiss when developing client-side applications. Here are five reasons why we should write unit tests when working on a JavaScript-based client-side application:

Proof of correctness
> Without unit tests, there is blind reliance on end-to-end manual tests to ensure that our feature or part of the application actually works. Unit tests act as proof that what we have developed actually does what it is supposed to, that we have handled all the edge cases correctly, and that it delivers the correct result in all these cases.

Lack of compiler

In JavaScript, there is nothing like the Java compiler to tell us that something doesn't work. It is up to the browser to ultimately tell us that something is broken, and even then, different browsers produce different results. Unit tests can be run well before our application makes it out to the browser to catch problems and warn us about our assumptions.

Catch errors early

Without unit tests, we would only know about an error in our application after we hit refresh in our browser and saw the live application. Unit tests can help us catch errors much earlier, reducing turnaround time and thus increasing our development speed.

Prevent regressions

At the end of the day, we are unlikely to be the only person working on our codebase. Other developers will inevitably rely on or actively change parts of the codebase that we developed. You can ensure that they don't change any fundamental assumptions by providing a set of unit tests that prevent regressions and bugs in the future.

Specification

Comments have a bad habit of becoming outdated. Unit tests in AngularJS, especially written using Jasmine, look and read like English. And because unit tests break when the underlying code changes, we are forced to keep comments updated. So unit tests can act as a living, breathing specification for our codebase.

An Introduction to TDD

Test-driven development, or TDD, is an AGILE methodology that flips the development life cycle by ensuring that tests are written, before the code is implemented, and that tests drive the development (and are not just used as a validation tool).

The tenets of TDD are simple:

- Code is written only when there is a failing test that requires the code to pass.
- The bare minimum amount of code is written to ensure that the test passes.
- Duplication is removed at every step.
- When all tests pass, the next failing test is added for the next required functionality.

These simple rules ensure that:

- Code develops organically, and that every line of code is purposeful.
- Code remains highly modular, cohesive, and reusable (because we need to be able to test it).

- We provide a comprehensive array of tests to prevent future breakages and bugs.

- The tests also act as specification, and thus documentation, for future needs and changes.

We at AngularJS have found these tenets and rules to be true, and the entire AngularJS codebase has been developed using TDD. For an uncompiled, dynamic language like JavaScript, we strongly believe that having a good set of unit tests reduces headaches in the future.

Introduction to Karma

Karma (*http://karma-runner.github.io/*) is the test runner that makes running tests painless and amazingly fast. It uses NodeJS (*http://www.nodejs.org*) and SocketIO (*http://www.socket.io*) to facilitate tests in multiple browsers at insanely fast speeds.

Test Runner Versus Testing Framework
We have often noticed that developers can sometimes get confused between the test runner and the testing framework. This could be because the same library often handles both responsibilities.

When working with JS (and AngularJS), we have two separate tools/libraries for each purpose. Karma, which is the test runner, is solely responsible for finding all the unit tests in our codebase, opening browsers, running the tests in them, and capturing results. It does not care what language or framework we use for writing the tests; it simply runs them.

Jasmine is the testing framework we will use. Jasmine defines the syntax with which we write our tests, the APIs, and the way we write our assertions. It is possible to not use Jasmine, and instead use something like mocha or some other framework to write tests for AngularJS.

Karma is a great test runner, and its aim is to make testing as simple and fast as possible. It makes it easy to set up tests and then gets out of the way, letting us developers get instant feedback on our code and tests.

These are the steps to install Karma (as of this writing):

1. Install NodeJS (*http://www.nodejs.org*). You can get the installers from here (*http://nodejs.org/download/*).

2. Install Karma CLI, which allows you to run Karma in an easier step. This is an npm (Node Package Manager) package, so you can install it with the following command:

```
sudo npm install -g karma-cli
```

Windows users can also run this from the command line after NodeJS has been installed successfully.

3. Install Karma locally in the folder where you need to run these tests:

```
npm install karma
```

4. Karma has a concept called plugins, which allow you to choose only the components you need for your project. These plugins allow you to choose which framework you use for writing your unit tests (Karma is framework agnostic), which browsers to launch, and so on. To start off, we will install the Jasmine plugin to write our tests in Jasmine, and the Chrome launcher to start Google Chrome automatically. Install these two with the following command:

```
npm install karma-jasmine karma-chrome-launcher
```

Be sure that you run the last two commands from inside the folder where you downloaded the code repository. These are specific to each project, and will need to be run for every new project.

 The recommended way to run Karma on our projects has changed with the newer releases of Karma, which recommend a local installation of Karma for each project as opposed to a global installation of the Karma package. Local installation is what we demonstrated in the installation instructions earlier.

This also means that instead of directly running Karma commands from the command line, we have to execute them with the path to Karma from the local npm installation folder. That is:

```
karma start myconf.js
```

would have to be written as:

```
node_modules/karma/bin/karma start myconf.js
```

To stop doing this, Karma has an npm package called karma-cli, which we installed. This allows us to execute Karma without the full path, because it will underneath pick up the local Karma installation.

Karma Plugins

We installed two plugins for Karma in the previous section. Let's explore the concept of Karma plugins a bit more. Karma plugins can be broadly split into the following categories:

Browser launchers

The first type of plugins for Karma are ones that help Karma launch browsers automatically as part of a test run. We installed the Chrome browser launcher plugin, and there are similar ones for Firefox, IE, and many more.

Testing frameworks

We can also choose the type of framework we want to use when we write unit tests. We will be using Jasmine, which we installed again in the previous section, but if you prefer a different style of writing unit tests, like mocha or qunit, there are plugins available for those as well.

Reporters

Karma can give us the results of the tests in various forms as well. The default progress reporter comes built in, but you might decide that you need the test results as *junit.xml* files. You can install a Karma plugin for that.

Integrations

One other major category of plugins allows us to integrate with existing JavaScript libraries or tools, like Google's Closure or RequireJS. Most of these have plugins for Karma as well that you can install if you need them.

Explaining the Karma Config

To use Karma, we need a configuration file that tells Karma how to operate. We will see how easy it is to generate this configuration file in the next section. But first, let's take a look at the Karma configuration and the options that we will use for our unit tests in this chapter. The default name for this file is *karma.conf.js*, and unless you tell Karma otherwise, it will automatically look for a file with this name in the directory you run Karma from:

```
// File:  chapter3/karma.conf.js
// Karma configuration

module.exports = function(config) {
  config.set({
    // base path that will be used to resolve files and exclude
    basePath: '',

    // testing framework to use (jasmine/mocha/qunit/...)
    frameworks: ['jasmine'],

    // list of files / patterns to load in the browser
    files: [
      'angular.min.js',
      'angular-mocks.js',
      'controller.js',
      'simpleSpec.js',
      'controllerSpec.js'
```

```
        ],

        // list of files / patterns to exclude
        exclude: [],

        // web server port
        port: 8080,

        // level of logging
        // possible values: LOG_DISABLE || LOG_ERROR ||
        //                  LOG_WARN || LOG_INFO || LOG_DEBUG
        logLevel: config.LOG_INFO,


        // enable / disable watching file and executing tests
        // whenever any file changes
        autoWatch: true,

        // Start these browsers, currently available:
        // - Chrome
        // - ChromeCanary
        // - Firefox
        // - Opera
        // - Safari (only Mac)
        // - PhantomJS
        // - IE (only Windows)
        browsers: ['Chrome'],


        // Continuous Integration mode
        // if true, it captures browsers, runs tests, and exits
        singleRun: false
    });
};
```

Let's take a look at each of the options in the preceding example, to see what effect they have on Karma:

basePath
> The base path from which all files for testing and the tests themselves need to be loaded. This is set relative to the location of the Karma config file.

frameworks
> Which frameworks to load, as an array. In our example, we loaded Jasmine (which requires that the karma-jasmine plugin be installed). You can select mocha, qunit, or something else as well here.

files
> The list of files (or file paths) to load, listed as an array. In the case of AngularJS, we first load the AngularJS library, and then the *angular-mocks.js* file, which AngularJS

provides as a helper for testing. Finally, we load the application source code followed by the actual unit tests.

exclude

A list of files (or file paths) to exclude. Useful if you are using a lot of glob rules (wildcard statements to include a set of files, like `**.js`) for the files, and want to exclude certain files (like the *karma.conf.js*).

port

This specifies which port the Karma test runner server runs on. By default, it is `8080`.

logLevel

Which levels of log (`console.log`, `console.info`) Karma needs to capture from the browser.

autoWatch

This is by far the coolest and most useful feature of Karma. This tells Karma to keep a watch on all the files included by the `files` config, and if any of them change, to run the affected unit tests. If this is set to `true`, you don't need to ever manually trigger a run of your unit tests; Karma will take care of that for you.

browsers

The browsers Karma should open when it is initially started. Most of these require a `karma-launcher` plugin (we installed the `chrome-launcher`, so we specify Chrome in this).

singleRun

This is a Boolean value, and tells Karma to shut down the server after one single run of the unit tests. This should be set to `true` for continuous integration environments, and can be ignored otherwise.

There are a lot more configurations that you can set and modify with Karma, but we won't get into that in this book. You can read about them at the Karma Configuration File Overview page (*http://bit.ly/1nySvJX*).

Generating the Karma Config

Now, you can of course copy and paste the contents of the config file from the previous section to get started, but Karma offers a much nicer way to get started with your own Karma config. Karma lets you autogenerate the config by running the following command:

```
karma init
```

This triggers an interactive shell, which prompts us with a series of questions. Each answer usually has a series of options that you can cycle through by using Tab on your keyboard. After we select all our options, the *karma.conf.js* file is generated for us.

Jasmine: Spec Style of Testing

In the previous section, we saw the test runner that we will use to run the unit tests we write for AngularJS. But the actual testing framework that we will use for the purpose of this book is Jasmine (*http://jasmine.github.io/*). The Jasmine framework uses what we call a behavior-driven style of writing tests.

That is, instead of writing a bunch of functions and asserts, we describe behaviors and set expectations. How does this translate into actual tests? Let's take a deeper look.

Jasmine Syntax

Before we jump down into Jasmine syntax and talk about the various concepts of a Jasmine test, let's take an example to make things clearer:

```
// A test suite in Jasmine
describe('My Function', function() {

  var t;
  // Similar to setup
  beforeEach(function() {
    t = true;
  });

  afterEach(function() {
    t = null;
  });

  it('should perform action 1', function() {
    expect(t).toBeTruthy();
  });
  it('should perform action 2', function() {
    var expectedValue = true;
    expect(t).toEqual(expectedValue);
  });
});
```

Let's go through the example one piece at a time:

describe

The very first line of our test creates a test suite of sorts. Think of it as a container for multiple unit tests. You would write a describe for a controller, for a service, and so on. You can also nest describes within a describe, in case you want a describe for a complex function inside a controller.

beforeEach

A beforeEach is similar to a setup function in the xUnit testing pattern. That is, the function you pass to beforeEach will be executed before each individual it block. In this case, the t = true; line will execute once before each of the it blocks in the `describe`. You can also have multiple `beforeEach` functions inside a `describe`, and they will each be executed once in the order in which they are declared.

afterEach

Similar to the `beforeEach`, the `afterEach` block gets executed after the individual `it` blocks are completed. If you use mocking libraries, this is the best place to check whether or not any expectations set on the mocks are satisfied.

it

These are the unit tests. Each `it` block should be self-contained, and independent of all the other `it` blocks. Inside the `it`, you would basically set up your state, execute the function, check its return value, and ensure that all expectations are met.

expect

These are the Jasmine equivalents of `assert` statements. Each `expect` takes a value, and then you can use one of the built-in matchers (or create your own) to check its value. In the preceding example, we use the Jasmine matcher `toBeTruthy`, which states that the value should match the JavaScript concept of truthy (nonnull, non-empty string, nonzero number, or Boolean `true`). In the second `it` block, we use the `toEqual` matcher, which takes another value and compares it with the first value for equality.

Useful Jasmine Matchers

Let's quickly run through some basic built-in Jasmine matchers that we use in the tests. All of these are used along with `expect`; that is, `expect(value).myMatcherHere`:

toEqual

The most basic of Jasmine matchers, the `toEqual` takes a second value and does a deep equality check between the two objects. In the case of an object, all the fields have to match. In the case of an array, all the array elements have to match.

toBe

The `toBe` matcher checks for reference, and expects both items passed to the `expect` and the matcher to be the exact same object reference.

toBeTruthy

Checks the value passed to the matcher to pass the JavaScript concept of `true`. Nonnull objects, nonempty strings, nonzero numbers, and the Boolean `true` all evaluate to be truthy in JavaScript.

toBeFalsy

Checks the value passed to the matcher to pass the JavaScript concept of `false`. Null values, undefined variables, empty strings, zero, and false all evaluate to be falsy in JavaScript.

toBeDefined

Ensures the reference passed to the `expect` is defined (a value is assigned to the reference, that is).

toBeUndefined

Checks if the reference passed to the `expect` is undefined or not set.

toBeNull

Checks if the reference passed to the `expect` is null.

toContain

Checks if the array passed to the `expect` contains the element passed to the matcher, `toContain`.

toMatch

Used for regular expression checks when the first argument to the `expect` is a string that needs to match a specific regular expression pattern.

We will be using some or all of these throughout this book. Of course, Jasmine is extensible, and allows you to write your own custom matchers as well. You can read all about it at the Jasmine Matcher page (*http://bit.ly/1pNj7LY*).

Writing a Unit Test for Our Controller

Now, with both Karma (our test runner) and Jasmine (our test framework) in place, let's see how we can write tests for the controllers we create in AngularJS. Let's take a very simple controller, something similar to what we saw in Chapter 2:

```
// File: chapter3/controller.js
angular.module('notesApp', [])
  .controller('ListCtrl', [function() {

    var self = this;
    self.items = [
      {id: 1, label: 'First', done: true},
      {id: 2, label: 'Second', done: false}
    ];

    self.getDoneClass = function(item) {
      return {
        finished: item.done,
        unfinished: !item.done
      };
    };
  }]);
```

We have a very simplistic controller in the preceding example. All it does is assign an array to its instance (to make it available to the HTML), and then has a function to figure out the presentation logic, which returns the classes to apply based on the item's done state. Given this controller, let's take a look at how a Jasmine spec for this might look:

```
// File: chapter3/controllerSpec.js
describe('Controller: ListCtrl', function() {
  // Instantiate a new version of my module before each test
  beforeEach(module('notesApp'));

  var ctrl;

  // Before each unit test, instantiate a new instance
  // of the controller
  beforeEach(inject(function($controller) {
    ctrl = $controller('ListCtrl');
  }));

  it('should have items available on load', function() {
    expect(ctrl.items).toEqual([
      {id: 1, label: 'First', done: true},
      {id: 2, label: 'Second', done: false}
    ]);
  });

  it('should have highlight items based on state', function() {
    var item = {id: 1, label: 'First', done: true};

    var actualClass = ctrl.getDoneClass(item);
    expect(actualClass.finished).toBeTruthy();
    expect(actualClass.unfinished).toBeFalsy();

    item.done = false;
    actualClass = ctrl.getDoneClass(item);
    expect(actualClass.finished).toBeFalsy();
    expect(actualClass.unfinished).toBeTruthy();
  });

});
```

In this example, we look at two specific unit tests for the ListCtrl controller. Let's take a look at each interesting bit one by one:

Instantiating a module

The very first thing we do as a part of our describe block for the ListCtrl is instantiate a new instance of the AngularJS module notesApp. This has the effect of freshly loading all the controllers, services, directives, and filters associated with that module before each specific unit test. The advantage of this is that the state you set up and modify in one unit test cannot affect another. Each unit test essentially becomes independent and contained. This module function is one of the helper methods that the *angular-mocks.js* AngularJS library file provides, as well as many others.

Injecting services

We then have a variable called ctrl, which will hold a controller instance across each of the unit tests. The beforeEach block after that uses something called in ject, which basically injects AngularJS services into the functions that befor eEach and it in Jasmine take. We will look into AngularJS services in Chapter 5, but just know that there is an AngularJS service called $controller that we can use to instantiate new instances of our controller. The function passed to inject can take multiple arguments, each of which is an AngularJS service that AngularJS then creates and injects into the function.

Creating our controller instance

We use the $controller service to create an instance of our ListCtrl. We do this by simply passing in the name of the controller as a string to the $controller service, and get back a new instance of the controller. We then assign this to the ctrl variable, which we will use in each individual test.

Writing a test for the constructor

Whatever we define in our controller function gets executed when the controller is instantiated. The only things we do in our controller function is set up the items array and the function. So the first it block tests the state of the items array to see if it is instantiated correctly with the right values. It uses the Jasmine toEqual matcher to check if the items array is exactly the same as what we specify.

Writing a test for the getDoneClass *function*

The last test we write is to check the getDoneClass function defined on the controller instance. We do this by instantiating some local state for the test (the item object), and then pass that to the getDoneClass function on the controller and store its return value. Next, we check for the truthiness and falsiness of the two classes on it, finished and unfinished. We then change the state of item from done to not done (by setting it to false), and then check if the function changes its return value correspondingly.

The order of execution in the previous example is as follows:

1. The beforeEach that loads the AngularJS module executes.

2. The beforeEach that creates our controller executes.

3. The it for the "items on load" executes.

4. The beforeEach that loads the AngularJS module executes.

5. The beforeEach that creates our controller executes.

6. The it for the getDoneClass executes.

Thus each unit test gets a clean slate when it executes, and ensures that modifications and state changes in one unit test don't affect the other.

Running the Unit Test

How do we actually run these unit tests? That is the simplest part—just execute the following command from the command line/terminal/console:

```
karma start
```

The command automatically looks for the *karma.conf.js* file in the directory you are executing the command from, and picks up the config from it. In case your config file is not named *karma.conf.js*, or if it is in a different folder, you can optionally pass it in as an argument to the command. That is:

```
karma start my.conf.js
```

This is not needed in our example.

Both of these will read the config file, grab the files that are under test, start a server on the port specified, and then try to open the browsers listed in the config (provided the launcher plugins for them are installed).

> The examples and tests in this book were run using version 0.12.16 of Karma, and version 1.2.19 of AngularJS (both the *angular.js* and *angular-mocks.js* files). If you are having trouble running them for any reason, make sure that you are using the same version.

The `karma` command starts a test server that is used for serving the test files. Each browser that you open and connect to the server gets a *green bar* at the top to signal that it is ready to run the tests. If you have not selected any browsers in the configuration, or there are some problems capturing the browsers automatically, you can still capture any browser manually (on any machine) by opening the URL specified in the browser.

The *results of the test* are printed in the console/command window from which the `karma start` command was executed. The captured browsers themselves do not print the results. This is because the browsers that are executing the test might be on a different machine altogether. We should see something like Figure 3-1 in the console/command window after a successful run.

```
Shyam-Seshadris-MacBook-Pro:chapter3 shyamseshadri$ karma start
INFO [karma]: Karma v0.12.16 server started at http://localhost:8080/
INFO [launcher]: Starting browser Chrome
INFO [Chrome 38.0.2096 (Mac OS X 10.9.4)]: Connected on socket ThBIJoGmk4SFpyMpB
SSv with id 71340095
Chrome 38.0.2096 (Mac OS X 10.9.4): Executed 1 of 4 SUCCESS (0 secs / 0.006 secs
Chrome 38.0.2096 (Mac OS X 10.9.4): Executed 2 of 4 SUCCESS (0 secs / 0.008 secs
Chrome 38.0.2096 (Mac OS X 10.9.4): Executed 3 of 4 SUCCESS (0 secs / 0.022 secs
Chrome 38.0.2096 (Mac OS X 10.9.4): Executed 4 of 4 SUCCESS (0 secs / 0.028 secs
Chrome 38.0.2096 (Mac OS X 10.9.4): Executed 4 of 4 SUCCESS (0.033 secs / 0.028
secs)
```

Figure 3-1. Test results for a Karma run

Now if you have autoWatch set to true in your configuration, Karma will automatically trigger a test run in all the browsers you have captured every time any of the files under test change. If you don't have autoWatch set to true, you can manually trigger a test run by executing the following command from the console/terminal:

```
karma run
```

This tells Karma to execute tests for the currently active server configuration, again based on the configuration.

Conclusion

We generated a Karma configuration, and then wrote our very first AngularJS unit test. In our unit test, we instantiated an instance of the controller using the $controller service, and leveraged Jasmine to set expectations on our controller.

One thing to note and remember is that Dependency Injection, which is heavily used throughout AngularJS, is something we leveraged in our unit tests as well. We did not need to worry about what the controller is, what it depends on, or how to instantiate it. AngularJS took care of that for us. This would be something that would continue for all the other unit tests we will write for the rest of the book.

In the next chapter, we will see how to do two-way data-binding and work with forms in AngularJS. We will also cover form validation and error handling with forms.

CHAPTER 4

Forms, Inputs, and Services

In the previous chapters, we first covered the most basic AngularJS directives and dealt with creating controllers and getting our data from the controllers into the UI. We then looked at how to write tests for the same, using Karma and Jasmine. In this chapter, we will build on the work from Chapter 2 and work on getting the user's data out of forms in the UI into our controller so that we can then send it to the server, validate it, or do whatever else we might need to.

We will then get into using AngularJS services, and see how we can leverage some of the common existing services as well as create our own. We will also briefly cover when and why you should create AngularJS services.

Working with ng-model

In the previous chapter, we saw the `ng-bind` directive, or its equivalent double-curly `{{ }}` notation, which allowed us to take the data from our controllers and display it in the UI. That gives us our one-way data-binding, which is powerful in its own regard. But most applications we develop also have user interaction, and parts where the user has to feed in data. From registration forms to profile information, forms are a staple of web applications, and AngularJS provides the `ng-model` directive for us to deal with inputs and two-way data-binding:

```
<!-- File: chapter4/simple-ng-model.html -->
<html ng-app="notesApp">
<head><title>Notes App</title></head>
<body ng-controller="MainCtrl as ctrl">

  <input type="text" ng-model="ctrl.username"/>
  You typed {{ctrl.username}}

<script
  src="https://ajax.googleapis.com/ajax/libs/angularjs/1.2.19/angular.js">
```

```
    </script>
    <script type="text/javascript">
      angular.module('notesApp', [])
        .controller('MainCtrl', [function() {
          this.username = 'nothing';
        }]);
    </script>
    </body>
    </html>
```

In this example, we define a controller with a variable exposed on its instance called username. Now, we get its value out into the HTML using the ng-controller and the double-curly syntax for one-way data-binding. What we have introduced in addition is an input element. It is a plain text box, but on it we have attached the ng-model directive. We pointed the value for the ng-model at the same username variable on the MainCtrl. This accomplishes the following things:

- When the HTML is instantiated and the controller is attached, it gets the current value (in this case, *nothing* as a string) and displays it in our UI.

- When the user types, updates, or changes the value in the input box, it updates the model in our controller.

- When the value of the variable changes in the controller (whether because it came from the server, or due to some internal state change), the input field gets the value updated automatically.

The beauty of this is twofold:

- If we need to update the form element in the UI, all we need to do is update the value in the controller. No need to go looking for input fields by IDs or CSS class selectors; just update the model.

- If we need to get the latest value that the user entered into the form or input to validate or send to the server, we just need to grab it from our controller. It will have the latest value in it.

Now let's add some complexity, and actually deal with forms. Let's see if we can bring this concept together with an example:

```
<!-- File: chapter4/simple-ng-model-2.html -->
<html ng-app="notesApp">
<head><title>Notes App</title></head>
<body ng-controller="MainCtrl as ctrl">

  <input type="text" ng-model="ctrl.username">
  <input type="password" ng-model="ctrl.password">
  <button ng-click="ctrl.change()">Change Values</button>
  <button ng-click="ctrl.submit()">Submit</button>
```

```
<script
  src="https://ajax.googleapis.com/ajax/libs/angularjs/1.2.19/angular.js">
</script>
<script type="text/javascript">
  angular.module('notesApp', [])
    .controller('MainCtrl', [function() {
      var self = this;
      self.change = function() {
        self.username = 'changed';
        self.password = 'password';
      };
      self.submit = function() {
        console.log('User clicked submit with ',
            self.username, self.password);
      };
    }]);
</script>
</body>
</html>
```

We introduced one more input field, which is bound to a field called `password` on the controller's instance. And we added two buttons:

- The first button, Change Values, is to simulate the server sending some data that needs to be updated in the UI. All it does is reassign the values to the username and password fields in the controller with the latest values.

- The second button, Submit, simulates submitting the form to the server. All it does for now is log the value to the console.

The most important thing in both of these is that the controller never reached out into the UI. There was no jQuery selector, no `findElementById`, or anything like that. When we need to update the UI, we just update the model fields in the controller. When we need to get the latest and greatest value, we just grab it from the controller. Again, this is the AngularJS way.

Let's now build on this, and see how we can integrate and work with forms in AngularJS.

Working with Forms

When we work with forms in AngularJS, we heavily leverage the `ng-model` directive to get our data into and out of the form. In addition to the data-binding, it is also recommended to structure your model and bindings in such a way to reduce your own effort, as well as the lines of code you write. Let's take a look at an example:

```
<!-- File: chapter4/simple-form.html -->
<html ng-app="notesApp">
<head><title>Notes App</title></head>
<body ng-controller="MainCtrl as ctrl">
```

```
<form ng-submit="ctrl.submit()">
  <input type="text" ng-model="ctrl.user.username">
  <input type="password" ng-model="ctrl.user.password">
  <input type="submit" value="Submit">
</form>

<script
  src="https://ajax.googleapis.com/ajax/libs/angularjs/1.2.19/angular.js">
</script>
<script type="text/javascript">
  angular.module('notesApp', [])
    .controller('MainCtrl', [function() {
      var self = this;
      self.submit = function() {
        console.log('User clicked submit with ', self.user);
      };
    }]);
</script>
</body>
</html>
```

We are still using the same two input fields as last time, but we made a few changes:

- We wrapped our text fields and button inside a form. And instead of an `ng-click` on the button, we added an `ng-submit` directive on the form itself. The `ng-submit` directive has a few advantages over having an `ng-click` on a button when it comes to forms. A form submit event can be triggered in multiple ways: clicking the Submit button, or hitting Enter on a text field. The `ng-submit` gets triggered on all those events, whereas the `ng-click` will only be triggered when the user clicks the button.

- Instead of binding to `ctrl.username` and `ctrl.password`, we bind to `ctrl.user.username` and `ctrl.user.password`. Notice that we did not declare a user object in the controller (that is, `self.user = {}`). When you use `ng-model`, AngularJS automatically creates the objects and keys necessary in the chain to instantiate a data-binding connection. In this case, until the user types something into the username or password field, there is no user object. The first letter typed into either the username or password field causes the user object to be created, and the value to be assigned to the correct field in it.

Leverage Data-Binding and Models

When designing your forms and deciding which fields to bind the `ng-model` to, you should always consider what format you need the data in. Let's take the following example to demonstrate:

```
<!-- File: chapter4/two-forms-databinding.html -->
<html ng-app="notesApp">
<head><title>Notes App</title></head>
<body ng-controller="MainCtrl as ctrl">

  <form ng-submit="ctrl.submit1()">
    <input type="text" ng-model="ctrl.username">
    <input type="password" ng-model="ctrl.password">
    <input type="submit" value="Submit">
  </form>

  <form ng-submit="ctrl.submit2()">
    <input type="text" ng-model="ctrl.user.username">
    <input type="password" ng-model="ctrl.user.password">
    <input type="submit" value="Submit">
  </form>

<script
  src="https://ajax.googleapis.com/ajax/libs/angularjs/1.2.19/angular.js">
</script>
<script type="text/javascript">
  angular.module('notesApp', [])
    .controller('MainCtrl', [function() {
      var self = this;
      self.submit1 = function() {
        // Create user object to send to the server
        var user = {username: self.username, password: self.password};
        console.log('First form submit with ', user);
      };
      self.submit2 = function() {
        console.log('Second form submit with ', self.user);
      };
    }]);
</script>
</body>
</html>
```

There are two forms in this example, both with the same fields. The first form is bound
to a username and password directly on the controller, while the second form is bound
to a username and password key on a user object in the controller. Both of them trigger
an ng-submit function on submission of a function. Now in the case of the first form,
we have to take those fields from the controller and put them into an object, or something
similar, before we can send it to the server. In the second case, we can directly take the
user object from the controller and pass it around.

The second flow makes more sense, because we are directly modeling how we want to
represent the form as an object in the controller. This removes any additional work we
might have to do when we work with the values of the form.

Form Validation and States

We have seen how to create forms, and enable (and leverage) data-binding to get our data in and out of the UI. Now let's proceed to see how else AngularJS can benefit us when working with forms, and especially with validation and various states of the forms and inputs:

```
<!-- File: chapter4/form-validation.html -->
<html ng-app="notesApp">
<head><title>Notes App</title></head>
<body ng-controller="MainCtrl as ctrl">

  <form ng-submit="ctrl.submit()" name="myForm">
    <input type="text"
           ng-model="ctrl.user.username"
           required
           ng-minlength="4">
    <input type="password"
           ng-model="ctrl.user.password"
           required>
    <input type="submit"
           value="Submit"
           ng-disabled="myForm.$invalid">
  </form>

<script
  src="https://ajax.googleapis.com/ajax/libs/angularjs/1.2.19/angular.js">
</script>
<script type="text/javascript">
  angular.module('notesApp', [])
    .controller('MainCtrl', [function() {
      var self = this;
      self.submit = function() {
        console.log('User clicked submit with ', self.user);
      };
    }]);
</script>
</body>
</html>
```

In this example, we reworked our old example to add some validation. In particular, we want to disable the Submit button if the user has not filled out all the required fields. How do we accomplish this?

1. We give the form a name, which we can refer to later. In this case, it is myForm.

2. We leverage HTML5 validation tags and add the required attribute on each input field.

3. We add a validator, ng-minlength, which enforces that the minimum length of the value in the input field for the username is four characters.

4. On the Submit button, we add an `ng-disabled` directive. This disables the element if the condition is true.

5. For the `disable` condition, we leverage the form, which exposes a controller with the current state of the form. In this case, we tell the button to disable itself if the form with the name `myForm` is `$invalid`.

When you use forms (and give them names), AngularJS creates a `FormController` that holds the current state of the form as well as some helper methods. You can access the `FormController` for a form using the form's name, as we did in the preceding example using `myForm`. Things that are exposed as the state and kept up to date with data-binding are shown in Table 4-1.

Table 4-1. Form states in AngularJS

Form state	Description
`$invalid`	AngularJS sets this state when any of the validations (`required`, `ng-minlength`, and others) mark any of the fields within the form as invalid.
`$valid`	The inverse of the previous state, which states that all the validations in the form are currently evaluating to correct.
`$pristine`	All forms in AngularJS start with this state. This allows you to figure out if a user has started typing in and modifying any of the form elements. Possible usage: disabling the reset button if a form is pristine.
`$dirty`	The inverse of `$pristine`, which states that the user made some changes (he can revert it, but the `$dirty` bit is set).
`$error`	This field on the form houses all the individual fields and the errors on each form element. We will talk more about this in the following section.

Each of the states mentioned in the table (except `$error`) are Booleans and can be used to conditionally hide, show, disable, or enable HTML elements in the UI. As the user types or modifies the form, the values are updated as long as you are leveraging `ng-model` and the form name.

Error Handling with Forms

We looked at the types of validation you can do at a form level, but what about individual fields? In our previous example, we ensured that both input fields were required fields, and that the minimum length on the username was four. What else can we do? Table 4-2 contains some built-in validations that AngularJS offers.

Table 4-2. Built-in AngularJS validators

Validator	Description
`required`	As previously discussed, this ensures that the field is required, and the field is marked invalid until it is filled out.
`ng-required`	Unlike `required`, which marks a field as always required, the `ng-required` directive allows us to conditionally mark an input field as required based on a Boolean condition in the controller.
`ng-minlength`	We can set the minimum length of the value in the input field with this directive.
`ng-maxlength`	We can set the maximum length of the value in the input field with this directive.
`ng-pattern`	The validity of an input field can be checked against the regular expression pattern specified as part of this directive.
`type="email"`	Text input with built-in email validation.
`type="number"`	Text input with number validation. Can also have additional attributes for min and max values of the number itself.
`type="date"`	If the browser supports it, shows an HTML datepicker. Otherwise, defaults to a text input. The `ng-model` that this binds to will be a `date` object. This expects the date to be in yyyy-mm-dd format (e.g., 2009-10-24).
`type="url"`	Text input with URL validation.

In addition to this, we can write our own validators, which we cover in Chapter 13.

Displaying Error Messages

What can we do with all these validators? We can of course check the validity of the form, and disable the Save or Update button accordingly. But we also want to tell the user what went wrong and how to fix it. AngularJS offers two things to solve this problem:

- A model that reflects what exactly is wrong in the form, which we can use to display nicer error messages
- CSS classes automatically added and removed from each of these fields allow us to highlight problems in the form

Let's first take a look at how to display specific error messages based on the problem with the following example:

```
<!-- File: chapter4/form-error-messages.html -->
<html ng-app="notesApp">
<head><title>Notes App</title></head>
<body ng-controller="MainCtrl as ctrl">

  <form ng-submit="ctrl.submit()" name="myForm">
    <input type="text"
           name="uname"
           ng-model="ctrl.user.username"
```

```
              required
              ng-minlength="4">
      <span ng-show="myForm.uname.$error.required">
        This is a required field
      </span>
      <span ng-show="myForm.uname.$error.minlength">
        Minimum length required is 4
      </span>
      <span ng-show="myForm.uname.$invalid">
        This field is invalid
      </span>
      <input type="password"
             name="pwd"
             ng-model="ctrl.user.password"
             required>
      <span ng-show="myForm.pwd.$error.required">
        This is a required field
      </span>
      <input type="submit"
             value="Submit"
             ng-disabled="myForm.$invalid">
    </form>

  <script
    src="https://ajax.googleapis.com/ajax/libs/angularjs/1.2.19/angular.js">
  </script>
  <script type="text/javascript">
    angular.module('notesApp', [])
      .controller('MainCtrl', [function () {
        var self = this;
        self.submit = function () {
          console.log('User clicked submit with ', self.user);
        };
      }]);
  </script>
  </body>
  </html>
```

Nothing in the controller has changed in this example. Instead, we can just focus on the form HTML. Let's see what changed with the form:

1. First, we added the name attribute to both the input fields where we needed validation: uname for the username box, and pwd for the password text field.

2. Then we leverage AngularJS's form bindings to be able to pick out the errors for each individual field. When we add a name to any input, it creates a model on the form for that particular input, with the error state.

3. So for the username field, we can access it if the field was not entered by accessing myForm.uname.$error.required. Similarly, for ng-minlength, the field would be

`myForm.uname.$error.minlength`. For the password, we look at `myForm.pwd.$er ror.required` to see if the field was filled out or not.

4. We also accessed the state of the input, similar to the form, by accessing `myForm.un ame.$invalid`. All the other form states (`$valid`, `$pristine`, `$dirty`) we saw earlier are also available similarly on `myForm.uname`.

With this, we now have an error message that shows only when a certain type of error is triggered. Each of the validators we saw in Table 4-2 exposes a key on the `$error` object, so that we can pick it up and display the error message for that particular error to the user. Need to show the user that a field is required? Then when the user starts typing, show the minimum length, and then finally show a message when he exceeds the maximum length. All these kinds of conditional messages can be shown with the AngularJS validators.

Styling Forms and States

We saw the various states of the forms (and the inputs): `$dirty`, `$valid`, and so on. We saw how to display specific error messages and disable buttons based on these conditions, but what if we want to highlight certain input fields or form states using UI and CSS? One option would be to use the form and input states along with the `ng-class` directive to, say, add a class `dirty` when `myForm.$dirty` is true. But AngularJS provides an easier option.

For each of the states we described previously, AngularJS adds and removes the CSS classes shown in Table 4-3 to and from the forms and input elements.

Table 4-3. Form state CSS classes

Form state	CSS class applied
$invalid	ng-invalid
$valid	ng-valid
$pristine	ng-pristine
$dirty	ng-dirty

Similarly, for each of the validators that we add on the input fields, we also get a CSS class in a similarly named fashion, as demonstrated in Table 4-4.

Table 4-4. Input state CSS classes

Input state	CSS class applied
$invalid	ng-invalid
$valid	ng-valid
$pristine	ng-pristine
$dirty	ng-dirty

Input state	CSS class applied
required	ng-valid-required or ng-invalid-required
min	ng-valid-min or ng-invalid-min
max	ng-valid-max or ng-invalid-max
minlength	ng-valid-minlength or ng-invalid-minlength
maxlength	ng-valid-maxlength or ng-invalid-maxlength
pattern	ng-valid-pattern or ng-invalid-pattern
url	ng-valid-url or ng-invalid-url
email	ng-valid-email or ng-invalid-email
date	ng-valid-date or ng-invalid-date
number	ng-valid-number or ng-invalid-number

Other than the basic input states, AngularJS takes the name of the validator (number, maxlength, pattern, etc.) and depending on whether or not that particular validator has been satisfied, adds the ng-valid-validator_name or ng-invalid-validator_name class, respectively.

Let's take an example of how this might be used to highlight the input in different ways:

```
<!-- File: chapter4/form-styling.html -->
<html ng-app="notesApp">
<head>
  <title>Notes App</title>
  <style>
    .username.ng-valid {
      background-color: green;
    }
    .username.ng-dirty.ng-invalid-required {
      background-color: red;
    }
    .username.ng-dirty.ng-invalid-minlength {
      background-color: lightpink;
    }
  </style>
</head>
<body ng-controller="MainCtrl as ctrl">

  <form ng-submit="ctrl.submit()" name="myForm">
    <input type="text"
           class="username"
           name="uname"
           ng-model="ctrl.user.username"
           required
           ng-minlength="4">
    <input type="submit"
           value="Submit"
           ng-disabled="myForm.$invalid">
```

```
    </form>

<script
  src="https://ajax.googleapis.com/ajax/libs/angularjs/1.2.19/angular.js">
</script>
<script type="text/javascript">
  angular.module('notesApp', [])
    .controller('MainCtrl', [function() {
      var self = this;
      self.submit = function() {
        console.log('User clicked submit with ', self.user);
      };
    }]);
</script>
</body>
</html>
```

In this example, we kept the existing functionality of the validators, though we removed the specific error messages. Instead, what we try to do is mark out the required field using CSS classes. So here is what the example accomplishes:

- When the field is correctly filled out, it turns the input box green. This is done by setting the background color when the CSS class ng-valid is applied to our input field.

- We want to display the background as dark red if the user starts typing in, and then undoes it. That is, we want to set the background as red, marking it as a required field, but only after the user modifies the field. So we set the background color to be red if the CSS classes ng-dirty (which marks that the user has modified it) and ng-invalid-minlength (which marks that the user has not typed in the necessary amount of characters) are applied.

Similarly, you could add a CSS class that shows a * mark in red if the field is required but not dirty. Using a combination of these CSS classes (and the form and input states) from before, you can easily style and display all the relevant and actionable things to the user about your form.

Nested Forms with ng-form

By this point, we know how to create forms and get data into and out of our controllers (by binding it to a model). We have also seen how to perform simple validation, and style and display conditional error messages in AngularJS.

The next part that we want to cover is how to deal with more complicated form structures, and grouping of elements. We sometimes run into cases where we need subsections of our form to be valid as a group, and to check and ascertain its validity. This is not possible with the HTML form tag because form tags are not meant to be nested.

AngularJS provides an ng-form directive, which acts similar to form but allows nesting, so that we can accomplish the requirement of grouping related form fields under sections:

```html
<!-- File: chapter4/nested-forms.html -->
<html ng-app>
<head>
  <title>Notes App</title>
</head>

<body>
  <form novalidate name="myForm">
    <input type="text"
           class="username"
           name="uname"
           ng-model="ctrl.user.username"
           required=""
           placeholder="Username"
           ng-minlength="4" />
    <input type="password"
           class="password"
           name="pwd"
           ng-model="ctrl.user.password"
           placeholder="Password"
           required="" />


    <ng-form name="profile">
      <input type="text"
             name="firstName"
             ng-model="ctrl.user.profile.firstName"
             placeholder="First Name"
             required>
      <input type="text"
             name="middleName"
             placeholder="Middle Name"
             ng-model="ctrl.user.profile.middleName">
      <input type="text"
             name="lastName"
             placeholder="Last Name"
             ng-model="ctrl.user.profile.lastName"
             required>
      <input type="date"
             name="dob"
             placeholder="Date Of Birth"
             ng-model="ctrl.user.profile.dob">
    </ng-form>

    <span ng-show="myForm.profile.$invalid">
        Please fill out the profile information
      </span>
```

```
    <input type="submit"
           value="Submit"
           ng-disabled="myForm.$invalid"/>
  </form>

<script
    src="https://ajax.googleapis.com/ajax/libs/angularjs/1.2.19/angular.js">
</script>
</body>

</html>
```

In this example, we nest a subform inside our main form, but because the HTML form element cannot be nested, we use the `ng-form` directive to do it. Now we can have substate within our form, evaluate quickly if each section is valid, and leverage the same binding and form states that we have looked at so far. A quick highlight of the features in the example:

- A subform using the `ng-form` directive. We can give this a name to identify and grab the state of the subform.

- The state of the subform can be accessed directly (`profile.$invalid`) or through the parent form (`myForm.profile.$invalid`).

- Individual elements of the form can be accessed as normal (`profile.firstName.$error.required`).

- Subforms and nested forms still affect the outer form (the `myForm.$invalid` is `true` because of the use of the required tags).

You could have subforms and groupings that have their own way of checking and deciding validity, and `ng-form` allows you to model that grouping in your HTML.

Other Form Controls

We have dealt with forms, `ng-models`, and bindings, but mostly we have only looked at regular text boxes. Let's see how to interact and work with other form elements in AngularJS.

Textareas

Textareas in AngularJS work exactly the same as text inputs. That is, to have two-way data-binding with a textarea, and make it a required field, you would do something like:

```
<textarea ng-model="ctrl.user.address" required></textarea>
```

All the data-binding, error states, and CSS classes remain as we saw it with text inputs.

Checkboxes

Checkboxes are in some ways easier to deal with because they can only have one of two values: true or false. So an `ng-model` two-way data-binding to the checkbox basically takes a Boolean value and assigns the checked state based on it. After that, any changes to the checkbox toggles the state of the model:

```
<input type="checkbox" ng-model="ctrl.user.agree">
```

But what if we didn't have just Boolean values? What if we wanted to assign the string YES or NO to our model, or have the checkbox checked when the value is YES? AngularJS gives two attribute arguments to the checkbox that allow us to specify our custom values for the true and false values. We could accomplish this as follows:

```
<input type="checkbox"
        ng-model="ctrl.user.agree"
        ng-true-value="YES"
        ng-false-value="NO">
```

This sets the value of the `agree` field to YES if the user checks the checkbox, and NO if the user unchecks it.

But what if we didn't want the two-way data-binding, and just want to use the checkbox to display the current value of a Boolean? That is, one-way data-binding where the state of the checkbox changes when the value behind it changes, but the value doesn't change on checking or unchecking the checkbox.

We can accomplish this using the `ng-checked` directive, which binds to an AngularJS expression. Whenever the value is true, AngularJS will set the checked property for the input element, and remove and unset it when the value is false. Let's use the following example to demonstrate all these together:

```
<!-- File: chapter4/checkbox-example.html -->
<html ng-app="notesApp">
<head><title>Notes App</title></head>
<body ng-controller="MainCtrl as ctrl">
  <div>
    <h2>What are your favorite sports?</h2>
    <div ng-repeat="sport in ctrl.sports">
      <label ng-bind="sport.label"></label>
      <div>
        With Binding:
        <input type="checkbox"
               ng-model="sport.selected"
               ng-true-value="YES"
               ng-false-value="NO">
      </div>
      <div>
        Using ng-checked:
        <input type="checkbox"
               ng-checked="sport.selected === 'YES'">
```

```
      </div>
      <div>
        Current state: {{sport.selected}}
      </div>
    </div>
  </div>

<script
  src="https://ajax.googleapis.com/ajax/libs/angularjs/1.2.19/angular.js">
</script>
<script type="text/javascript">
  angular.module('notesApp', [])
    .controller('MainCtrl', [function() {
      var self = this;
        self.sports = [
          {label: 'Basketball', selected: 'YES'},
          {label: 'Cricket', selected: 'NO'},
          {label: 'Soccer', selected: 'NO'},
          {label: 'Swimming', selected: 'YES'}
        ];
    }]);
</script>
</body>
</html>
```

With this example, we have an ng-repeat, which has a checkbox with ng-model, a checkbox with ng-checked, and a div with the current state bound to it. The first checkbox uses the traditional two-way data-binding with the ng-model directive. The second checkbox uses ng-checked. This means that:

- When the user checks the first checkbox, the value of selected becomes YES because the true value, set using ng-true-value, is YES. This triggers the ng-checked and sets the second box as checked (or unchecked).

- When the user unchecks the first box, the value of selected is set to NO because of the ng-false-value.

- The second checkbox in each repeater element displays the state of the ng-model using ng-checked. This updates the state of the checkbox whenever the model backing ng-model changes. Checking or unchecking the second checkbox itself has no effect on the value of the model.

So if you need two-way data-binding, use ng-model. If you need one-way data-binding with checkboxes, use ng-checked.

Radio Buttons

Radio buttons behave similarly to checkboxes, but are slightly different. You can have multiple radio buttons (and you normally do) that each assigns a different value to a model depending on which one is selected. You can specify the value using the traditional value attribute of the input element. Let's see how that would look:

```
<div ng-init="user = {gender: 'female'}">
    <input type="radio"
           name="gender"
           ng-model="user.gender"
           value="male">
    <input type="radio"
           name="gender"
           ng-model="user.gender"
           value="female">
</div>
```

In this example, we have two radio buttons. We gave them both the same name so that when one is selected, the other gets deselected. Both of them are bound to the same ng-model (user.gender). Next, each of them has a value, which is the value that gets stored in user.gender (male if it is the first radio button; female, otherwise). Finally, we have an ng-init block surrounding it, which sets the value of user.gender to be female by default. This has the effect of ensuring that the second checkbox is selected when this snippet of HTML loads.

But what if our values are dynamic? What if the value we needed to assign was decided in our controller, or some other place? For that, AngularJS gives you the ng-value attribute, which you can use along with the radio buttons. ng-value takes an AngularJS expression, and the return value of the expression becomes the value that is assigned to the model:

```
<div ng-init="otherGender = 'other'">
    <input type="radio"
           name="gender"
           ng-model="user.gender"
           value="male">Male
    <input type="radio"
           name="gender"
           ng-model="user.gender"
           value="female">Female
    <input type="radio"
           name="gender"
           ng-model="user.gender"
           ng-value="otherGender">{{otherGender}}
</div>
```

In this example, the third option box takes a dynamic value. In this case, we assign it as part of the initialization block (ng-init), but in a real application, the initialization could be done from within a controller instead of in the HTML directly. When we say ng-value="otherGender", it doesn't assign otherGender as a string to user.gender, but the value of the otherGender variable, which is *other*.

Combo Boxes/Drop-Downs

The final HTML form element (which can be used outside forms as well) is the select box, or the drop-down/combo box as it is commonly known. Let's take a look at the simplest way you can use select boxes in AngularJS:

```
<div ng-init="location = 'India'">
    <select ng-model="location">
      <option value="USA">USA</option>
      <option value="India">India</option>
      <option value="Other">None of the above</option>
    </select>
</div>
```

In this example, we have a simple select box that is data-bound to the variable `location`. We also initialize the value of `location` to India, so when the HTML loads, India is the selected option. When the user selects any of the other options, the value of the value attribute gets assigned to the `ng-model`. The standard validators and states also apply to this field, so those can be applied (`required`, etc.).

This has a few restrictions, though:

- You need to know the values in the drop-down up front.
- They need to be hardcoded.
- The values can only be strings.

In a truly dynamic app, one or none of these might be true. In such a case, the `select` HTML element also has a way of dynamically generating the list of options, and working with objects instead of pure string `ng-models`. This is done through the `ng-options` directive. Let's take a look at how this might work:

```
<!-- File: chapter4/select-example.html -->
<html ng-app="notesApp">
<head><title>Notes App</title></head>
<body ng-controller="MainCtrl as ctrl">

<div>
  <select ng-model="ctrl.selectedCountryId"
          ng-options="c.id as c.label for c in ctrl.countries">
  </select>
  Selected Country ID : {{ctrl.selectedCountryId}}
</div>

<div>
  <select ng-model="ctrl.selectedCountry"
          ng-options="c.label for c in ctrl.countries">
  </select>

  Selected Country : {{ctrl.selectedCountry}}
```

```
    </div>

    <script
      src="https://ajax.googleapis.com/ajax/libs/angularjs/1.2.19/angular.js">
    </script>
    <script type="text/javascript">
      angular.module('notesApp', [])
        .controller('MainCtrl', [function() {
          this.countries = [
            {label: 'USA', id: 1},
            {label: 'India', id: 2},
            {label: 'Other', id: 3}
          ];
          this.selectedCountryId = 2;
          this.selectedCountry = this.countries[1];
        }]);
    </script>
    </body>
    </html>
```

In this example, we have two select boxes, both bound to different models in our controller. The first `select` element is bound to `ctrl.selectedCountryId` and the second
one is bound to `ctrl.selectedCountry`. Note that one is a number, while the other is
an actual object. How do we achieve this?

- We use the `ng-options` attribute on the select dialog, which allows us to repeat an
  array (or object, similar to `ng-repeat` from "Working with and Displaying Arrays" on page 22) and display dynamic options.

- The syntax is similar to `ng-repeat` as well, with some additional ability to select
  what is displayed as the label, and what is bound to the model.

- In the first select box, we have `ng-options="c.id as c.label for c in
  ctrl.countries"`. This tells AngularJS to create one option for each country in the
  array of countries. The syntax is as follows: `modelValue as labelValue for item
  in array`. In this case, we tell AngularJS that our `modelValue` is the ID of each
  element, the label value is the label key of each array item, and then our typical `for
  each` loop.

- In the second select box, we have `ng-options="c.label for c in ctrl.coun
  tries"`. Here, when we omit the `modelValue`, AngularJS assumes that each item in
  the repeat is the actual model value, so when we select an item from the second
  select box, the country object (c) of that option box gets assigned to `ctrl.selec
  tedCountry`.

- Because the backing model for the two select boxes are different, changing one does
  not affect the value or the selection in the other drop-down.

- You can also optionally give a grouping clause, for which the syntax would be `ng-options="modelValue as labelValue group by groupValue for item in array"`. Similar to how we specified the model and label values, we can point the `groupValue` at another key in the object (say, continent).

- When you use objects, the clause changes as follows: `modelValue as labelValue group by groupValue for (key, value) in object`.

 AngularJS compares the `ng-options` individual values with the `ng-model` by reference. Thus, even if the two are objects that have the same keys and values, AngularJS will not show that item as selected in the drop-down unless and until they are the same object. We accomplished this in our example by using an item from the array `countries` to assign the initial value of the model.

There is a better way to accomplish this, which is through the use of the track by syntax with `ng-options`. We could have written the `ng-options` as:

```
ng-options="c.label for c in ctrl.countries track by c.id"
```

This would ensure that the object `c` is compared using the ID field, instead of by reference, which is the default.

Conclusion

We started with the most common requirements, which is getting data in and out of UI forms. We played around with `ng-model`, which gives us two-way data-binding to remove most of the boilerplate code we would write when working with forms. We then saw how we could leverage form validation, and show and style error messages. Finally, we saw how to deal with other types of form elements, and the kinds of options AngularJS gives to work with them.

In the next chapter, we start dealing with AngularJS services and then jump into server communication using the `$http` service in AngularJS.

CHAPTER 5

All About AngularJS Services

Until now, we have dealt with data-binding in AngularJS. We have seen how to take data from our controllers and get it into the UI, and ensure that whenever the user interacts with or types in any data, we get it back into our controllers. We used and worked with some common directives, and dealt with forms and error handling.

In this chapter, we dive into AngularJS services. By the end of the chapter, we will have a thorough understanding of AngularJS services and get some hands-on experience in using core built-in AngularJS services. After that, we will learn why and when we should create AngularJS services, and actually create a simple service ourselves.

AngularJS Services

AngularJS services are functions or objects that can hold behavior or state across our application. Each AngularJS service is instantiated only once, so each part of our application gets access to the same instance of the AngularJS service. Repeated behavior, shared state, caches, factories, etc. are all functionality that can be implemented using AngularJS services.

Service Versus Service

In AngularJS, when we say service, we are actually referring to the conceptual service that is a reusable API or substitutable objects, which can be shared across our applications. A service in AngularJS can be implemented as a factory, service, or provider.

This is one of the badly named concepts in AngularJS and thus can lead to confusion. We end up calling all of the above services. We will see the difference between them in a bit.

Let's first take a look at why we need them.

Why Do We Need AngularJS Services?

So far we have only created AngularJS controllers, which create state and functions that our HTML then uses for a variety of tasks. AngularJS controllers are great for tasks that relate to the following:

- Which model and data fields to fetch and show in the HTML
- User interaction, as in what needs to happen when a user clicks something
- Presentation logic, such as how a particular UI element should be styled, or whether it should be hidden

Controllers are stateful, but ephemeral. That is, they can be destroyed and re-created multiple times throughout the course of navigating across a Single Page Application. Let's take a look at an example to clarify this:

```
<!-- File: chapter5/need-for-service/index.html -->
<html ng-app="notesApp">

<head>
  <script
    src="https://ajax.googleapis.com/ajax/libs/angularjs/1.2.19/angular.js">
  </script>
  <script src="app.js"></script>
</head>

<body ng-controller="MainCtrl as mainCtrl">
  <h1>Hello Controllers!</h1>
  <button ng-click="mainCtrl.open('first')">Open First</button>
  <button ng-click="mainCtrl.open('second')">Open Second</button>
  <div ng-switch on="mainCtrl.tab">

    <div ng-switch-when="first">
      <div ng-controller="SubCtrl as ctrl">
        <h3>First tab</h3>
        <ul>
          <li ng-repeat="item in ctrl.list">
            <span ng-bind="item.label"></span>
          </li>
        </ul>

        <button ng-click="ctrl.add()">Add More Items</button>
      </div>

    </div>
    <div ng-switch-when="second">
      <div ng-controller="SubCtrl as ctrl">
        <h3>Second tab</h3>
        <ul>
          <li ng-repeat="item in ctrl.list">
            <span ng-bind="item.label"></span>
```

```
        </li>
      </ul>

      <button ng-click="ctrl.add()">Add More Items</button>
    </div>
  </div>
</div>
</body>

</html>
// File: chapter5/need-for-service/app.js
angular.module('notesApp', [])
  .controller('MainCtrl', [function() {
    var self = this;
    self.tab = 'first';
    self.open = function(tab) {
      self.tab = tab;
    };
  }])
  .controller('SubCtrl', [function() {
    var self = this;
    self.list = [
      {id: 1, label: 'Item 0'},
      {id: 2, label: 'Item 1'}
    ];

    self.add = function() {
      self.list.push({
        id: self.list.length + 1,
        label: 'Item ' + self.list.length
      });
    };
  }]);
```

In this example, we introduced two controllers for the first time: a `MainCtrl` and a `SubCtrl`. The `MainCtrl` controls the overall page, and the `SubCtrl` controls a subsection of the page and holds the data we want to display.

We also have two tabs, which are shown and hidden depending on which button the user clicks. This is accomplished using a new directive, `ng-switch`. `ng-switch` acts like a `switch` statement in the HTML. It takes a variable (using the on attribute, which in this case is `MainCtrl`'s tab), and then, depending on the state, hides and shows elements (using the `ng-switch-when` attribute, used as children of the `ng-switch`). The `ng-switch-when` takes the value that the variable should take.

Finally, the `SubCtrl` has a function to add more items to the array, which is triggered by a button in the UI.

Now, moving on to our HTML, the body is controlled by the `MainCtrl`, and holds state on which tab in the HTML is shown. We then have two buttons that allow us to change which tab is currently shown. Notice again that this is done by changing the model and letting AngularJS update the UI automatically.

Finally, we have a div element on which we have the ng-switch. Both tabs (each one has the ng-switch-when) are exactly the same except for the header. They show the list of items, and add items when the button in that tab is clicked.

With this out of the way, let's take a look at some key behaviors:

- Both of the tabs, First and Second, are using the same controller, SubCtrl. But each one has its own instance of the list variable. Adding items in one tab does not add them to the other, and vice versa.

- If we add items to the first tab and then switch to the second tab, we will see the items the controller starts with. But then if we navigate back to the first tab, we will see that those items disappear from the first controller as well.

 We could still achieve the functionality we were aiming for by having a parent-level controller, and moving our list variable into the parent controller (such as MainCtrl). Each SubCtrl would then have to access the variable through the top controller explicitly. This solves our problem but adds global, implicit state, which is never ideal for a large, maintainable application.

When we use controllers, they are instances that get created and destroyed as we navigate across our application. This is especially true when we start working on routing and multiple URLs in a Single Page Application in Chapter 6. Also, one controller cannot directly communicate with another controller to share state or behavior.

Services Versus Controllers

In the applications we develop, we will end up using both controllers as well as services. Now, when we say "services" in AngularJS, we include factories, services, and providers. We'll see the difference between the three in "The Difference Between Factory, Service, and Provider" on page 82.

That said, both controllers and services fill a certain need in our application, and attempting to do too much or do in one what ideally belongs in the other can lead to bloated, unmaintainable, and untestable code. Table 5-1 gives a quick overview of the types of responsibilites and needs for which we would use controllers versus services.

Table 5-1. Controllers versus services

Controllers	Services
Presentation logic	Business logic
Directly linked to a view	Independent of views
Drives the UI	Drives the application
One-off, specific	Reusable
Responsible for decisions like what data to fetch, what data to show, how to handle user interactions, and styling and display of UI	Responsible for making server calls, common validation logic, application-level stores, and reusable business logic

We'll dive into AngularJS services next, including how to use existing services and create our own. After we finish that, we'll come back to some examples of what belongs in services.

Dependency Injection in AngularJS

The entire service concept in AngularJS is heavily dependent on and driven by its Dependency Injection system. Any service known to AngularJS (internal or our own) can be simply injected into any other service, directive, or controller by stating it as a dependency. AngularJS will automatically figure out what the service is, what it further depends on, and create the entire chain before injecting a fully instantiated service.

Dependency Injection is a concept that started more on the server side, to basically propagate reuse, modularity, and testability of code. Dependency Injection states that instead of creating an instance of a dependent service when we need it, the class or function should ask for it instead. Something else (usually known as an injector) would then be responsible for figuring out how to create it and pass it in.

Consider a case where we had a service called `$http` that could make server calls. Now let's take two cases, with and without Dependency Injection:

```
// Without Dependency Injection
function fetchDashboardData() {
  var $http  = new HttpService();
  return $http.get('my/url');
}

// With Dependency Injection
function fetchDashboardData($http) {
  return $http.get('my/url');
}
```

In the first function, a new instance of `$http` is created whenever a server call needs to happen. In the second, the `$http` service instance itself gets passed in.

What are the disadvantages of the former?

- Because it creates a new instance using the new keyword, any test we write for this function is dependent on HttpService implicitly.

- If we need to extend HttpService to provide for offline functionality, or change it to sockets, we will be forced to change each implementation where new is called.

- It is inherently tied to HttpService, making it hard to reuse for other cases, such as with sockets or offline as mentioned previously.

Dependency Injection allows us to:

- Change the underlying implemention of a dependency without manually changing each dependent function

- Change the underlying implementation just for the test, to prevent it from making server calls

- Explicitly state what needs to be included and present before this function or constructor can execute

AngularJS guarantees that the function we provide to the service declaration will be executed only once (*lazily*, the first time something that needs the dependency is loaded), and future dependents will get that very same instance. That is, AngularJS services are singletons for the scope of our application. Two controllers or services that ask for ServiceA will get the very same instance, instead of two different instances.

Using Built-In AngularJS Services

Before we go off and try to create our own services, let's take a look at some existing core AngularJS services and how we might use them in our own applications. The simplest one we can start working with is the $log service.

The $ Prefix in AngularJS
AngularJS prefixes all the services that are provided by the AngularJS library with the $ sign. So you will see services like $log, $http, $window, and so on. This is used as a namespacing technique so that when you see a service, you can immediately figure out whether a service is coming from AngularJS or somewhere else. Conversely, when you create your own services, do not prefix them with a $ sign. It will just end up confusing you and your team at some point in time.

Before we can use any AngularJS service (in a controller, service, or otherwise), we need to inject it in. Let's see how we can write a very simple controller that pulls in the $log service:

```
<!-- File: chapter5/log-example.html -->
<html ng-app="notesApp">
<body ng-controller="MainCtrl as mainCtrl">
  <h1>Hello Services!</h1>
  <button ng-click="mainCtrl.logStuff()">Log something</button>

<script
  src="https://ajax.googleapis.com/ajax/libs/angularjs/1.2.19/angular.js">
</script>
<script type="text/javascript">
  angular.module('notesApp', [])
    .controller('MainCtrl', ['$log', function($log) {
      var self = this;
      self.logStuff = function() {
        $log.log('The button was pressed');
      };
    }])
</script>
</body>
</html>
```

In this example, the HTML has been simplified down to a single button, which triggers MainCtrl.logStuff(). It uses the ng-click directive that we've seen before.

Our first major change is in the controller definition. So far, we have had the name of the controller as the first argument to the controller() function, and an array with the controller definition inside it. Now when we depend on a service, we first add the dependency as a string in the array (this is what we call the safe style of Dependency Injection). After we declare it as a string, we then inject it as a variable (the name of our choosing) into the function that is passed as the last argument in the array.

AngularJS will pick up the individual strings in the array, look up the services internally, and inject them into the function in the order in which we have defined the strings.

As soon as we have the service, we can use it as the API permits within our controller, so our logStuff function just logs a string to the console.

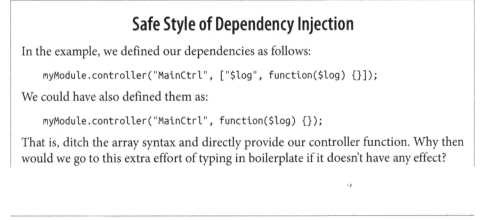

Safe Style of Dependency Injection

In the example, we defined our dependencies as follows:

```
myModule.controller("MainCtrl", ["$log", function($log) {}]);
```

We could have also defined them as:

```
myModule.controller("MainCtrl", function($log) {});
```

That is, ditch the array syntax and directly provide our controller function. Why then would we go to this extra effort of typing in boilerplate if it doesn't have any effect?

The reason for preferring the first syntax over the latter is that when we build our application for deployment, we often run our JavaScript through a step known as minification or uglification. In this step, our JavaScript is globbed into one single file, comments are dropped, spaces are removed, and finally, variables are renamed to make them shorter. So the $log variable might get renamed to xz (or some other random, shorter name).

When we normally run our application and use the latter syntax (without the arrays), AngularJS is able to look at the name of the variable and figure out what service we need. When the uglification has finished, AngularJS has no clue what the variable xz previously referred to.

The uglification and minification processes do not touch string constants. Therefore, the first example would get translated to something like:

```
myModule.controller("MainCtrl", ["$log", function(xz) {}]);
```

while the latter example would translate to something like:

```
myModule.controller("MainCtrl", function(xz) {});
```

In the former, AngularJS still has the string "$log" to tell it what the service originally was, while it doesn't have that in the latter.

Recent developments like the ng-min library (https://github.com/btford/ngmin) allow us to write code in the latter way and have it automatically convert to the former, but it can have edge cases. So it might be preferable to always use the safer style of Dependency Injection in case you don't want to risk it.

In this book, we will always use the safer style of Dependency Injection.

Order of Injection

We define our dependencies as strings. AngularJS inspects the strings, and injects the dependencies in the order in which they are listed:

```
myModule.controller("MainCtrl",
    ["$log", "$window", function($l, $w) {}]);
```

In this line of code, the $log service would be injected into the $l variable in the function, and the $window service would get injected into the $w variable:

```
myModule.controller("MainCtrl",
    ["$log", "$window", function($w, $l) {}]);
```

In this line of code, it is almost the exact same thing, except the $w and $l variables have been switched inside the function. AngularJS will ignore this and take its cue from the strings. So the $w variable will actually hold the $log service, and the $l variable would in fact hold the $window service.

So just be careful to keep the strings and the variables in sync and in the same order, or expect some craziness with your code.

Common AngularJS Services

Some other AngularJS services that we will see or use on a common basis are:

$window

The $window service in AngularJS is nothing but a wrapper around the global window object. The sole reason for its existence is to avoid global state, especially in tests. Instead of directly working with the window object, we can ask for and work with $window. In the unit tests, the $window service can be easily mocked out (available for free with the AngularJS mocking library).

$location

The $location service in AngularJS allows us to interact with the URL in the browser bar, and get and manipulate its value. Any changes made to the $location service get reflected in the browser, and any changes in the browser are immediately captured in the $location service. The $location service has the following functions, which allow us to work with the URL:

absUrl

A getter that gives us the absolute URL in the browser (called $location.absUrl()).

url

A getter and setter that gets or sets the URL. If we give it an argument, it will set the URL; otherwise, it will return the URL as a string.

path

Again, a getter and setter that sets the path of the URL. Automatically adds the forward slash at the beginning. So $location.path() would give us the current path of the application, and $location.path("/new") would set the path to /new.

search

Sets or gets the search or query string of the current URL. Calling $location.search() without any arguments returns the search parameter as an object. Calling $location.search("test") removes the search parameter from the URL, and calling $location.search("test", "abc"); sets the search parameter test to abc.

$http

We will deal with $http extensively in Chapter 6, but it is the core AngularJS service used to make XHR requests to the server from the application. Using the $http service, we can make GET and POST requests, set the headers and caching, and deal with server responses and failures.

Creating Our Own AngularJS Service

We saw how to use AngularJS services through the use of some built-in AngularJS services. We will be using the ones previously mentioned extensively throughout the book going forward, so don't worry that we didn't get to see them all in action yet.

The core AngularJS services only touch the tip of the iceberg in terms of the functionality we will need when we start creating our own AngularJS applications. But how do we decide between embedding our functionality right in the controller or putting it in a service? We should consider creating an AngularJS service if what we are implementing falls into one of the following broad criteria:

It needs to be reusable
More than one controller or service will need to access the particular function that is being implemented.

Application-level state
Controllers get created and destroyed. If we need state stored across our application, it belongs in a service.

It is independent of the view
If what we are implementing is not directly linked to a view, it probably belongs in a service.

It integrates with a third-party service
We need to integrate a third-party service (think SocketIO (*http://socket.io*), BreezeJS (*http://www.breezejs.com/*), etc.), but we want to be able to mock or replace it in our unit tests. A service makes that easy.

Caching/factories
Do we need an object cache? Or something that creates model objects? Services are our best bet.

Services themselves can depend on other built-in services or our own services. So traditional software engineering concepts like modularity, composite services, and even hierarchy of services are still applicable.

Creating a Simple AngularJS Service

Let's take an example of how to create a simple service. We will take the very first example from this chapter, which demonstrated the problem with using just controllers, and use a service to share the state between the two views:

```
<!-- File: chapter5/simple-angularjs-service/index.html -->
<html ng-app="notesApp">
<body ng-controller="MainCtrl as mainCtrl">
  <h1>Hello Controllers!</h1>
  <button ng-click="mainCtrl.open('first')">
    Open First
  </button>
  <button ng-click="mainCtrl.open('second')">
    Open Second
  </button>
  <div ng-switch on="mainCtrl.tab">
    <div ng-switch-when="first">
      <div ng-controller="SubCtrl as ctrl">
        <h3>First tab</h3>
        <ul>
          <li ng-repeat="item in ctrl.list()">
            <span ng-bind="item.label"></span>
          </li>
        </ul>

        <button ng-click="ctrl.add()">
          Add More Items
        </button>
      </div>

    </div>
    <div ng-switch-when="second">
      <div ng-controller="SubCtrl as ctrl">
        <h3>Second tab</h3>
        <ul>
          <li ng-repeat="item in ctrl.list()">
            <span ng-bind="item.label"></span>
          </li>
        </ul>

        <button ng-click="ctrl.add()">
          Add More Items
        </button>
      </div>
    </div>
  </div>

<script
  src="https://ajax.googleapis.com/ajax/libs/angularjs/1.2.19/angular.js">
</script>
<script src="app.js"></script>
</body>

</html>
```

The *app.js* file, which houses the controllers and services, looks something like this:

```
// File: chapter5/simple-angularjs-service/app.js

angular.module('notesApp', [])
  .controller('MainCtrl', [function() {
    var self = this;
    self.tab = 'first';
    self.open = function(tab) {
      self.tab = tab;
    };
}])
  .controller('SubCtrl', ['ItemService',
      function(ItemService) {
    var self = this;
    self.list = function() {
      return ItemService.list();
    };

    self.add = function() {
      ItemService.add({
        id: self.list().length + 1,
        label: 'Item ' + self.list().length
      });
    };
}])
  .factory('ItemService', [function() {
    var items = [
      {id: 1, label: 'Item 0'},
      {id: 2, label: 'Item 1'}
    ];
    return {
      list: function() {
        return items;
      },
      add: function(item) {
        items.push(item);
      }
    };
}]);
```

We changed the following things in the previous example:

- Instead of the list being instantiated and stored in the SubCtrl (and getting destroyed and re-created), we are storing the list in a service called ItemService.

- The SubCtrl has a function called list(), which just delegates and returns the value of ItemService.list() function.

- The SubCtrl has a function called add() that delegates and adds an item to the ItemService.

- The HTML now binds the `ng-repeat` to `ctrl.list()` instead of `ctrl.list`. So it calls the function and uses its return value to display the array in the UI.

We created the `ItemService` using an AngularJS module function called `factory`:

- The `factory` function follows a similar declaration style like the controller. So we declare the name of the service, `ItemService`, in the first argument and then the array syntax for Dependency Injection with our actual service function as the second argument.

- In the service definition function, we return an object, which becomes the API for the service. In this case, the `ItemService` defines two functions, `list` and `add`, which all users of the service can access.

- In the service definition function, we also declare some local variables (in this case, the `items` array). These are private to the service, and cannot be accessed directly (though they are accessible through the `list` function here) by any users of the service. Therefore, no controller can access `ItemService.items` directly.

The `ItemService` gets instantiated once when the application loads and the `SubCtrl` is loaded, at which point AngularJS decides it needs an instance of the `ItemService`. After it is created, all other controllers that ask for the `ItemService` will get the exact same instance that was returned the very first time.

This is why both the tabs in our example show the exact same list, and if we click Add in one tab and then move to the other tab, the items still show up.

To summarize, when we create our own AngularJS service:

- Use the `angular.module().factory` function to declare the service's name and dependencies.

- Return an object, or a function from within the service definition, which becomes the public API for our service.

- Hold internal state as local variables inside the service. This is important because in a Single Page Application where controllers can get created and destroyed, the service can act as an application-level store.

AngularJS guarantees the following:

- The service will be lazily instantiated. The very first time a controller, service, or directive asks for the service, it will be created.

- The service definition function will be called once, and the instance stored. Every caller of this service will get this same, singleton instance handed to them.

This is important because in a Single Page Application, the HTML and controllers can get destroyed and created multiple times in an application.

In this way, we can create our own AngularJS service, and define the API of how someone interacts with our own service. Notice that we call ItemService a service, even though we defined it using a function called factory. We will touch upon this in the next section.

The Difference Between Factory, Service, and Provider

AngularJS provides a few different ways in which we can to create and register services (and constants and values), depending on our preference and style of programming. In the previous section, we used the factory function to define our services.

You should use module.factory() to define your services if:

- You follow a functional style of programming
- You prefer to return functions and objects

JavaScript (and AngularJS) also allow us to follow a Class/OO style of programming, where we define classes and types instead of functions and objects. When we use a service, AngularJS assumes that the function definition passed in as part of the array of dependencies is actually a JavaScript type/class. So instead of just invoking the function and storing its return value, AngularJS will call new on the function to create an instance of the type/class.

Let's see how the service we defined in the previous example changes if we use the service() function:

```
// File: chapter5/item-service-using-service/app.js

function ItemService() {
  var items = [
    {id: 1, label: 'Item 0'},
    {id: 2, label: 'Item 1'}
  ];
  this.list = function() {
    return items;
  };
  this.add = function(item) {
    items.push(item);
  };
}

angular.module('notesApp', [])
  .service('ItemService', [ItemService])
  .controller('MainCtrl', [function() {
    var self = this;
    self.tab = 'first';
```

```
    self.open = function(tab) {
      self.tab = tab;
    };
  }])
  .controller('SubCtrl',
    ['ItemService', function(ItemService) {
    var self = this;
    self.list = function() {
      return ItemService.list();
    };

    self.add = function() {
      ItemService.add({
        id: self.list().length + 1,
        label: 'Item ' + self.list().length
      });
    };
  }]);
```

In this example, we can use the exact same controllers and HTML from before. We can use this *app.js* with the *index.html* from the previous example. We only display the part that is changed, which is the service definition:

- The first thing of note is that we now use `service` instead of `factory` for defining our AngularJS service.

- Our service definition function is now a JavaScript class function. It doesn't return anything.

- Our service defines the public API by defining methods (`add`, `list`) on its instance (using the `this` keyword).

- Private state for the service is still defined as local variables inside the function definition.

- AngularJS will perform `new ItemService()` (with possible dependencies injected in) and then return that instance to all functions that depend on `ItemService`.

The third and final way of defining services is using the `provider` function. This is not a very common approach, but can be useful when we need to set up some configuration for our service before our application loads. We will deal with application-level configuration in Chapter 6, but with the provider, we can have functions that can be called to set up how our service works based on the language, environment, or other things that are applicable to our service. Let's see how that might look:

```
// File: chapter5/item-service-using-provider/app.js

function ItemService(opt_items) {
  var items = opt_items || [];

  this.list = function() {
```

```
      return items;
    };
    this.add = function(item) {
      items.push(item);
    };
  }

  angular.module('notesApp', [])
    .provider('ItemService', function() {
      var haveDefaultItems = true;

      this.disableDefaultItems = function() {
        haveDefaultItems = false;
      };

      // This function gets our dependencies, not the
      // provider above
      this.$get = [function() {
        var optItems = [];
        if (haveDefaultItems) {
          optItems = [
            {id: 1, label: 'Item 0'},
            {id: 2, label: 'Item 1'}
          ];
        }
        return new ItemService(optItems);

      }];
    })
    .config(['ItemServiceProvider',
      function(ItemServiceProvider) {
        // To see how the provider can change
        // configuration, change the value of
        // shouldHaveDefaults to true and try
        // running the example
        var shouldHaveDefaults = false;

        // Get configuration from server
        // Set shouldHaveDefaults somehow
        // Assume it magically changes for now
        if (!shouldHaveDefaults) {
          ItemServiceProvider.disableDefaultItems();
        }
    }])
    .controller('MainCtrl', [function() {
      var self = this;
      self.tab = 'first';
      self.open = function(tab) {
        self.tab = tab;
      };
    }])
    .controller('SubCtrl',
```

```
    ['ItemService', function(ItemService) {
  var self = this;
  self.list = function() {
    return ItemService.list();
  };

  self.add = function() {
    ItemService.add({
      id: self.list().length + 1,
      label: 'Item ' + self.list().length
    });
  };
}]);
```

We introduced two new concepts in this example. The rest of the controllers and HTML remain the same as before, so use the same *index.html* from the factory example:

- ItemService now takes in the list of default items as an argument to the constructor.

- ItemService is declared using a provider. We define a function in the provider called disableDefaultItems. This can be called in the configuration phase of an AngularJS application. That is, this can be called before the AngularJS app has loaded and the service has been initialized.

- Note that the provider does not use the same notation as factory and service. It doesn't take an array as the second argument because providers cannot have dependencies on other services.

- The provider also declares a $get function on its instance, which is what gets called when the service needs to be initialized. At this point, it can use the state that has been set up in the configuration to instantiate the service as needed.

Let's take a look at the config function that we have defined:

- The config function executes before the AngularJS app executes. So we can be assured that this executes before our controllers, services, and other functions.

- The config function follows the same Dependency Injection pattern, but gets providers injected in. In this case, we ask for the ItemServiceProvider.

- At this point, we can now call functions and set values that the provider exposes. We are able to the call the disableDefaultItems function that we defined in the provider.

- The config function could also set up URL endpoints, locale information, routing configuration for our application, and so on: things that need to be executed and initialized before our application starts.

- We can try changing the value of `shouldHaveDefaults` to `true` (this would come from the server or URL, or some other way usually) to see the effect it has on our application.

Conclusion

We saw the limitations of just using controllers for our entire application, and saw how and when to use AngularJS services. We saw the Dependency Injection syntax in AngularJS when we used the built-in `$log` service. We then covered some of other built-in services before diving into creating our own AngularJS services.

We then created the same AngularJS service (a data store for an array of items) in three different ways, depending on the need and preference. We created the functional form using the factory method, the OO style using the service method, and the configurable version using the provider method.

In the next chapter, we will build on these concepts and start working with server communication in the context of AngularJS.

CHAPTER 6

Server Communication Using $http

In Chapter 5, we looked at AngularJS services and how they differ from controllers. We also explored some basic core AngularJS built-in services, and saw how to create our own AngularJS service as well.

In this chapter, we explore how to start creating applications that can communicate with a server to fetch and store data. In particular, we will work with the $http service and save and update information. By the end of the chapter, we as developers should be extremely comfortable working with asynchronous tasks in AngularJS and with server communication, because we have built the infrastructure we might need for a full-fledged application.

Fetching Data with $http Using GET

The traditional way of making a request to the server from AJAX applications (using XMLHttpRequests) involves getting a handle on the XMLHttpRequest object, making the request, reading the response, checking the error codes, and finally processing the server response. It goes something like this:

```
var xmlhttp = new XMLHttpRequest();

xmlhttp.onreadystatechange = function() {
 if (xmlhttp.readystate == 4 && xmlhttp.status == 200) {
   var response = xmlhttp.responseText;
 } else if (xmlhttp.status == 400) { // or really anything in the 4 series
   // Handle error gracefully
 }
};

// Set up connection
xmlhttp.open("GET", "http://myserver/api", true);
```

```
// Make the request
xmlhttp.send();
```

This is a lot of work for such a simple, common, and often repeated task. More often than not, we will likely end up creating wrappers or using a library.

$http is a core AngularJS service that allows us to communicate with server endpoints using XHR. The AngularJS XHR API follows what is commonly known as the *Promise interface*. Because XHRs are asynchronous method calls, the response from the server will come back at an unknown future date and time (hopefully almost immediately). The Promise interface guarantees how such responses will be dealt with, and allows consumers of the Promise to use them in a predictable manner.

Reducing Code with ngResource

In case you have a RESTFUL API on your server, you can further reduce the amount of code you write by using AngularJS's optional module, ngResource. ngResource allows us to take an API endpoint and create an AngularJS service around it. For example, consider an API for projects on the server side that behaves like the following:

- GET request to */api/project/* returned an array of projects
- GET request to */api/project/17* returned the project with ID 17
- POST request to */api/project/* with a project object as JSON created a new project
- POST request to */api/project/19* with a project object as JSON updated the project with ID 19
- DELETE request to */api/project/* deleted all the projects
- DELETE request to */api/project/23* deleted the project with ID 23

If we have such an API, then instead of manually creating a project resource, and wrapping up $http requests individually, we could just create a service as follows:

```
angular.module('resourceApp', ['ngResource'])
  .factory('ProjectService', ['$resource', function($resource) {
    return $resource('/api/project/:id');
}]);
```

This would automatically give us methods on ProjectService like:

- ProjectService.query() to get a list of projects
- ProjectService.save({id: 15}, projectObj) to update a project with ID 15
- ProjectService.get({id: 19}) to get an individual project with ID 19

---

and so on. You can read more about the configuration and options you get with `ngRe source` at the official AngularJS docs for `ngResource` (*http://bit.ly/1pNofzA*).

We have a simple server that we can use to create and list some notes that we have made available at our GitHub repository (*http://bit.ly/1pNohaB*). To set up the server, clone the repository, open the *chapter6* folder, and execute the following commands in succession:

- `npm install`
- `node server.js`

Then navigate to *http://localhost:8000* and click the first link to see this in action.

We need to serve the HTML and the JavaScript for this chapter from this server so that it can make GET and POST requests successfully. The browser prevents us from making XHR requests to any other domain for security reasons.

Our server exposes the following endpoints:

/api/note
> GET request gives back an array of notes present on the server.

/api/note
> POST request creates a note.

/api/note/:id
> GET request with the `:id` replaced with a numeric ID returns the note with given ID.

/api/note/:id
> POST request with the `id` updates the note with the given ID.

The entire data is stored in memory so if we kill and restart the server, any data we might have added will be destroyed.

Given this, let's see how our app would fetch the list of notes from the server and display them:

```html
<!-- File: chapter6/public/http-get-example.html -->
<html ng-app="notesApp">

<head>
  <title>$http get example</title>
  <style>
    .item {
      padding: 10px;
    }
  </style>
```

```
    </head>

    <body ng-controller="MainCtrl as mainCtrl">
      <h1>Hello Servers!</h1>
      <div ng-repeat="todo in mainCtrl.items" class="item">
        <div><span ng-bind="todo.label"></span></div>
        <div>- by <span ng-bind="todo.author"></span></div>
      </div>

    <script
      src="https://ajax.googleapis.com/ajax/libs/angularjs/1.2.19/angular.js">
    </script>
    <script>
      angular.module('notesApp', [])
        .controller('MainCtrl', ['$http', function($http) {
          var self = this;
          self.items = [];
          $http.get('/api/note').then(function(response) {
            self.items = response.data;
          }, function(errResponse) {
            console.error('Error while fetching notes');
          });
        }]);
    </script>
    </body>
    </html>
```

In this example, our HTML is quite simple. We have a `div` that has the `MainCtrl` attached to it. Inside the `div`, we have an `ng-repeat` over the `items` array in our controller in which we `ng-bind` to the *label* and *author* fields.

Our controller has a dependency on `$http` as a service. Then, when the controller loads, we make a GET request to the */api/notes* server endpoint. `$http.get()` returns what we call a *Promise object* (more on this in just a bit), which allows us to chain functions as if they were synchronous. Our server call might execute in a jiffy, or might take a few seconds to execute. With a Promise object, we can say, when the server returns a response (whether it is a success or failure), then execute the following function.

This is important because promises (just like callbacks) allow us to deal with scalability issues. Both of these concepts keep JavaScript nonblocking and event-driven, which allows us to let the browser continue to do its work while the server request is in flight. Now, regardless of whether the server has only one request, ten requests, or even a million requests, the client is not stuck waiting for the response. It can continue to do other stuff without making the UI hang.

The then function takes two arguments, a *success handler* and an *error handler*. If the server returns a non-200 response, the error handler is called. Otherwise, the success handler is triggered. Both these handlers get passed in a response object, which has the following keys:

headers

> The headers for the call

status

> The status code for the response

config

> The configuration with which the call was made

data

> The body of the response from the server

In the case of success, we just assign the data from the server to the items array and let AngularJS take care of updating the UI through data-binding. In the case of an error, we just log it to the console.

A Deep Dive into Promises

At this point, let's quickly dive into the powerful concept that are *promises*. Promises in AngularJS are based on Kris Kowal's Q proposal (*https://github.com/kriskowal/q*), which is a standardized, convenient way of dealing with asynchronous calls in JavaScript.

The traditional way to deal with asynchronous calls in JavaScript has been with callbacks. Say we had to make three calls to the server, one after the other, to set up our application. With callbacks, the code might look something like the following (assuming a xhrGET function to make the server call):

```
// Fetch some server configuration
xhrGET('/api/server-config', function(config) {
    // Fetch the user information, if he's logged in
    xhrGET('/api/' + config.USER_END_POINT, function(user) {
        // Fetch the items for the user
        xhrGET('/api/' + user.id + '/items', function(items) {
            // Actually display the items here
        });
    });
});
```

In this example, we first fetch the server configuration. Then based on that, we fetch information about the current user, and then finally get the list of items for the current user. Each xhrGET call takes a callback function that is executed when the server responds.

Now of course the more levels of nesting we have, the harder the code is to read, debug, maintain, upgrade, and basically work with. This is generally known as callback hell. Also, if we needed to handle errors, we need to possibly pass in another function to each xhrGET call to tell it what it needs to do in case of an error. If we wanted to have just one common error handler, that is not possible.

The Promise API was designed to solve this nesting problem and the problem of error handling. The Promise API proposes the following:

1. Each asynchronous task will return a `promise` object.

2. Each `promise` object will have a `then` function that can take two arguments, a success handler and an error handler.

3. The success or the error handler in the `then` function will be called only once, after the asynchronous task finishes.

4. The `then` function will also return a `promise`, to allow chaining multiple calls.

5. Each handler (success or error) can return a value, which will be passed to the next function in the chain of promises.

6. If a handler returns a promise (makes another asynchronous request), then the next handler (success or error) will be called only after that request is finished.

So the previous example code might translate to something like the following, using promises and the `$http` service:

```
$http.get('/api/server-config').then(function(configResponse) {
    return $http.get('/api/' + configResponse.data.USER_END_POINT);
}).then(function(userResponse) {
    return $http.get('/api/' + userResponse.data.id + '/items');
}).then(function(itemResponse) {
    // Display items here
}, function(error) {
    // Common error handling
});
```

In this example, we use the `$http` service to make a series of server calls. Each server call using `$http.get` returns a `promise`, and we use the `then` function to add a success handler. In the first two success handlers, we use the response from the server to make another server call.

Each success handler in the promise returns another promise using `$http.get`. AngularJS then waits for that server call to return before proceeding to the next function in the promise chain. Also, the server response value for that promise will be passed as an argument to the next success handler in the chain. So, the first `then` will get the `config Response`. The second `then` will get the return value of the `configResponse` success handler, which is the `userResponse`, and so on.

Also, we have one error handler, which we pass as the second argument to the very last function in the promise chain. Because of this, if any error happens in any of the functions in the promise chain, AngularJS will find the next closest error handler and trigger it. So regardless of whether the error happens in the config request or the user request, the common error handling function will get called.

Propagating Success and Error

Chaining promises is a very powerful technique that allows us to accomplish a lot of functionality, like having a service make a server call, do some postprocessing of the data, and then return the processed data to the controller. But when we work with promise chains, there are a few things we need to keep in mind.

Consider the following hypothetical promise chain with three promises, P1, P2, and P3. Each promise has a success handler and an error handler, so S1 and E1 for P1, S2 and E2 for P2, and S3 and E3 for P3:

```
xhrCall()
    .then(S1, E1) //P1
    .then(S2, E2) //P2
    .then(S3, E3) //P3
```

In the normal flow of things, where there are no errors, the application would flow through S1, S2, and finally, S3. But in real life, things are never that smooth. P1 might encounter an error, or P2 might encounter an error, triggering E1 or E2.

Now, depending on the return value of any of these handlers, AngularJS will decide which function in the chain to execute next. At each of these handlers, we as developers have control. We can decide, given the current handler, which function in the chain to execute next. Consider the following cases:

- We receive a successful response from the server in P1, but the data returned is not correct, or there is no data available on the server (think empty array). In such a case, for the next promise P2, it should trigger the error handler E2.

- We receive an error for promise P2, triggering E2. But inside the handler, we have data from the cache, ensuring that the application can load as normal. In that case, we might want to ensure that after E2, S3 is called.

So each time we write a success or an error handler, we need to make a call—given our current function, is this promise a success or a failure for the next handler in the promise chain?

If we want to trigger the success handler for the next promise in the chain, we can just return a value from the success or the error handler, and AngularJS will treat it as us successfully resolving any errors.

If, on the other hand, we want to trigger the error handler for the next promise in the chain, we can leverage the $q service in AngularJS. Just ask for $q as a dependency in our controller and service, and return $q.reject(data) from the handler. This will ensure that the next promise in the chain goes into the error condition, and will get the data passed to it as an argument.

The $q Service

The $q service in AngularJS has the following APIs for us to use in our application:

`$q.defer()`
> Creates a deferred object when we need to create a promise for our own asynchronous task. Most asynchronous tasks in AngularJS (server calls, timeouts, and intervals) return a promise, but if we are integrating with a third-party library, then we might need our own promise. The `$q.defer()` is useful in those times because the deferred object has a `promise` attribute that can be returned from a function.

`deferredObject.resolve`
> The deferred object created by the previous function can be resolved successfully at any point by calling the `resolve()` function on it with the argument being the data passed to the success handler in the promise chain.

`deferredObject.reject`
> The deferred object can also be rejected, thus denoting that the promise was a failure and triggering the failure handler in the promise. Again, the argument passed to it will be passed to the error handler as is.

`$q.reject`
> The `$q.reject()` can be called from within any of the promise handlers (success or error) with an optional argument that denotes the value to be passed along in the promise chain. The return value of this should be returned to ensure that the promise continues to the next error handler instead of the success handler in the promise chain.

Making POST Requests with $http

Given this background, let's now build out the rest of the UI for this server communication example. We will now add a section that allows users to add notes to display in this list:

```
<!-- File: chapter6/public/http-post-example.html -->
<html ng-app="notesApp">

<head>
  <title>HTTP Post Example</title>
  <style>
    .item {
      padding: 10px;
    }
  </style>
</head>

<body ng-controller="MainCtrl as mainCtrl">
  <h1>Hello Servers!</h1>
```

```
<div ng-repeat="todo in mainCtrl.items"
     class="item">
  <div><span ng-bind="todo.label"></span></div>
  <div>- by <span ng-bind="todo.author"></span></div>
</div>

<div>
  <form name="addForm"
        ng-submit="mainCtrl.add()">
    <input type="text"
           placeholder="Label"
           ng-model="mainCtrl.newTodo.label"
           required>
    <input type="text"
           placeholder="Author"
           ng-model="mainCtrl.newTodo.author"
           required>
    <input type="submit"
           value="Add"
           ng-disabled="addForm.$invalid">
  </form>
</div>

<script
  src="https://ajax.googleapis.com/ajax/libs/angularjs/1.2.19/angular.js">
</script>
<script>
  angular.module('notesApp', [])
    .controller('MainCtrl', ['$http', function($http) {
      var self = this;
      self.items = [];
      self.newTodo = {};
      var fetchTodos = function() {
        return $http.get('/api/note').then(
            function(response) {
          self.items = response.data;
        }, function(errResponse) {
          console.error('Error while fetching notes');
        });
      };

      fetchTodos();

      self.add = function() {
        $http.post('/api/note', self.newTodo)
            .then(fetchTodos)
            .then(function(response) {
              self.newTodo = {};
            });
      };

    }]);
```

```
      </script>
      </body>
      </html>
```

In this example, we added a new section to the HTML that has a standard form with two input fields. We bind these two input fields to our model, newTodo, in the controller. On submit of the form, we trigger the add() function in our controller.

Our controller has slightly changed from the previous example as well. The fetching of notes from the server is now wrapped inside the fetchTodos() function, which in addition to making the $http.get server call also returns the promise for the async call. This function is triggered once when the controller loads.

The add function also uses the $http service, and calls $http.post. Unlike the GET, which takes one argument, the URL of the server, the POST request takes two arguments: the URL and the post data. We chain this server call to call fetchTodos on a successful creation of the todo. We then finally add another promise to the chain, which will clear the newTodo object. This last promise handler will only get triggered after the server call to create the todo, and the server call to get the list of todos (because of the promise returned by the fetchTodos function) both finish.

$http API

We have been using $http to get and save data, so let's take a look at the actual API that the $http service in AngularJS provides.

$http provides the following convenience methods to make certain types of requests:

- GET
- HEAD
- POST
- DELETE
- PUT
- JSONP

So just like $http.get, we can use $http.put or $http.delete. Each of these method signatures are in one of two patterns:

- For requests without any post data (think GET), the function takes two arguments: the URL as the first argument, and a configuration object as the second.
- For requests with post data (POST, PUT), the function takes three arguments: the URL as the first argument, the post data as the second, and a configuration object as the third and final argument.

Each of these is a convenience method, and can actually be directly called through $http itself. That is:

```
$http.get(url, config)
```

can be replaced with:

```
$http(config)
```

where the url and the method (GET, in this case) become part of the configuration object itself. In each of the convenience methods ($http.get, $http.post, etc.), the config object, which is the last parameter, is optional. So we can call $http.get with only the URL like we did in these examples.

Configuration

We have been mentioning this configuration object for the past few paragraphs, so let's take a look at some acceptable parameters and values for it. The following is a basic pseudocode template for the configuration object, which details the keys that are acceptable and the type of value that it expects:

```
{
  method: string,
  url: string,
  params: object,
  data: string or object,
  headers: object,
  xsrfHeaderName: string,
  xsrfCookieName: string,
  transformRequest: function transform(data, headersGetter) or
                    an array of functions,
  transformResponse: function transform(data, headersGetter) or
                     an array of functions,
  cache: boolean or Cache object,
  timeout: number,
  withCredentials: boolean
}
```

The GET, POST, and other convenience methods set the method parameter, so we don't need to. Similarly, if we give the GET or POST requests a URL, it gets set in the config automatically.

We can change the request or how it behaves by passing the config object set with the following keys:

method

A string representing the HTTP request type, like GET or POST.

url

A URL string representing the absolute or relative URL of the resource being requested.

params

A JavaScript object with keys and values translating to URL query parameter keys and values. For example:

```
[{key1: 'value1', key2: 'value2'}]
```

would be converted to:

```
?key1=value1&key2=value2
```

after the URL. If we use an object instead of a string or a number for the value, the object will be converted to a JSON string.

data

A string or an object that will be sent as the request message data. This basically becomes the POST data for the server.

headers

An object (or map) with each key being the name of the header, and the value being the value of that particular header. So passing {'Content-Type': 'text/csv'} would set the Content-Type header to be text/csv.

xsrfHeaderName

We can set the XSRF header that the server will be setting to prevent XSRF attacks on our website. This will then be used in the request to ensure the XSRF handshake happens with our server.

xsrfCookieName

The name of the cookie that has the xsrf token to be used for the XSRF handshake.

transformRequest *and* **transformResponse**

These provide a way for us to change the data for the request going out or the response coming in. These take a single function (which gets passed the data and a way to get the headers) or an array of these functions. Each of these functions can take the data (which is either the post data being sent, or the data of the response), and then return the converted, transformed data from it. A simple transformRequest that takes the JSON post data and converts it into jQuery like a post data string is as follows:

```
transformRequest: function(data, headers) {
  var requestStr;
  for (var key in data) {
    if (requestStr) {
      requestStr += '&' + key + '=' + data[key];
    } else {
      requestStr = key + '=' + data[key];
    }
  }
}
```

```
        return requestStr;
    }
```

cache

> A Boolean or a cache object to use for an application-level caching mechanism. This would be over and above the browser-level caching. If set to true, AngularJS will automatically cache server responses and return them for subsequent requests to the same URL.

timeout

> The time in milliseconds to wait before the request is treated as timed out. This can also be a promise object, which when rejected tells AngularJS to abandon the server call.

Advanced $http

Until now, we have seen how to make simple GET and POST requests using the $http service and have looked into some of the configuration we can do at a request level. Until this point though, we have been dealing with the $http service on a request level. The $http service also allows us to configure defaults, or intercept each and every request going out and response coming in to have some common handling. We will deal with these in this section.

Configuring $http Defaults

The first thing we want to look at is how to configure $http defaults. We saw how to add transformations and headers as part of the config of a single $http request in the previous section. If we needed to add a caching header as part of each and every request, it could quickly become annoying if we did it each time we call $http. For these kinds of requirements, we can use the config section of our module, and use the $httpProvider to configure these defaults. Let's see how we might configure some headers and a default transformRequest using the $httpProvider:

```
// File: chapter6/public/http-defaults.js

angular.module('notesApp', [])
  .controller('LoginCtrl', ['$http', function($http) {
    var self = this;
    self.user = {};
    self.message = 'Please login';
    self.login = function() {
      $http.post('/api/login', self.user).then(
        function(resp) {
          self.message = resp.data.msg;
      });
    };
  }])
```

```
.config(['$httpProvider', function($httpProvider) {
  // Every POST data becomes jQuery style
  $httpProvider.defaults.transformRequest.push(
      function(data) {
    var requestStr;
    if (data) {
      data = JSON.parse(data);
      for (var key in data) {
        if (requestStr) {
          requestStr += '&' + key + '=' + data[key];
        } else {
          requestStr = key + '=' + data[key];
        }
      }
    }

    return requestStr;
  });
  // Set the content type to be FORM type for all post requests
  // This does not add it for GET requests.
  $httpProvider.defaults.headers.post['Content-Type'] =
      'application/x-www-form-urlencoded';
}]);
```

In this example, we set up some application-level configuration for the $http service. We do this by creating a config section for our module and getting the $httpProvid er injected into it. As part of the configuration, we first add a global request transformer, which changes the post data for any outgoing request from a JSON object into a jQuery post string format. Notice that we push this transformation function into the default transformers.

We would do something like the preceding example when we are dealing with a backend that is configured to accept Content-Type *text/www-form-urlencoded*, which is what jQuery defaults to. AngularJS defaults to *application/json*, which is recommended for web applications. If you can't change your backend to accept *application/json*, then you can add a transformer and header to get your AngularJS application talking to your backend.

We can have multiple transformers for requests and responses, both at an individual request level as well as a global level, so the transformRequest and transformRes ponse are arrays by default. We just push (and unshift) as necessary the functions we want to add.

Then we also add a default header to all outgoing GET requests. The $httpProvid er.defaults.headers object allows us to set default headers for common, get, post, and put requests. Each one ($httpProvider.defaults.headers.post, for example) is an object, where the key is the header name and the value is the value of the header. In this example, we set the Content-Type for all outgoing POST requests.

The following is the list of keys and values that can have defaults set using `$httpPro`
`vider` (using `$httpProvider.defaults`):

- `headers.common`

- `headers.get`

- `headers.put`

- `headers.post`

- `transformRequest`

- `transformResponse`

- `xsrfHeaderName`

- `xsrfCookieName`

`transformRequest` and `transformResponse` are arrays of functions. The XSRF-related
keys take pure string values. The headers are all object maps with keys being the header
names and the values being the value of the header.

Interceptors

Handling request-level actions (such as logging, authentication check, and handling
certain types of responses) globally has always been challenging. It usually required
planning to create a layer through which all requests would be channeled so that we
could add global hooks.

AngularJS immensely simplifies this using `$httpProvider` to set up *interceptors*. AngularJS interceptors allow us to hook and check each request and response and handle
certain events (like the server returning 403s for authorization issues) in a common way.

 Do note that the old style of creating response interceptors has been
deprecated and is not expected to be available in future versions of
AngularJS. Therefore, do not use `$httpProvider.responseInter`
`ceptors` in your code anymore.

When we create an interceptor (and we can create multiple), AngularJS makes sure that
it is called before any request is made to the server. Similarly, AngularJS makes sure that
it is called first before the controller or service that makes the `$http` call. So it gives us
a common pipe to work with. Let's take a quick look at how we implement one:

```
// File: chapter6/public/logging-interceptor.js
angular.module('notesApp', [])
  .controller('MainCtrl', ['$http', function($http) {
    var self = this;
    self.items = [];
```

```
    self.newTodo = {};
    var fetchTodos = function() {
      return $http.get('/api/note').then(function(response) {
        self.items = response.data;
      }, function(errResponse) {
        console.log('Error while fetching notes');
      });
    };

    fetchTodos();

    self.add = function() {
      $http.post('/api/note', self.newTodo)
        .then(fetchTodos)
        .then(function(response) {
          self.newTodo = {};
        });
    };

}]).factory('MyLoggingInterceptor', ['$q', function($q) {
  return {
    request: function(config) {
      console.log('Request made with ', config);
      return config;
      // If an error, not allowed, or my custom condition,
      // return $q.reject('Not allowed');
    },
    requestError: function(rejection) {
      console.log('Request error due to ', rejection);
      // Continue to ensure that the next promise chain
      // sees an error
      return $q.reject(rejection);
      // Or handled successfully?
      // return someValue
    },
    response: function(response) {
      console.log('Response from server', response);
      // Return a promise
      return response || $q.when(response);
    },
    responseError: function(rejection) {
      console.log('Error in response ', rejection);
      // Continue to ensure that the next promise chain
      // sees an error
      // Can check auth status code here if need to
      // if (rejection.status === 403) {
      //    Show a login dialog
      //    return a value to tell controllers it has
      //    been handled
      // }
      // Or return a rejection to continue the
      // promise failure chain
```

```
        return $q.reject(rejection);
      }
    };
  }])
  .config(['$httpProvider', function($httpProvider) {
    $httpProvider.interceptors.push('MyLoggingInterceptor');
  }]);
```

In this example, we implement an interceptor that simply logs every single outgoing request and incoming response from the server. We implement interceptors in AngularJS as factories, which return an object with any or all of the following four methods:

request

Any outgoing request passes through the request function, which is also passed the configuration with which the request is being made. At this point, we can take a look at the URL, the post data, the method (whether it is a GET or POST), etc., and then decide to continue with the request (in which case we return the config), or we can decide to reject it to prevent the request from being made (using return $q.reject, which rejects the promise).

requestError

This is triggered if there are multiple interceptors and one of them rejected the request going out. In that case, the reason for the rejection (the argument to $q.reject) is passed to this function.

response

When the server eventually returns, this function is called with the response object (which holds the configuration, status code, headers, and data). If we need to check the validity of the data or a particular header, or log the response, this is the place to do it.

responseError

If the server returns with a non-200 series status code, AngularJS treats it as a response error. We get the same response configuration handled here, where we can check the status, do additional work (like show a login dialog if the status is a 403), and then finally continue returning a rejection (to tell future promises to treat it as a failure), or return a value to say all errors have been handled successfully.

This factory basically dictates how our interceptor works, and how it handles each of these four cases. In any interceptor, we might decide that we only care about responseErrors, so we can implement a factory that returns an object with only that function.

We finally hook it up with the $http service through the $httpProvider in the con
fig function. The $httpProvider has an interceptors array on which we can push in-
terceptors by name. So we simply push the MyLoggingInterceptor onto it, and that
automatically adds the interceptor after the AngularJS app has finished loading.

Best Practices

We have dived through the depths of $http, seen how to configure requests, intercept
all responses, and much more. With all that behind us, here are a few things we should
keep in mind when we work with $http:

Wrap $http in services

In the previous examples, we directly called $http.get or post in our controllers.
In a real application, we should do this: instead of calling $http.get(*/api/
notes*) directly from our controller, we should wrap that call in a service so that we
can do something like NoteService.query(), which in turn would do the
$http.get call. This service call can then return the promise so that the controller
can chain and handle the response correctly:

```
angular.module('notesApp', [])
    .factory('NoteService', ['$http', function($http) {
        return {
            query: function() {
                return $http.get('/api/notes');
            }
        };
    }]);
```

This example code shows how such a NoteService might look. All it does is wrap
the $http call inside a service method, and return the promise from it to which
controllers and other services can add their functionality on the chain.

Use interceptors

There are some common tasks that we might want to do every time a request goes
out from the client, such as logging the request or adding some authorization headers to the request. Or tasks we might need accomplished or conditions we might
want to check on every response. In such a case, interceptors are our best bet. A
simple interceptor that handles 403s, as well as adds the authorization header on
every request, might look something like the following:

```
angular.module('notesApp', [])
  .factory('AuthInterceptor',
    ['AuthInfoService', '$q', function(AuthInfoService, $q) {
      return {
        request: function(config) {
          if (AuthInfoService.hasAuthHeader()) {
            config.headers['Authorization'] =
                AuthInfoService.getAuthHeader();
```

```
      }
      return config;
    },
    responseError: function(responseRejection) {
      if (responseError.status === 403) {
        // Authorization issue, access forbidden
        AuthInfoService.redirectToLogin();
      }
      return $q.reject(responseRejection);
    }
  };
}])
.config(['$httpProvider', function($httpProvider) {
  $httpProvider.interceptors.push('AuthInterceptor');
}]);
```

In this example, we added an interceptor that only intercepts outgoing requests and incoming responses with a non-200 status code. In the case of an outgoing request, we add the authorization header if it is present in a service called AuthInfoSer vice. In the case of the responses, we check if the status is a 403 and if so, redirect the user to the login page. We ensure that the promise is rejected so that the controller or service still sees a failure. The implementation of AuthInfoService can be as per the project's needs.

Chain interceptors

Instead of creating one giant interceptor to do all our intercepting work, we create multiple tiny interceptors, each with individual responsibility. We have a separate interceptor for authorization, a separate one for logging, and so on. The interceptors will be called in the order we add them to the provider, so we can also control the order in which they are called.

Leverage defaults

If we find ourselves setting the same headers again and again, or adding the same request or response transformation, then we should heavily consider using defaults. If all our endpoints return XML instead of JSON, add a default transformRes ponse to the $httpProvider that takes the XML and converts it into JSON (or vice versa if our server only accepts XML). We can also set defaults for only GET or POST requests, so we can be as specific or generic with our defaults as needed.

Conclusion

We saw how to do the very simple task of making GET and POST requests to the server using the $http service in AngularJS. We used the $http service to fetch a list of notes from the server as well as add notes to be persisted on the server. We then dove into some of the configuration parts of AngularJS, to see how to change request options such as headers and transformers. We then looked at how to set defaults for HTTP requests, as well how and when to use interceptors and transformers. We demonstrated a few examples of interceptors, incuding logging interceptors and even authorization interceptors. At this point, any task using $http should be straightforward.

In the next chapter, we will leverage $http and start building out a full-fledged application with multiple URLs and routes, and show views depending on the context. We will use the core AngularJS ngRoute module to accomplish this.

CHAPTER 7

Unit Testing Services and XHRs

In Chapters 5 and 6, we learned how to leverage existing AngularJS services, as well as create our very own AngularJS services. We created simple AngularJS services that we used to store state and communicate across different parts of the application, and services to allow for HTTP communication with our servers.

In Chapter 3, we saw how we might unit test our controllers. Now that we have started creating our own AngularJS services, we will look at how to unit test them. In particular, we will test controllers that use built-in AngularJS services, as well as our very own services. Finally, we will write unit tests for services and controllers that make HTTP requests, and see how we can mock out and leverage the AngularJS Dependency Injection.

Dependency Injection in Our Unit Tests

In Chapter 3, we saw how to leverage AngularJS Dependency Injection in our unit tests to test controllers. We asked for the $controller service, and then created controller instances as and when we needed them. $controller is actually an AngularJS service that we ask for in the unit test.

Similary, we can ask for any service that AngularJS knows about in our unit test, whether it comes from core AngularJS or is one of our own creations. AngularJS will figure out how to create it, what its dependencies are, and give us a fully instantiated service for testing.

Don't forget that to run these tests, you need to:

1. Switch to the *chapter7* folder.

2. Run `npm install karma karma-jasmine karma-chrome-launcher`.

3. Run `karma start`.

This will ensure that all the dependencies are installed correctly for you to run the Karma unit tests.

The examples and tests in this book were run using Karma version 0.12.16 and AngularJs version 1.2.19 (both the *angular.js* and *angular-mocks.js* files). If you are having trouble running them for any reason, ensure that you are using the same versions.

We will use the following Karma configuration for this chapter:

```
// File: chapter7/karma.conf.js
// Karma configuration

module.exports = function(config) {
  config.set({
    basePath: '',
    frameworks: ['jasmine'],
    files: [
      'angular.min.js',
      'angular-mocks.js',
      '*.js'
    ],
    exclude: [],
    port: 8080,
    logLevel: config.LOG_INFO,
    autoWatch: true,
    browsers: ['Chrome'],
    singleRun: false
  });
};
```

Let's see how we might test whether the controller redirects us to a new URL when a function is called in the controller:

```
// File: chapter7/simpleCtrl1.js

angular.module('notesApp', [])
  .controller('SimpleCtrl', ['$location', function($location) {
    var self = this;
    self.navigate = function() {
      $location.path('/some/where/else');
    };
  }]);
```

This controller is as simplistic as it can get while depending on a core AngularJS service. All it does is provide a function called `navigate`, which changes the current location in the browser to *some/where/else*. Now let's see how its unit test might look:

```
// File: chapter7/simpleCtrl1Spec.js

describe('SimpleCtrl', function() {
  beforeEach(module('notesApp'));

  var ctrl, $loc;
  beforeEach(inject(function($controller, $location) {
    ctrl = $controller('SimpleCtrl');
    $loc = $location;
  }));

  it('should navigate away from the current page', function() {
    $loc.path('/here');
    ctrl.navigate();
    expect($loc.path()).toEqual('/some/where/else');
  });
});
```

This code snippet is a simple unit test for the `SimpleCtrl` that we defined earlier. All we attempt to do is to test the `navigate` function in the controller. All the navigate function does is redirect the user to *some/where/else*. Now, if this were a real live browser, the URL would change in the browser bar and an actual page navigation would happen. We don't want this happening in our unit test, so the *angular-mocks.js* file that we included as part of the Karma configuration provides mocked-out versions of services like `$location` and `$window`. This allows us to unit test without worrying about affecting the browser or things like global state that might affect our unit tests.

The mocked-out version of the `$location` (for which we did not have to change a single line of production code, thanks to Dependency Injection!) allows us to set an initial state of the browser's location (*/here* in this case). After executing the `ctrl.navigate()` function, we can then set an expectation that the `$location.path` be set to */some/where/else*. Neither of these will change the browser's actual URL, so the unit tests will complete as normal.

State Across Unit Tests

Let's modify the previous code and unit tests to add two functions and two tests to demonstrate how state is shared (or not shared) between tests:

```
// File: chapter7/simpleCtrl2.js

angular.module('simpleCtrl2App', [])
  .controller('SimpleCtrl2', ['$location', '$window',
    function($location, $window) {
      var self = this;
```

```
      self.navigate1 = function() {
        $location.path('/some/where');
      };
      self.navigate2 = function() {
        $location.path('/some/where/else');
      };
    }]);

// File: chapter7/simpleCtrl2Spec.js

describe('SimpleCtrl2', function() {
  beforeEach(module('simpleCtrl2App'));

  var ctrl, $loc;
  beforeEach(inject(function($controller, $location) {
    ctrl = $controller('SimpleCtrl2');
    $loc = $location;
  }));

  it('should navigate away from the current page', function() {
    expect($loc.path()).toEqual('');
    $loc.path('/here');
    ctrl.navigate1();
    expect($loc.path()).toEqual('/some/where');
  });

  it('should navigate away from the current page', function() {
    expect($loc.path()).toEqual('');
    $loc.path('/there');
    ctrl.navigate2();
    expect($loc.path()).toEqual('/some/where/else');
  });
});
```

We added two functions to our controller. Both the navigate1 and navigate2 functions in the controller navigate to a URL. If we call navigate1 first, it navigates to */some/ where*. If we call navigate2 next, the URL changes to */some/where/else*. The change from the first navigate1 function (the redirected URL) is visible at the beginning of the navigate2 function call.

With this context, let's now look at our unit tests. There are two unit tests, one for each of the two functions. And each one checks that the $location path changes to the correct URL after the function is called. What is noteworthy is the pre-function call check we do. In both cases, we can expect that the browser URL is an empty string.

The reason we can do that is because there is no global state in our unit test. If we execute the first test in a real live application, that changes the value of the browser URL. The second test would then see that. This makes the order of the tests important, because something that sets a variable that the other test uses could cause the tests to fail if they are in a certain order, but pass in another.

AngularJS avoids that by getting rid of global state in the unit tests. The $location service is destroyed and created between our unit tests. All of this happens because we instantiate our module before each unit test. This is responsible for creating a fresh version of each of the service that our test uses.

Mocking Out Services

What if we had a service that was really heavy, or we did not want to test the service? We saw mocked-out versions of $location and $window that the AngularJS mock file provides. In this section, we see how to create our own mocks. Let's consider the very simple ItemService from Chapter 5:

```
// File: chapter7/notesApp1.js
angular.module('notesApp1', [])
  .factory('ItemService', [function() {
    var items = [
      {id: 1, label: 'Item 0'},
      {id: 2, label: 'Item 1'}
    ];
    return {
      list: function() {
        return items;
      },
      add: function(item) {
        items.push(item);
      }
    };
  }])
  .controller('ItemCtrl', ['ItemService', function(ItemService) {
    var self = this;
    self.items = ItemService.list();
  }]);
```

This code snippet uses the ItemService we defined in Chapter 5, and has a simple controller that fetches the list of items when it loads. Now for the purpose of our unit test, we want to mock out ItemService so that we can override the default implementation for our unit test. There are two ways to accomplish this.

The first way is to override the service during the unit test, as an inline mock:

```
// File: chapter7/notesApp1Spec.js

describe('ItemCtrl with inline mock', function() {
  beforeEach(module('notesApp1'));

  var ctrl, mockService;

  beforeEach(module(function($provide) {
    mockService = {
      list: function() {
```

```
      return [{id: 1, label: 'Mock'}];
    }
  };

  $provide.value('ItemService', mockService);
}));

beforeEach(inject(function($controller) {
  ctrl = $controller('ItemCtrl');
}));

it('should load mocked out items', function() {
  expect(ctrl.items).toEqual([{id: 1, label: 'Mock'}]);
});

});
```

In this unit test, the start of the test is similar, where we instantiate our module, the notesApp1. After that, we have another beforeEach, which is where we override the ItemService with our own mock. We use the module function, but instead of giving it the name of the module, we give it a function that gets injected with a $provide. This provider shares its namespace with the modules loaded before. So now we create our mockService and tell the provider that when any controller or service asks for ItemSer vice, give it our value. Because we do this *after* the notesApp1 module is loaded, it overwrites the original ItemService definition.

The rest of the unit test proceeds the same as before, except we now check that the value of items in the controller is returned by our mock instead of the original service.

The second option to override services would be at a global level instead of a unit test level. To decide whether to create the mocks as we did in the previous example using a local variable and the $provide.value function, or whether to do it globally like An- gularJS does it, the question we need to answer is whether or not other tests could reuse the mock.

The mock we created before would only be usable within this particular describe block. To change the preceding to be a more reusable, general-purpose mock of the ItemSer vice, we could do the following:

```
// File: chapter7/notesApp1-mocks.js

angular.module('notesApp1Mocks', [])
  .factory('ItemService', [function() {
    return {
      list: function() {
        return [{id: 1, label: 'Mock'}];
      }
    };
  }]);
```

What we had hardcoded in the mockService has been extracted out into a service with the same name, but in a different module named notesApp1Mocks. This file will reside in the test folder, and be included by *karma.conf.js*, but not in our live application. Our tests would now change as follows:

```
// File: chapter7/notesApp1SpecWithMock.js

describe('ItemCtrl With global mock', function() {

  var ctrl;
  beforeEach(module('notesApp1'));
  beforeEach(module('notesApp1Mocks'));

  beforeEach(inject(function($controller) {
    ctrl = $controller('ItemCtrl');
  }));

  it('should load mocked out items', function() {
    expect(ctrl.items).toEqual([{id: 1, label: 'Mock'}]);
  });

});
```

This ensures that after notesApp1 is loaded, we load the notesApp1Mocks module, which overrides the ItemService. After that, when our test loads the controller, which then calls the service, it defers to the mocked-out ItemService that we created.

We can use this approach when we need a global reusable mock, and defer to the describe-level mock when we need to mock just one particular test.

Spies

But what if we didn't want to implement an entire mocked-out service? What if we just wanted to know in the case of ItemService whether or not the list function was called, and not worry about the actual value from it? For those kinds of cases, we have *Jasmine spies*. Spies allow us to hook into certain functions, and check whether they were called, how many times they were called, what arguments they were called with, and so on.

So let's see how to change our mock to use spies instead:

```
// File: chapter7/notesApp1SpecWithSpies.js

describe('ItemCtrl with spies', function() {
  beforeEach(module('notesApp1'));

  var ctrl, itemService;

  beforeEach(inject(function($controller, ItemService) {
    spyOn(ItemService, 'list').andCallThrough();
    itemService = ItemService;
```

```
    ctrl = $controller('ItemCtrl');
  }));

  it('should load mocked out items', function() {
    expect(itemService.list).toHaveBeenCalled();
    expect(itemService.list.callCount).toEqual(1);
    expect(ctrl.items).toEqual([
      {id: 1, label: 'Item 0'},
      {id: 2, label: 'Item 1'}
    ]);
  });
});
```

We call the spyOn function with an object as the first argument, and a string with the function name that we want to hook on to as the second argument. In this example, we tell Jasmine to spy on the list function of the ItemService. We also tell it to continue calling the actual service underneath by calling andCallThrough on the spy. This means we can use Jasmine to check whether or not the function was called, and have the function work as it used to underneath.

This adds a wrapper around the existing ItemService.list function. Jasmine lets the existing code continue as is while giving us a window into what is happening, and letting us know whether the right functions were called. The data that is returned is still from the original service, as we can see in the expectation on the controllers items. Note that it is recommended that you set up all your mocks and spies before instantiating your controllers.

What if we wanted to not have the existing method execute as normal? Let's see how we might override the method using spies:

```
// File: chapter7/notesApp1SpecWithSpyReturn.js

describe('ItemCtrl with SpyReturn', function() {
  beforeEach(module('notesApp1'));

  var ctrl, itemService;

  beforeEach(inject(function($controller, ItemService) {

    spyOn(ItemService, 'list')
        .andReturn([{id: 1, label: 'Mock'}]);
    itemService = ItemService;
    ctrl = $controller('ItemCtrl');
  }));

  it('should load mocked out items', function() {
    expect(itemService.list).toHaveBeenCalled();
    expect(itemService.list.callCount).toEqual(1);
    expect(ctrl.items).toEqual([{id: 1, label: 'Mock'}]);
```

```
  });
});
```

In this example, we override the `list` method in the `ItemService`, and replace it with our Jasmine spy. The `spyOn` function returns a spy that's called with the `andReturn` function on the spy created by `createSpy`, and gives it the value to return. Note that we do this before creating our controller, which is *recommended*. Then, in our unit test, we can check if `ItemService.list` was called, and if it was called once. Also, we specify that our spy return the value in the controller's `items` array (specified with the `andRe turn` on the `createSpy` function).

Unit Testing Server Calls

We covered how to unit test simple services, as well as mock services and functions depending on our need. With this in our toolbelt, now let's explore how we might test controllers and services using the `$http` service to make server calls.

In unit tests, we focus on testing a single unit of code and checking whether it behaves correctly under all conditions. In a unit test, we want to mock out the larger system at play, whether that be a server, other third-party dependencies, the DOM and browser, or whatever.

With AngularJS, as long as we include the *angular-mocks.js* file as part of the Karma configuration, AngularJS takes care of ensuring that when we use the `$http` service, it doesn't actually make server calls. All server calls are intercepted, and we can test them all within the context of a unit test. Because they are intercepted and mocked out, our unit tests remain fast and stable.

Let's take a sample controller that makes server calls using `$http`, and see how we might unit test it:

```
// File: chapter7/serverApp.js

angular.module('serverApp', [])
  .controller('MainCtrl', ['$http', function($http) {
    var self = this;
    self.items = [];
    self.errorMessage = '';

    $http.get('/api/note').then(function(response) {
      self.items = response.data;
    }, function(errResponse) {
      self.errorMessage = errResponse.data.msg;
    });
  }]);
```

In this code snippet, we have a very simple controller, which makes a GET request to */api/note* when it loads, and saves the response into the `items` array on the controller.

In case of an error, it saves the error message on the controller's instance. Now, let's see how we might test this:

```
// File: chapter7/serverAppSpec.js

describe('MainCtrl Server Calls', function() {
  beforeEach(module('serverApp'));

  var ctrl, mockBackend;

  beforeEach(inject(function($controller, $httpBackend) {

    mockBackend = $httpBackend;
    mockBackend.expectGET('/api/note')
        .respond([{id: 1, label: 'Mock'}]);
    ctrl = $controller('MainCtrl');
    // At this point, a server request will have been made
  }));

  it('should load items from server', function() {
    // Initially, before the server responds,
    // the items should be empty
    expect(ctrl.items).toEqual([]);

    // Simulate a server response
    mockBackend.flush();

    expect(ctrl.items).toEqual([{id: 1, label: 'Mock'}]);
  });

  afterEach(function() {
    // Ensure that all expects set on the $httpBackend
    // were actually called
    mockBackend.verifyNoOutstandingExpectation();

    // Ensure that all requests to the server
    // have actually responded (using flush())
    mockBackend.verifyNoOutstandingRequest();
  });
});
```

To unit test our controller that makes XHR calls, we leverage a service called $httpBack end. The $http service internally uses the $httpBackend to make the actual XHR requests. The *angular-mocks.js* file provides a mock $httpBackend service that prevents server calls, and gives us hooks to set expectations and trigger responses.

As part of beforeEach, we ask for the $httpBackend service to be injected into the test. Because our controller makes a server call as part of the loading behavior, it is important for us to set our expectations on what server calls will be made before the controller is instantiated.

There are two ways to set expectations on what server calls will be made on the $httpBackend:

expect

> The expect function is used when we want to control exactly how many requests will be made and to what URLs, and then control the response. The expect function has a series of functions, one for each method of HTTP, such as expectGET or expectPOST. The first argument to the function is the URL and the second argument, if provided, acts as the POST data. So expectGET('/api/notes') in the previous example says that there will be a GET request to the given URL. Similarly, expectPOST('/api/notes', {label: 'Hi'}) tells the service to expect a POST request, and that the POST data should exactly match what is passed as the second argument.

when

> Similar to expect, when also takes a URL and potential POST data. The syntax is also exactly the same. The difference is that the when does not care about the order of requests or how many times the call was made. It simply sees a request and sends a response. With the expect, a test can fail if the expectation was not satisfied. With when, even if the test never makes the call, the test will pass.

The difference really comes down to the fact that expect is more fine-grained and sets expectations. when stubs out the backend (a stub is something that returns the same response, regardless of the request), allowing it to respond in a consistent manner without any expectations for any and all requests.

After we use either expect (like expectGET) or when, we can define the response for that particular server call by chaining the respond function on it. If respond is given one argument, it is treated as the server response. You can optionally give it two arguments, in which case the first argument will be the status code, and the second argument will be the body of the response (like respond(404, {msg: 'Invalid'})). In our example, we respond with a list of items from the server.

Now, on to our actual unit test. When the controller loads, the items array is initialized to an empty array. Our first expectation in the test is whether the items array is empty. If we consider a server request in a real live application, a request is made first, and then the response comes back at some later point in time. The server requests are asynchronous in nature. To simulate this, AngularJS gives a flush method on the backend service. So by default, when a server request happens, AngularJS tracks it against the expectations and holds on to the request without returning the response. Then, when you as a developer finally call flush() on the $httpBackend, AngularJS sends back the responses for all the requests that the client has received so far.

`flush` allows us to test asynchronous behavior without actually writing asynchronous tests. `$httpBackend.flush()` also takes an integer argument, which can tell the mock backend how many server requests it needs to return. This is useful if we want to check that the controller makes four server calls, but does some work only after at least three of them return. In such a case, we can flush the requests one at a time (using `$httpBackend.flush(1)`), or flush three of them (`$httpBackend.flush(3)`) at once.

At this point, now we can check whether the data that the server responded with has been stored in the right variable in the controller (the `items` array).

As a good practice, it is *recommended* that when you write tests using the `$httpBackend` service, you add an `afterEach` block with the two function calls in the previous code snippet:

- The first function, `verifyNoOutstandingExpectations()`, checks whether you specified any expects on the `$httpBackend` that were not satisfied as part of your test. So if you added another expectation but the controller never made that server call, your test fails. This adds a good check to ensure that everything that you expected actually happened

- The second function, `verifyNoOutstandingRequests()`, is to ensure that you fully tested all the cases. As mentioned earlier, AngularJS splits all server requests into a request and a response. And we trigger the responses using the `flush()` function. `verifyNoOutstandingRequests` ensures that for each server call made, the response has also been triggered using `flush()`. If not, the test fails.

Integration-Level Unit Tests

What if we followed the best practices, and didn't have our `$http` calls right in our controller? Instead, we had our `$http` calls in a `NoteService`, and our controller delegated the `NoteService` to fetch the list of notes.

In such a case, we have two options:

- Option 1 is to write a focused unit test and mock out (or spy on) the `NoteService`, and ensure that our controller delegates to the correct APIs on the `NoteService` and that the flow and arguments are correct.

- Option 2 is to write an integration-level unit test that only focuses on mocking out the backend (using `$httpBackend`) and checking the entire flow.

Let's try our hand at Option 2 with the following code snippet:

```
// File: chapter7/serverAppWithService.js

angular.module('serverApp2', [])
  .controller('MainCtrl', ['NoteService', function(NoteService) {
    var self = this;
    self.items = [];
    self.errorMessage = '';

    NoteService.query().then(function(response) {
      self.items = response.data;
    }, function(errResponse) {
      self.errorMessage = errResponse.data.msg;
    });
  }])
  .factory('NoteService', ['$http', function($http) {
    return {
      query: function() {
        return $http.get('/api/note');
      }
    };
  }]);
```

This example is almost the same as the one in the previous section, except that the $http call has been extracted into the NoteService service. Functionally, it behaves exactly the same way.

Now let's look at how we might test this, while also getting an idea for the error condition test:

```
// File: chapter7/serverAppWithServiceSpec.js
describe('Server App Integration', function() {
  beforeEach(module('serverApp2'));

  var ctrl, mockBackend;

  beforeEach(inject(function($controller, $httpBackend) {

    mockBackend = $httpBackend;
    mockBackend.expectGET('/api/note')
        .respond(404, {msg: 'Not Found'});
    ctrl = $controller('MainCtrl');
    // At this point, a server request will have been made
  }));

  it('should handle error while loading items', function() {
    // Initially, before the server responds,
    // the items should be empty
    expect(ctrl.items).toEqual([]);

    // Simulate a server response
```

```
    mockBackend.flush();

    // No items from server, only an error
    // So items should still be empty
    expect(ctrl.items).toEqual([]);
    // and check the error message
    expect(ctrl.errorMessage).toEqual('Not Found');
  });

  afterEach(function() {
    // Ensure that all expects set on the $httpBackend
    // were actually called
    mockBackend.verifyNoOutstandingExpectation();

    // Ensure that all requests to the server
    // have actually responded (using flush())
    mockBackend.verifyNoOutstandingRequest();
  });
});
```

In this test, very little has changed even though our code has added a new service and extracted it out. For the unit test, we are only ensuring that when the controller loads, it makes a server call to */api/notes*. We don't care whether it is through NoteService or directly. This makes it much more of an integration test, where it is independent of the underlying implementation.

Also, we are now changing the server to respond with a 404. Under such a condition, we expect the items array to still be empty, but now the errorMessage variable should be updated in the controller with the server's response. We added an expect to make sure this happens. The afterEach blocks remains as it was.

Conclusion

We expanded our understanding of unit testing controllers, and walked through how to unit test controllers that depend on built-in AngularJS services (like $location and $window). After that, we created our own services and learned how to unit test those as well. In both cases, it was as simple as asking for the service to be injected into our test, and then interacting with that as need be.

We then covered unit testing XHRs, using the mocked-out $httpBackend service that the *angular-mocks.js* file provides. We saw how to set expectations, and handle the asynchronous behavior of the server calls using the flush() method. We also covered how to handle and test both the error and the success cases.

In the next chapter, we will look at AngularJS filters. We will see how to apply common built-in AngularJS filters, as well as create new filters to perform our own formatting tasks.

CHAPTER 8

Working with Filters

In the previous few chapters, we have explored two of the four cornerstones of AngularJS applications: controllers and services. With controllers, we looked at how to get the data we want out into the UI, and how to handle simple styling and presentation logic. We used services to create common business logic, and a layer that would be common across all our controllers.

In this chapter, we work with AngularJS filters. By the end of the chapter, we will get a sense of how and when to use AngularJS filters, as well as how to create a very simple but useful custom AngularJS filter. We end the chapter with a section on best practices and how to get the most out of AngularJS filters.

What Are AngularJS Filters?

AngularJS filters are used to process data and format values to present to the user. They are applied on expressions in our HTML, or directly on data in our controllers and services. Mostly, they are used as that final level of formatting to convert data from the way it is stored to a user-readable format. Some common examples where we would use filters are to take a timestamp and make it human-readable, or to add the currency symbol to a number.

Another feature of AngularJS filters, when they are used in the view, is that they give us dynamic, on-the-fly data that doesn't need to be stored. When we apply filters in the HTML, the filtered values are shown to the user but do not modify the original value on which they are applied.

Let's look at some common AngularJS filters that come with the core AngularJS codebase and how we might use them under various scenarios.

Using AngularJS Filters

AngularJS has some built-in filters to work with dates, numbers, strings, and arrays. A common use case for filters is to use them directly in the view as a last level for formatting of the data that the user sees. Let's look at the example to see some common filters in action:

```html
<!-- File: chapter8/filter-example-1.html -->
<html>
<head>
  <title>Filters in Action</title>
</head>
<body ng-app="filtersApp">

<div ng-controller="FilterCtrl as ctrl">
  <div>
    Amount as a number: {{ctrl.amount | number}}
  </div>
  <div>
    Total Cost as a currency: {{ctrl.totalCost | currency}}
  </div>
  <div>
    Total Cost in INR: {{ctrl.totalCost | currency:'INR '}}
  </div>
  <div>
    Shouting the name: {{ctrl.name | uppercase}}
  </div>
  <div>
    Whispering the name: {{ctrl.name | lowercase}}
  </div>
  <div>
    Start Time: {{ctrl.startTime | date:'medium'}}
  </div>
</div>

<script
  src="https://ajax.googleapis.com/ajax/libs/angularjs/1.2.19/angular.js">
</script>

<script type="text/javascript">
  angular.module('filtersApp', [])
    .controller('FilterCtrl', [function() {
      this.amount = 1024;
      this.totalCost = 4906;
      this.name = 'Shyam Seshadri';
      this.startTime = new Date().getTime();
    }]);
</script>
</body>
</html>
```

This example code translates into Figure 8-1.

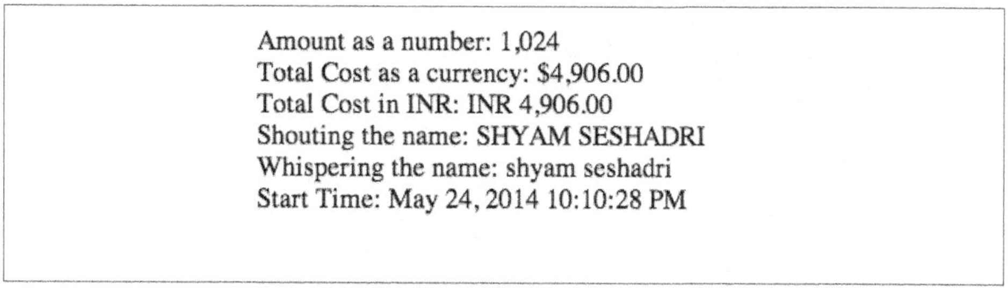

Amount as a number: 1,024
Total Cost as a currency: $4,906.00
Total Cost in INR: INR 4,906.00
Shouting the name: SHYAM SESHADRI
Whispering the name: shyam seshadri
Start Time: May 24, 2014 10:10:28 PM

Figure 8-1. AngularJS filter output

We will go over the AngularJS filters one by one, but before that, let's talk about their usage and syntax. The general syntax to use filters is to use the Unix syntax of piping the result of one expression to another. That is:

```
{{expression | filter}}
```

The filter will take the value of the expression (a string, number, or array) and convert it into some other form. For example, the currency filter used in the previous code snippet takes the totalCost number and converts it into a string, with commas, decimals, and the currency symbol added. The uppercase and lowercase filters take the string name and convert it into uppercase and lowercase, respectively.

 Do note that when we say something like:

```
{{ctrl.name | lowercase}}
```

we are formatting data on the fly. This means that the value of ctrl.name does not change, whereas the user still sees the final low-ercase result.

We can also chain multiple filters together by piping one filter after another. The syntax would be:

```
{{expression | filter1 | filter2}}
```

For example, say we want to take our name variable from the previous controller, convert it to lowercase, and display only the first five letters. We could accomplish that like this:

```
{{ctrl.name | lowercase | limitTo:5}}
```

Each filter takes the value from the previous expression and applies its logic on it. In this example, the name would first be lowercased, and then the lowercase name would be provided to the limitTo filter. The limitTo filter would just return the first five characters from the string, thus returning "shyam" to the HTML. As you can see, we can pass arguments to filters as well, which we use to tell the limitTo filter how many characters to limit the string to.

Common AngularJS Filters

Let's go over each of the filters we mentioned in passing, as well as some additional ones with some examples to see how and when to use each one. We'll talk about the available filters before giving a comprehensive example that demos all of them in a single app:

currency
> The currency filter formats a given number as currency with the commas, decimals, and currency symbol added as needed. The filter takes an optional currency symbol as the second argument; if none exists, it takes the default symbol for the current browser.

number
> The number filter takes a number and converts it to a human-readable string with comma separation. The number filter also takes an optional decimal size that tells it how many digits to keep after the decimal point.

lowercase
> A very simple string filter that takes any string and converts all the characters to lowercase.

uppercase
> A very simple string filter that takes any string and converts all the characters to uppercase.

json
> The json filter is a great tool for debugging, or for any time we need to display the contents of a JSON object or an array in the UI. It takes a JSON object or array (or even primitives) and displays it as a string in the UI.

date
> The date filter is a customizable and powerful filter that takes a date object or a long timestamp and displays it as a human-readable string in the UI. It can take a user-defined format or one of the built-in *short*, *medium*, or *long* formats. The detailed documentation for various formatting options is available in the Date Filter API page (*https://docs.angularjs.org/api/ng/filter/date*).

The following example demonstrates these filters used in combination with strings and numbers:

```
<!-- File: chapter8/filter-number-string.html -->
<html>
<head>
  <title>Filters in Action</title>
</head>
<body ng-app="filtersApp">

<ul ng-controller="FilterCtrl as ctrl">
```

```html
<li>
  Amount - {{ctrl.amount}}
</li>
<li>
  Amount - Default Currency: {{ctrl.amount | currency}}
</li>
<li>
  <!-- Using the English pound sign -->
  Amount - INR Currency: {{ctrl.amount | currency:'&#163 '}}
</li>

<li>
  Amount - Number: {{ctrl.amount | number}}
</li>
<li>
  Amount - No. with 4 decimals: {{ctrl.amount | number:4}}
</li>

<li>
  Name with no filters: {{ctrl.name}}
</li>
<li>
  Name - lowercase filter: {{ctrl.name | lowercase}}
</li>
<li>
  Name - uppercase filter: {{ctrl.name | uppercase}}
</li>

<li>
  The JSON Filter: {{ctrl.obj | json}}
</li>

<li>
  Timestamp: {{ctrl.startTime}}
</li>
<li>
  Default Date filter: {{ctrl.startTime | date}}
</li>
<li>
  Medium Date filter: {{ctrl.startTime | date:'medium'}}
</li>
<li>
  Custom Date filter: {{ctrl.startTime | date:'M/dd, yyyy'}}
</li>
</ul>

<script
  src="https://ajax.googleapis.com/ajax/libs/angularjs/1.2.19/angular.js">
</script>

<script type="text/javascript">
  angular.module('filtersApp', [])
```

```
    .controller('FilterCtrl', [function() {
      this.amount = 1024;
      this.name = 'Shyam Seshadri';
      this.obj = {test: 'value', num: 123};
      this.startTime = new Date().getTime();
    }]);
  </script>
  </body>
  </html>
```

In this code snippet, four values are defined in the controller:

- A number, amount
- A string, name
- A JSON object, obj
- A timestamp, startTime

Then, in the HTML (shown in Figure 8-2) we have the following bindings and filters, in order:

1. The amount variable itself.
2. The amount variable, using the default currency filter. This uses the current browser to grab the currency symbol.
3. The amount variable using the currency filter with a defined symbol (in this case, the English pound sign).
4. The amount variable using the default number filter, which is like the currency filter but without decimals and the currency symbol by default.
5. The amount variable using the number filter, and forcing four digits after the decimal point.
6. The name variable itself.
7. The name variable using the lowercase filter, which ensures that the output becomes "shyam seshadri".
8. The name variable using the uppercase filter, which ensures that the output becomes "SHYAM SESHADRI".
9. The obj variable, printed as a string {"test": "value", "num": 123}
10. The timestamp used for the date filters.
11. The timestamp used with the default date filter (which prints something like "Jan 3, 2007": the medium date format).
12. The timestamp with the medium date filter, which prints the medium date in the filter, along with the time (something like "Jan 3, 2007 12:04:45 pm").

13. The `timestamp` with a custom `date` filter specified using a date format (something like 1/23, 2014).

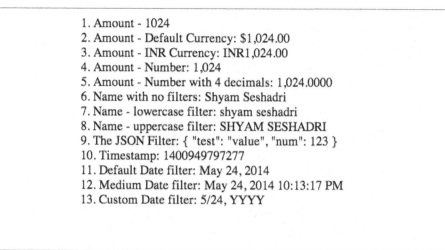

1. Amount - 1024
2. Amount - Default Currency: $1,024.00
3. Amount - INR Currency: INR1,024.00
4. Amount - Number: 1,024
5. Amount - Number with 4 decimals: 1,024.0000
6. Name with no filters: Shyam Seshadri
7. Name - lowercase filter: shyam seshadri
8. Name - uppercase filter: SHYAM SESHADRI
9. The JSON Filter: { "test": "value", "num": 123 }
10. Timestamp: 1400949797277
11. Default Date filter: May 24, 2014
12. Medium Date filter: May 24, 2014 10:13:17 PM
13. Custom Date filter: 5/24, YYYY

Figure 8-2. Screenshot of number and string filters

Next, let's look at the filters that work mostly with arrays and give ways to slice and dice and change the order as per our needs:

limitTo

The `limitTo` is a simple AngularJS filter that takes either a string (as we saw in the example on chaining) or an array and returns a subset from the beginning or the end of the array, depending on the argument passed to it. If the `limitTo` is given only a number (say, 3), it returns only that many elements from the array or characters from the string (in this case, 3 again). If it is a negative number, it picks up those elements or characters from the end of the array.

orderBy

One of the two more complicated filters (the other being `filter`, which we cover next), `orderBy` allows us to take an array and order it by a predicate expression (or a series of predicate expressons). It also takes a second optional Boolean argument, which decides whether or not the sorted array is reversed. The simplest form of a predicate expression is a string, which is the name of the field (the key of each object) to order the array by, with an optional + or – sign before the field name to decide whether to sort ascending or descending by the field. The predicate expression can also be passed a function, in which case the return value of the function will be used (with simple <, >, = comparisons) to decide the order. Finally, the predicate expression can be an array, in which case each element of the array is either a string or a function. AngularJS will then sort it by the first element of the array, and keep cascading to the next element if it is equal.

filter

By far one of the most flexible filters in AngularJS is `filter` (confused yet?). While named slightly confusingly, the `filter` filter in AngularJS is used to filter an array based on predicates or functions, and decide which elements of an array are included. This filter is most commonly used along with the `ng-repeat` to do dynamic filtering of an array. The expression to filter the array can be one of the following:

string

If provided a string expression, AngularJS will look for the string in the keys of each object of the array, and if it is found, the element is included. The string can optionally be prefixed with an ! to negate the match.

object

A pattern object can also be provided, in which case AngularJS takes each key of the object and makes sure that its value is present in the corresponding key of each object of the array. For example, an object expression like {size: "M"} would check each item of the array and ensure that the objects have a key called `size` and that they contain the letter "M" (not necessarily an exact match).

function

The most flexible and powerful of the options, the filter can take a function to implement arbitrary and custom filters. The function gets called with each item of the array, and uses the return value of the function to decide whether to include the item in the end result. Any item that returns a false gets dropped from the result.

Let's use an example to demonstrate how these might work:

```
<!-- File: chapter8/filter-arrays.html -->
<html>
<head>
  <title>Filters in Action</title>
</head>
<body ng-app="filtersApp">

<div ng-controller="FilterCtrl as ctrl">

  <button ng-click="ctrl.currentFilter = 'string'">
    Filter with String
  </button>
  <button ng-click="ctrl.currentFilter = 'object'">
    Filter with Object
  </button>
  <button ng-click="ctrl.currentFilter = 'function'">
```

```
      Filter with Function
    </button>
    Filter Text
    <input type="text"
           ng-model="ctrl.filterOptions['string']">
    Show Done Only
    <input type="checkbox"
           ng-model="ctrl.filterOptions['object'].done">
    <ul>
      <li ng-repeat="note in ctrl.notes |
                     filter:ctrl.filterOptions[ctrl.currentFilter] |
                     orderBy:ctrl.sortOrder |
                     limitTo:5">
        {{note.label}} - {{note.type}} - {{note.done}}
      </li>
    </ul>
  </div>

  <script
    src="https://ajax.googleapis.com/ajax/libs/angularjs/1.2.19/angular.js">
  </script>

  <script type="text/javascript">
    angular.module('filtersApp', [])
      .controller('FilterCtrl', [function() {
        this.notes = [
          {label: 'FC Todo', type: 'chore', done: false},
          {label: 'FT Todo', type: 'task', done: false},
          {label: 'FF Todo', type: 'fun', done: true},
          {label: 'SC Todo', type: 'chore', done: false},
          {label: 'ST Todo', type: 'task', done: true},
          {label: 'SF Todo', type: 'fun', done: true},
          {label: 'TC Todo', type: 'chore', done: false},
          {label: 'TT Todo', type: 'task', done: false},
          {label: 'TF Todo', type: 'fun', done: false}
        ];
        this.sortOrder = ['+type', '-label'];

        this.filterOptions = {
          "string": '',
          "object": {done: false, label: 'C'},
          "function": function(note) {
            return note.type === 'task' && note.done === false;
          }
        };

        this.currentFilter = 'string';
      }]);
  </script>
</body>
</html>
```

In this example, we are using all the array-related filters in one example. We have an array of notes, with three keys (label, type, and done). We also define an array of sorting predicates, sortOrder, to tell AngularJS to first sort by the type, and if they are equal, to sort in reverse by label.

In the HTML, we are sorting by sortOrder and limiting the results to five elements. Before either of these, we are filtering the array by our filterOptions. By default, we are using the string filter, which is bound to the text box. If we type in anything, it will match against all the fields in each note and display only the items that match. Clicking the buttons will switch our filtering mode from string to object or function.

The object filter shows all notes that are not done, and which have the character C in the label. The checkbox in the UI allows us to toggle the done filter to show only the done notes, or only the notes that are not done.

The function filter only shows notes that are tasks and not done.

In a real application, we could bind checkboxes, select boxes, and text boxes to various fields of an object (using ng-model) and use the object to filter the list dynamically. The function filter could be expanded and made more complex based on the business logic. The beauty of the filter filter is that it is dynamic when used in the HTML directly, so the minute the underlying model changes, the entire list gets filtered automatically.

Using Filters in Controllers and Services

Filters are well and great in the HTML and UI, but what if we need to apply these transformations to our controller or service? Thankfully, AngularJS allows us to use the filters wherever we want or need through the power of Dependency Injection. So without ever needing to access the DOM or the UI, we can use the business logic of the filter right in our JavaScript code.

Any filter, whether built-in or our own, can be injected into any service or controller by affixing the word "Filter" at the end of the name of the filter, and asking it to be injected. For example, if we need the currency filter in our controller, we can do something like this:

```
angular.module('myModule', [])
    .controller('MyCtrl', ['currencyFilter',
        function(currencyFilter) {
}]);
```

Similarly, the number filter becomes numberFilter and filter of course becomes the convoluted filterFilter. Attaching the word "Filter" after any AngularJS filter allows us to inject it into our controllers or services.

Now, in the HTML, we use the pipe syntax to give it some input to work with, followed by optional arguments. When we get a handle on it in our controller or service, we get a function. The first argument to the function is the value the filter needs to act upon: a string, number, or array. All additional parameters are the arguments we mentioned earlier, in order as needed.

So if we wanted to filter our array `self.notes` using the `filterFilter` with just a string, we could do something like:

```
self.filteredArray = filterFilter(self.notes, 'ch');
```

There are three main things to note:

- The first argument to the filter is the value it needs to act upon.
- Further arguments are the arguments that the filter needs (optional for some), in the order mentioned in the documentation.
- The return value of the filter is the final output that we need.

Creating AngularJS Filters

We saw how we can use some of the existing built-in AngularJS filters, but what if they are not enough? The date filter might be good, but we want our own formatting and behavior. We might want a filter for localization. In this section, we will go about creating our own filter.

We are going to write a very simple filter called `timeAgo`. In production, we might use something like MomentJS (*http://momentjs.com*), but here, we are going to craft a very simplistic one ourselves. All we want to do is take a timestamp and display in the UI messages like "seconds ago," "minutes ago," "days ago," and "months ago." We are displaying only the message, without any numbers. So regardless of whether it was 5 or 15 seconds ago, the message would read "seconds ago." How might we go about doing this?

```
<!-- File: chapter8/custom-filters.html -->
<html>
<head>
  <title>Custom Filters in Action</title>
</head>
<body ng-app="filtersApp">

<div ng-controller="FilterCtrl as ctrl">
  <div>
    Start Time (Timestamp): {{ctrl.startTime}}
  </div>
  <div>
    Start Time (DateTime): {{ctrl.startTime | date:'medium'}}
  </div>
  <div>
    Start Time (Our filter): {{ctrl.startTime | timeAgo}}
  </div>
```

```
  <div>
    someTimeAgo : {{ctrl.someTimeAgo | date:'short'}}
  </div>
  <div>
    someTimeAgo (Our filter): {{ctrl.someTimeAgo | timeAgo}}
  </div>
</div>

<script
  src="https://ajax.googleapis.com/ajax/libs/angularjs/1.2.19/angular.js">
</script>

<script type="text/javascript">
  angular.module('filtersApp', [])
    .controller('FilterCtrl', [function() {
      this.startTime = new Date().getTime();
      this.someTimeAgo = new Date().getTime() -
          (1000 * 60 * 60 * 4);
    }])
    .filter('timeAgo', [function() {
      var ONE_MINUTE = 1000 * 60;
      var ONE_HOUR = ONE_MINUTE * 60;
      var ONE_DAY = ONE_HOUR * 24;
      var ONE_MONTH = ONE_DAY * 30;

      return function(ts) {
        var currentTime = new Date().getTime();
        var diff = currentTime - ts;
        if (diff < ONE_MINUTE) {
          return 'seconds ago';
        } else if (diff < ONE_HOUR) {
          return 'minutes ago';
        } else if (diff < ONE_DAY) {
          return 'hours ago';
        } else if (diff < ONE_MONTH) {
          return 'days ago';
        } else {
          return 'months ago';
        }
      };
    }]);
</script>
</body>
</html>
```

In this example, we defined our own custom filter called timeAgo. We define a filter in a very similar manner to controllers and services, and we can also inject any services that our filter might depend on into it.

Every filter returns a function, which is what gets called for every usage of the filter. This function gets called with the value that the filter is being applied on. In this case, it is the `timestamp` as a number. The filter can then act upon this value, and slice and dice it in whichever way it wants. We just take the difference of the timestamp and the current time, and then return a string based on the difference.

If we want to take optional arguments, like the `currency` filter or the `number` filter, we just have to add them as additional parameters to the function we return. Suppose we want to take a Boolean to say only show minutes, or `ignoreSeconds`, then we could change the return to something like this:

```
return function(ts, ignoreSeconds) {
```

This would then be passed in from the HTML as follows, with the optional argument set to `true`:

```
{{ctrl.startTime | timeAgo:true}}
```

If you need multiple arguments, keep adding them and pass them in the same order in the HTML:

```
return function(ts, arg1, arg2, arg3) {
```

and:

```
{{ctrl.startTime | timeAgo:arg1:arg2:arg3}}
```

We will see how to test these filters in Chapter 9.

Things to Remember About Filters

We saw how to use existing filters in AngularJS, as well as how to customize them and pass them arguments. We then saw how we could use them in controllers and services, before finally creating our own custom filter. Now in this section, we cover some best practices and things to remember about working with filters in AngularJS:

View filters are executed every digest cycle
    The first and foremost thing we should know and remember about AngularJS filters is that if we are using them directly in the view (which is quite often), they are re-evaluated every time a digest cycle happens (we cover this in depth in "The Digest Cycle" on page 206). Therefore, as the data we are working on grows, we need to be aware of the extra computation we might be performing when we extensively use filters across our UI.

Filters should be blazingly fast
    Because of the previous point, whenever we write our own filters, we should write them in such a way that makes their execution blazingly fast. Ideally, our filter functions should be capable of executing multiple times in milliseconds. So things like DOM manipulation, asynchronous calls, and other slow activities should be avoided when we write filters.

Prefer filters in services and controllers for optimization

If you are working with large and complex arrays and data structures but still want to leverage filters because they are contained, modular, and reusable, then consider using filters directly in the controller or service. Inject the filter into your controller and service, and trigger the filter function as needed (like we saw in "Using Filters in Controllers and Services" on page 130). This will lead to a snappier and responsive UI, and is recommended over directly applying filters to large arrays. You can also prevent the filter from executing even when it has not changed, which will save some CPU cycles.

Conclusion

In this chapter, we explored AngularJS filters, which are great for formatting and converting data and values from one format to another. We then looked at the general way of using and chaining filters before digging into each of the built-in core AngularJS filters and the variety of ways to use and customize them. We then created our own `timeAgo` filter to display how long ago some time was. Finally, we talked about some general best practices and things to consider when working with or creating our own filters.

In the next chapter, we will cover how to unit test these filters that we have created.

CHAPTER 9

Unit Testing Filters

In Chapter 8, we covered how we could use existing AngularJS filters, as well as create our own filters. Filters are a great way of separating out common formatting and conversion logic into separate reusable components. In previous chapters, we saw how easy it was to create our own controllers and services, as well as unit test them.

In this chapter, we will work with the timeAgo filter we created in the previous chapter. We will first add complexity by adding optional parameters to the filter. Then we will unit test it step by step. By the end of the chapter, we will have Jasmine unit tests for all possible cases of our timeAgo filter.

The Filter Under Test

Let's use the timeAgo filter from "Creating AngularJS Filters" on page 131 as a base, and then add an optional argument to decide whether it should show the "seconds ago" message, or if it should start from the "minutes ago" message level only:

```
// File: chapter9/timeAgoFilter.js
angular.module('filtersApp', [])
  .filter('timeAgo', [function() {
    var ONE_MINUTE = 1000 * 60;
    var ONE_HOUR = ONE_MINUTE * 60;
    var ONE_DAY = ONE_HOUR * 24;
    var ONE_MONTH = ONE_DAY * 30;

    return function(ts, optShowSecondsMessage) {
      if (optShowSecondsMessage !== false) {
        optShowSecondsMessage = true;
      }

      var currentTime = new Date().getTime();
      var diff = currentTime - ts;
      if (diff < ONE_MINUTE && optShowSecondsMessage) {
```

```
      return 'seconds ago';
    } else if (diff < ONE_HOUR) {
      return 'minutes ago';
    } else if (diff < ONE_DAY) {
      return 'hours ago';
    } else if (diff < ONE_MONTH) {
      return 'days ago';
    } else {
      return 'months ago';
    }
  };
}]);
```

The `timeAgo` filter is almost unchanged, but now has a configuration option to allow the user to decide if he wants the messages to start at "seconds ago" or from "minutes ago" only. The default shows the seconds message. One might use the above filter as follows:

```
{{ myCtrl.ts | timeAgo }}
```

If we decided to only show messages from minutes, we might use it as follows with the optional argument set to `false`:

```
{{ myCtrl.ts | timeAgo:false }}
```

Testing the timeAgo Filter

We saw in Chapter 8 how to create filters, and how to use them in HTML, controllers, and services. In our unit tests, we'll use the same flow as we would in our controllers (i.e., we will inject our filter into our unit test, and then execute them directly as functions). We can then check the return values to see if they are executing correctly and our logic is as expected:

```
// File: chapter9/timeAgoFilterSpec.js
describe('timeAgo Filter', function() {
  beforeEach(module('filtersApp'));

  var filter;
  beforeEach(inject(function(timeAgoFilter) {
    filter = timeAgoFilter;
  }));

  it('should respond based on timestamp', function() {
    // The presence of new Date().getTime() makes it slightly
    // hard to unit test deterministicly.
    // Ideally, we would inject a dateProvider into the timeAgo
    // filter, but we are trying to keep it simple here.
    // So we will assume that our tests are fast enough to
    // execute in mere milliseconds.

    var currentTime = new Date().getTime();
```

```
    currentTime -= 10000;
    expect(filter(currentTime)).toEqual('seconds ago');
    var fewMinutesAgo = currentTime - 1000 * 60;
    expect(filter(fewMinutesAgo)).toEqual('minutes ago');
    var fewHoursAgo = currentTime - 1000 * 60 * 68;
    expect(filter(fewHoursAgo)).toEqual('hours ago');
    var fewDaysAgo = currentTime - 1000 * 60 * 60 * 26;
    expect(filter(fewDaysAgo)).toEqual('days ago');
    var fewMonthsAgo = currentTime - 1000 * 60 * 60 * 24 * 32;
    expect(filter(fewMonthsAgo)).toEqual('months ago');
  });
});
```

This example test is nothing very new or out of the ordinary. As part of beforeEach, we instantiate our module and then inject our filter into the test (using timeAgoFilter; don't forget that AngularJS automatically adds the word Filter after the filter). We then write our unit test, where we directly call the filter with the value it needs to filter. In this case, we create the current timestamp and then modify it slightly so that we can hit each of the if conditions in the filter.

This of course tests the filter without the optional argument. How would we modify this to test with the additional Boolean?

```
// File: chapter9/timeAgoFilterOptionalArgumentSpec.js
describe('timeAgo Filter', function() {
  beforeEach(module('filtersApp'));

  var filter;
  beforeEach(inject(function(timeAgoFilter) {
    filter = timeAgoFilter;
  }));

  it('should respond based on timestamp', function() {
    // The presence of new Date().getTime() makes it slightly
    // hard to unit test deterministicly.
    // Ideally, we would inject a dateProvider into the timeAgo
    // filter, but we are trying to keep it simple here.
    // So we will assume that our tests are fast enough to
    // execute in mere milliseconds.

    var currentTime = new Date().getTime();
    currentTime -= 10000;
    expect(filter(currentTime, false)).toEqual('minutes ago');
    var fewMinutesAgo = currentTime - 1000 * 60;
    expect(filter(fewMinutesAgo, false)).toEqual('minutes ago');
    var fewHoursAgo = currentTime - 1000 * 60 * 68;
    expect(filter(fewHoursAgo, false)).toEqual('hours ago');
    var fewDaysAgo = currentTime - 1000 * 60 * 60 * 26;
    expect(filter(fewDaysAgo, false)).toEqual('days ago');
    var fewMonthsAgo = currentTime - 1000 * 60 * 60 * 24 * 32;
    expect(filter(fewMonthsAgo, false)).toEqual('months ago');
```

```
        });
    });
```

We can pass optional or other arguments to the filter as additional parameters to the filter function. In this case, we pass `false` to tell the filter not to show the seconds message. Our test changes minutely, such that both the `currentTime` and the `fewMinu tesAgo` conditions return the `"minutes ago"` string as compared to `"seconds ago"` and `"minutes ago"` previously.

Conclusion

Unit testing filters is quite simple, and simply requires us to inject the filter as we would any other service dependency. After that, it's a matter of calling the filter with various arguments and seeing if it performs as expected under all the conditions.

In the next chapter, we will look at how AngularJS simplifies routing and allows us to declaratively set up various routes in our application. We will use the optional `ngRoute` module, as well as see how we can use it to perform access control in our application.

CHAPTER 10

Routing Using ngRoute

Until this point, we have dealt with various parts of AngularJS, including controllers, services, and filters. But we have not yet moved beyond having just one HTML template that changes behavior depending on the service or the controller. In a real Single-Page Application, we would usually have multiple views that would be loaded when the user clicks certain links or goes to a URL in the browser. Replicating that in a pure JavaScript framework is difficult, because implementing routing always involves:

- Creating a state machine
- Adding and removing items from the browser's history
- Loading and unloading templates and relevant JS as the state changes
- Handling the various idiosyncrasies across different browsers

More often than not, these get wrapped into reusable plugins or reimplemented from scratch. And we as developers are left hunting across the codebase to figure out how it is implemented and how to deal with it.

AngularJS provides us with an optional module called ngRoute, which can be used to do routing in an AngularJS application. Following the AngularJS philosophy, routing in AngularJS is declarative, so all routes are defined in a single configuration section where we can specify what the route is and what AngularJS needs to do when that route is encountered.

In this chapter, we will implement our own multiview AngularJS application with different routes while getting a detailed look at the various options that can be used to configure AngularJS routing. We will also dive deep into the concept of resolve, and add a page that can only be accessed by certain users under certain conditions. Finally, we will look at some other alternatives that can be used for routing in AngularJS, like ui-router.

Routing in a Single-Page Application

First of all, when we talk about routing in a Single-Page Application, we are not talking standard URLs, but what we call hashbang URLs. For example, a traditional URL might look something like *http://www.myawesomeapp.com/first/page*. In a Single-Page Application, it would usually look like *http://www.myawesomeapp.com/#/first/page* or *http://www.myawesomeapp.com/#!/first/page*.

This is because the browser treats URLs with hashes differently than URLs without. When the browser sees *http://www.myawesomeapp.com/first/page*, it makes a server request to *http://www.myawesomeapp.com/first/page* to fetch the relevant HTML and JavaScript for that particular URL. And when the user navigates from there to, say, *http://www.myawesomeapp.com/second/page*, it makes a full request to the server again to fetch the entire HTML contents.

In a Single-Page Application, we want to avoid this and prevent a full page reload. We only want to load the relevant data and HTML snippet instead of fetching the entire HTML again and again, especially if most of it does not change between pages. When the browser encounters a URL like *http://www.myawesomeapp.com/#/first/page* or *http://www.myawesomeapp.com/#!/first/page*, it makes a server request to *http://www.myawesomeapp.com/*. Any URL fragment after the # sign gets ignored by the browser in the server call. It falls upon the client to then take that part of the URL and deal with it. When the user navigates from *http://www.myawesomeapp.com/#/first/page* to *http://www.myawesomeapp.com/#/second/page*, the browser does not make any additional requests. There is no page reload happening. This flow is illustrated in Figure 10-1.

Thus, Single-Page Applications take advantage of this fact and use the hash fragment (the URL after the hash) to handle navigation. When the hash fragment changes, the JavaScript responds and loads only the relevant data and HTML instead of reloading the entire HTML. This makes the application faster and snappier because less data is fetched from the server.

AngularJS leverages hash URLs for routing, so all AngularJS routes that we define will be hash URLs. So if we defined a /first route, the /first would be added after the # in the URL.

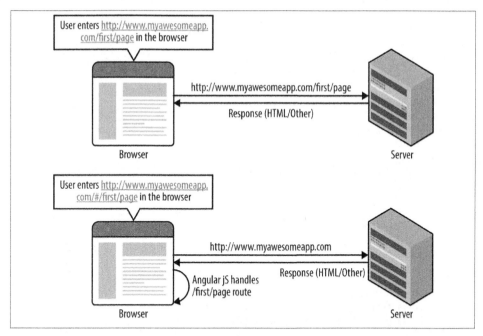

Figure 10-1. Flow of normal URLs versus hash URLs

Using ngRoute

AngularJS routing used to be part of the core AngularJS library before being split off into an optional module that needs to be included if it is being used. This was done because there were a lot of open source alternatives to routing that started being used heavily. With AngularJS version 1.2, routing became an optional module for AngularJS. To use AngularJS's routing module (or technically any other routing module that follows the AngularJS routing paradigm), the steps are as follows:

1. Include the optional module source code in the application's HTML. Most of the time, it's as simple as:

   ```
   <script type="text/javascript" src="/path/to/angular-route.min.js"></script>
   ```

2. Include the module as a dependency of our main AngularJS app module, like so:

   ```
   angular.module("myApp", ["ngRoute"])
   ```

3. Mark which section of the page AngularJS should change when the route changes. With the ngRoute module, this is done using the ng-view directive in the HTML.

4. Define our routes in the config section (which we saw in Chapter 6 while configuring the $http service) using the $routeProvider service.

Let's look at a very simple example that loads two different templates when the route changes:

```html
<!-- File: chapter10/simple-routing.html -->
<html>
<head>
  <title>AngularJS Routing</title>
  <script
  src="https://ajax.googleapis.com/ajax/libs/angularjs/1.2.19/angular.js">
  </script>
  <script
  src="https://ajax.googleapis.com/ajax/libs/angularjs/1.2.19/angular-route.js">
  </script>
</head>

<body ng-app="routingApp">

  <h2>AngularJS Routing Application</h2>

  <ul>
    <li><a href="#/">Default Route</a></li>
    <li><a href="#/second">Second Route</a></li>
    <li><a href="#/asdasdasd">Nonexistent Route</a></li>
  </ul>

  <div ng-view></div>

  <script type="text/javascript">
    angular.module('routingApp', ['ngRoute'])
      .config(['$routeProvider', function($routeProvider) {

        $routeProvider.when('/', {
          template: '<h5>This is the default route</h5>'
        })
        .when('/second', {
          template: '<h5>This is the second route</h5>'
        })
        .otherwise({redirectTo: '/'});
      }]);
  </script>
</body>
</html>
```

This example shows a very simple AngularJS application that enables routing. As already mentioned, before the code snippet, we do the following:

1. Include the *angular-route.js* file *after angular.js* is loaded to make the `ngRoute` module available.

2. We mark in our HTML where we want the routing to take effect with the `ng-view` directive.

3. When we create our module, we specify that it depends on the `ngRoute` module (using `angular.module("routingApp", ["ngRoute"])`).

4. We then define our routes in AngularJS's `config` section using the `$routeProvider`.

5. Routing inside this application can be done via simple anchor tags (like the ones we have) or by manually editing the URL in the browser. In fact, try it out, and see if you can directly get to the second route via a URL.

6. It takes care of the browser history, so you can actually use back and forward buttons in your browser to navigate within the application.

The `$routeProvider` allows us to define our routes in one place using the `when()` function. The `when` function takes two arguments:

- The first is a URL or a URL regex that specifies when this particular route is applicable.

- The second is a configuration object that specifies what needs to happen when the particular route is encountered.

We keep the previous example simple by telling AngularJS to load only a certain HTML template that we specify inline. Both of these are very simple, but could include AngularJS bindings and all the other components we've seen so far in this book. We will cover what else we can do with routing in the following section.

We also call an `otherwise` function on the `$routeProvider` that specifies what AngularJS needs to do if the user tries to go to a URL that is not specified in the configuration. That is, if the user tries to go to `/#/asdasdsa`, it redirects the user to `/`, which loads the default route template. Without the `otherwise`, the user would see an empty page because AngularJS does not know what template or HTML to load for that particular URL.

Routing Options

In the previous section, we saw how to define a very simple AngularJS application that leverages routing. We simply loaded different templates for different routes, and nothing else. The AngularJS route definition allows us to define more complex templates. The `$routeProvider.when` function takes a URL or URL regular expression as the first argument, and the route configuration object as the second. The syntax is as follows:

```
$routeProvider.when(url, {
        template: string,
        templateUrl: string,
        controller: string, function or array,
        controllerAs: string,
        resolve: object<key, function>
});
```

The following are the options we can specify and define when specifying route definitions with the `$routeProvider` service:

`url`

This is the first argument passed to the `$routeProvider` when function. This specifies the URL (or URLs, in case it is a regular expression) for which the route configuration must be triggered. It also allows us to specify variables in the route that could be used to have the ID or relevant information needed for the page. For example, valid routes are */list, /recipe/:recipeId*, and so on. In the case of the latter, it tells the `$routeProvider` that the URL will have some variable content after / *recipe/*, and the value of that needs to be picked up and passed to the controller using the `$routeParams` service. We explore that in the next section.

`template`

In cases where the HTML to be displayed is not very large, it can directly be inlined as a string as part of the route configuration object that is passed as the second argument to the `$routeProvider.when` function. AngularJS directly inserts this template HTML into the `ng-view` directive.

`templateUrl`

Often, the HTML for individual views will be significantly complex and large. In these cases, we can extract the HTML into separate files, and give the URL to the HTML file as the `templateUrl`. AngularJS loads the HTML file from the server when it needs to display the particular route. Future requests for that template are served from a local cache to prevent repeated calls to the server. An example of this follows:

```
$routeProvider.when('/test', {
        templateUrl: 'views/test.html',
});
```

This fetches *views/test.html* from the server and loads it into the `ng-view`.

`controller`

There are two ways in which we can define the controller for a particular route. This is an optional argument in the `$routeProvider.when` definition, in case we have not directly defined the controller in the HTML using the `ng-controller` directive. If the controller has already been declared using the `angularApp.con troller("MyCtrl")` syntax, we can specify the name of the controller as a string. The controller key can also use the `ng-controller`'s `controllerAs` syntax, so we can use it like `MyCtrl as ctrl` in the controller key for the route definition.

The other option is to define the controller inline, in which case we pass the controller function directly to the controller key. We can also use the array syntax to inject our dependencies in a way that is uglification-safe. The code might look something like:

```
$routeProvider.when('/test', {
  template: '<h1>Test Route</h1>',
  controller: ['$window', function($window) {
    $window.alert('Test route has been loaded!');
  }]
});
```

In this example, we define a route that has an inline controller with a dependency on the $window service. All the route does is show a window alert on load. It is *recommended* that we use the controller syntax to define our controllers; defining it inline will make it hard to write unit tests or reuse it in other routes.

controllerAs

The controllerAs key is there as a convenience in case we don't want to define what the controller should be named inline in the controller key. The two route definitions in the following example are equivalent in terms of functionality:

```
$routeProvider.when('/test', {
    template: '<h1>Test Route</h1>',
    controller: 'MyCtrl as ctrl'
});
$routeProvider.when('/test', {
    template: '<h1>Test Route</h1>',
    controller: 'MyCtrl',
    controllerAs: 'ctrl'
});
```

Whether we use the controller key and define the renaming in it, or define it separately using the controllerAs key, there is no functional difference. It is purely a personal preference.

redirectTo

There are cases where some routes that used to exist have been renamed or cases where multiple URLs in the application are actually the same page underneath. In such cases, the redirectTo key can be used to specify the URL to which that particular route must navigate when it is encountered. It can be used for error handling and common route handling. For example:

```
$routeProvider.when('/new', {
    template: '<h1>New Route</h1>'
});
$routeProvider.when('/old', {
    redirectTo: '/new'
});
```

In this example, AngularJS opens the */new* URL when the user enters either */#/new* or */#/old* in the browser.

resolve

> The final configuration, and most versatile and complex of the route configuration options, is the `resolve`. In the next section, we cover how to implement resolves. At a conceptual level, resolves are a way of executing and finishing asynchronous tasks before a particular route is loaded. This is a great way to check if the user is logged in and has authorization and permissions, and even preload some data before a controller and route are loaded into the view.

Using Resolves for Pre-Route Checks

As mentioned in the previous section, when we define a resolve, we can define a set of asynchronous tasks to execute before the route is loaded. A resolve is a set of keys and functions. Each function can return a value or a promise. A sample resolve, which makes a server call and returns a hardcoded value, is shown here:

```
angular.module('resolveApp', ['ngRoute'])
  .value('Constant', {MAGIC_NUMBER: 42})
  .config(['$routeProvider', function($routeProvider) {
    $routeProvider.when('/', {
      template: '<h1>Main Page, no resolves</h1>'
    }).when('/protected', {
      template: '<h2>Protected Page</h2>',
      resolve: {
        immediate: ['Constant', function(Constant) {
          return Constant.MAGIC_NUMBER * 4;
        }],
        async: ['$http', function($http) {
          return $http.get('/api/hasAccess');
        }]
      },
      controller: ['$log', 'immediate', 'async',
        function($log, immediate, async) {
          $log.log('Immediate is ', immediate);
          $log.log('Server returned for async', async);
        }]
    });
  }]);
```

This example expects that there is a server-side API available at */api/hasAccess*, which on a GET request returns a status 200 response if the user has access, and a nonstatus 200 response if the user does not have access.

There are two routes in this example. The first route is a very standard route that loads an HTML template when the route definition is encountered. We have no resolves on this route, so it always loads properly.

The second definition contains a resolve defined with two keys, `immediate` and `async`. Note that these are keys of our own choosing, so this could very well be `myKey1` and `myKey2`. AngularJS does not expect or force us to use any particular key. Each key takes an array, which is the AngularJS Dependency Injection syntax. We define the dependencies for the `resolve` in the array, and get it injected into the `resolve` function. The first resolve key, `immediate`, gets the `Constant` dependency injected into it, and returns a constant value multiplied by some number. The second resolve key, `async`, gets the `$http` dependency injected into it, and makes a server call to */api/hasAccess*. It then returns the promise for that particular server call. AngularJS guarantees the following:

- If the `resolve` function returns a value, AngularJS immediately finishes executing and treats it as a successful resolve.

- If the `resolve` function returns a promise, AngularJS waits for the promise to return and treats the resolve as successful if the promise is successful. If the promise is rejected, the resolve is treated as a failure.

- Because of the `resolve` function, AngularJS ensures that the route does not load until all the `resolve` functions are finished executing. If there are multiple `re solve` keys that make asynchronous calls, AngularJS executes all of them in parallel and waits for all of them to finish executing before loading the page.

- If any of the resolves encounter an error or any of the promises returned are rejected (is a failure), AngularJS doesn't load the route.

In the previous example, because the `immediate` resolve key is returning only a value, it is treated as a successful resolve every time. The `async` resolve key makes a server call, and if it is successful, the route is loaded. If the server returns a non-200 status response, AngularJS doesn't load the page. AngularJS still loads and caches the template if any of the resolves fail, but the controller associated with the route isn't loaded and the HTML doesn't make it into the `ng-view`.

In these cases, the user still sees the last page he was on. So it might not be a great user experience, because the user won't know that something went wrong. In "A Full AngularJS Routing Example" on page 150, we'll see a full-fledged AngularJS routing example that uses resolves in a more comprehensive pattern.

One other interesting thing about resolves is that we can get the value from each of the `resolve` keys injected into our controller, if we want or need the data. Each key can directly be injected into the controller by adding it as a dependency. This is over and above any AngularJS service dependency we might have. The following items are injected into the controller:

- The value itself, if the `resolve` function was returning a value

- The resolution of a promise, if the `resolve` function was returning a promise

In the case of the async resolve, we get the resolved value of the promise, which is the response object from the server, with the config, status, headers, and data. This is what's normally passed to the success function of the then of the promise:

```
$http.get('/api/hasAccess').then(function(response) {
    console.log('I am passed to the controller', response);
    return response;
});
```

In this case, response is the value that async will take when it is injected into the controller.

Using the $routeParams Service

The other thing to note, and which is often required in Single-Page Applications, is the context for a route. For example, we might want to load a certain email thread or view the details of a certain recipe. We want this information reflected in the URL so the user can bookmark it or directly come back to it. In such cases, it is recommended that controllers look up the IDs and information from the URL instead of relying on global state. It uses this information to load the necessary details from the server.

That is, in an ideal Single-Page Application, a controller and a route should be able to independently bootstrap themselves and not expect that the user first goes to a list page and then to the details page. These URL parameters don't have to be parsed from the URL, but can directly be accessed from a convenient service that AngularJS provides, called $routeParams:

```
angular.module('resolveApp', ['ngRoute'])
  .config(['$routeProvider', function($routeProvider) {
    $routeProvider.when('/', {
        template: '<h1>Main Page</h1>'
    }).when('/detail/:detId', {
        template: '<h2>Loaded {{myCtrl.detailId}}' +
          ' and query String is {{myCtrl.qStr}}</h2>',
        controller: ['$routeParams', function($routeParams) {
          this.detailId = $routeParams.detId;
          this.qStr = $routeParams.q;
        }],
        controllerAs: 'myCtrl'
    });
}]);
```

In this example, the / route is pretty standard in terms of what we have seen so far. It just loads a template when it is seen. The second route is defined as /detail/:detId. This tells the AngularJS routing that there will be a value after the /detail in the URL that needs to be picked up, stored, and provided as detId to the controller. For example, URLs like /detail/123 will match the route, with detId taking the value 123. Even the URL /detail/shyam will also match the route, with detId taking the value shyam. The

URL regex does not impose any restrictions on what kinds of values the parameters can take.

We can access these values in our controllers by asking for the $routeParams service. The $routeParams service is responsible for reading the URL, parsing it, and finding all these variables and making them accessible to the controller in a nice way. If we go to a URL like *detail/123?q=MySearchParam*, AngularJS will parse this URL and the $routeParams service will have the following value:

```
{
    detId: '123',
    q: 'MySearchParam'
}
```

Nowhere do we have to manually call parseURL or anything like that. Our controller can directly access these keys from the $routeParams service and do what it needs to from there. We can then make a server call to load the details, or process data and hide and show UI elements as need be.

Things to Watch Out For

Before we jump into a full-fledged AngularJS routing example hooked up to an end-to-end server, let's quickly talk about a few things that are not well documented, but that can cause headaches while developing an application:

Empty templates

> AngularJS requires that each route be associated with a nonempty template or templateUrl. That means if we leave out both template and templateUrl as part of a route, AngularJS silently drops that route and doesn't allow us to navigate to it in the UI. If we have a route that does some work before navigating away from the page (a logout route is an example), where the user will not be seeing any UI, make sure we specify at least a template for the route that is nonempty. Even an empty string will be treated the same as not specifying the template!

Resolve injection into controller

> If we use resolves and want to inject the values of the dependency into our controller, make sure we are defining our controller as part of the route definition, and not directly in our controller with the ng-controller directive. Otherwise, AngularJS does not know which controller needs those dependencies, and thus cannot inject it properly.

$routeParam variable type

> One potential problem when using the $routeParams service is when comparing the values we get from $routeParams with objects from our database. For example, if we're storing IDs as numbers in our database and trying to compare that with data from the $routeParams service, we'd better watch out! $routeParam returns

string values by default for all keys. A === comparison of something from $rou
teParams with something from our database, which is a number, fails. We need to
make sure we convert both values into the same format before we do any comparisons with data from $routeParams.

One `ng-view` *per application*

This is the last thing we should keep in mind when working with `ngRoute`. For every
AngularJS application that uses `ngRoute`, there can be one and only one `ng-view`
directive for that application. We cannot have multiple or nested `ng-views`. And
this is because the `ng-view` directive is quite simple in that it notices a URL change
and updates its content as per the route definition. If we have multiple `ng-views`,
we will see the same content multiple times. If we nest `ng-views`, we'll see the content
inside the content, which won't serve the purpose we are trying to solve.

A Full AngularJS Routing Example

We will now take a full end-to-end example that uses both AngularJS routing and the
`$http` service to communicate with our server. The next example is a FIFA Teams app,
which shows a list of some of the teams that play soccer.

Before we jump into the code, let's lay out how the application works:

- A landing page shows a list of teams. Anybody can access this page.
- A login page allows users to log in to the application. Anybody can access this page.
- Details pages for teams are access-controlled. Only logged-in users can access the
  details page. This is true whether the user logged in right before accessing, or logged
  in and then closed the window and came back at any later point. The latter works
  because the login session is maintained on the server, not on the client.

For the purpose of keeping the application simple and focused, the server has already
been created in NodeJS, which allows us to focus on the routing and server communication aspects of the client-side application. You can grab the source code from *chap-
ter10* of the GitHub repository (*http://bit.ly/1CqINTG*).

Run:

```
npm install
```

from the *chapter10/routing-example* folder to install its dependencies. Then execute:

```
node server.js
```

to get the server up and running. We can then navigate to *http://localhost:8000* to view
the application in action.

The following is the *index.html* for our application:

```
<!-- File: chapter10/routing-example/app/index.html -->
<html>
<head>
  <title>FIFA Teams</title>
  <link rel="stylesheet" href="styles/bootstrap.css">
  <link rel="stylesheet" href="styles/main.css">
</head>
<body ng-app="fifaApp" class="landing">
  <div class="top-bar"  ng-controller="MainCtrl as mainCtrl">
    <div class="pull-left">
      <span><a href="#/">FIFA TEAMS</a></span>
    </div>
    <div class="pull-right">
      <span ng-hide="mainCtrl.userService.isLoggedIn">
        <a href="#/login">Login</a>
      </span>
      <span ng-show="mainCtrl.userService.isLoggedIn">
        <!-- server-side route, not a client-side route -->
        <a href="/api/logout">Logout</a>
      </span>
    </div>
  </div>

  <div ng-view></div>

  <script src="scripts/vendors/jquery-1.11.1.js"></script>
  <script src="scripts/vendors/angular.js"></script>
  <script src="scripts/vendors/angular-route.js"></script>

  <script src="scripts/app.js"></script>
  <script src="scripts/services.js"></script>
  <script src="scripts/controllers.js"></script>
</body>
</html>
```

Our *index.html* file is noteworthy in the following ways:

- ng-app is on the body tag that dictates where to find the controllers, configuration, etc.

- A top bar with a controller of its own is used to show a logo, as well as login and logout links. To ensure that we don't show both links at the same time, and that the login state is handled at an application level, we have a UserService (which we'll look at in a bit) that holds the user's logged-in state. The login and logout links are then shown and hidden based on this service.

- An ng-view is the part of the HTML that responds to URL changes.

- We then load jQuery and AngularJS, followed by our own app code.

The most noteworthy thing is the login/logout links, which are shown and hidden using ng-show and ng-hide, respectively. They are backed by the UserService instead of a controller, so that regardless of which page or screen the user is on, login and logouts are reflected across the application.

Before we look at *app.js*, which is used to define our routes and configuration, let's take a look at the services we defined for our application in *services.js*:

```
// File: chapter10/routing-example/app/scripts/services.js
angular.module('fifaApp')
  .factory('FifaService', ['$http',
    function($http) {
      return {
        getTeams: function() {
          return $http.get('/api/team');
        },

        getTeamDetails: function(code) {
          return $http.get('/api/team/' + code);
        }
      }
  }])
  .factory('UserService', ['$http', function($http) {
    var service = {
      isLoggedIn: false,

      session: function() {
        return $http.get('/api/session')
              .then(function(response) {
          service.isLoggedIn = true;
          return response;
        });
      },

      login: function(user) {
        return $http.post('/api/login', user)
          .then(function(response) {
            service.isLoggedIn = true;
            return response;
        });
      }
    };
    return service;
  }]);
```

We define two services, FifaService and UserService. FifaService is used to fetch the list of teams, and the details of each team from the server using HTTP GET requests. UserService also has two methods, one to check if the current user has an active session on the server, and the second to log in the user. The server defines the following endpoints:

- GET on /api/team returns the list of teams in the system as an array.

- GET on /api/team/:code, with code being the code of the team, returns the details of a particular team as a single object.

- GET on /api/session returns either a 400 status if the user is not logged in, or an object with the user details if he is logged in. This enables the client (the web application) to verify that the user is logged in to the server.

- POST on /api/login with POST data containing {username: 'myuser', password: 'mypassword'} will try to log in the user. If successful, it returns what the session call returns. Otherwise, it returns a status 400 error if the user authentication fails with the msg field in the object containing the reason for the failure.

All the service APIs that make HTTP requests return promises that allow controllers or other services to chain and perform their own postcompletion work.

The *controllers.js* file is next:

```
// File: chapter10/routing-example/app/scripts/controllers.js
angular.module('fifaApp')
  .controller('MainCtrl', ['UserService',
    function(UserService) {
      var self = this;
      self.userService = UserService;

      // Check if the user is logged in when the application
      // loads
      // User Service will automatically update isLoggedIn
      // after this call finishes
      UserService.session();
  }])

  .controller('TeamListCtrl', ['FifaService',
    function(FifaService) {
      var self = this;
      self.teams = [];

      FifaService.getTeams().then(function(resp) {
        self.teams = resp.data;
      });
  }])

  .controller('LoginCtrl', ['UserService', '$location',
    function(UserService, $location) {
      var self = this;
      self.user = {username: '', password: ''};

      self.login = function() {
        UserService.login(self.user).then(function(success) {
          $location.path('/team');
```

```
      }, function(error) {
        self.errorMessage = error.data.msg;
      })
    };
})

.controller('TeamDetailsCtrl',
  ['$location', '$routeParams', 'FifaService',
  function($location, $routeParams, FifaService) {
    var self = this;
    self.team = {};
    FifaService.getTeamDetails($routeParams.code)
        .then(function(resp){
      self.team = resp.data;
    }, function(error){
      $location.path('/login');
    });
}]);
```

Four controllers are defined for this application:

- MainCtrl is used to handle the top navigation bar, and basically exposes the User Service to the view so that the HTML can hide and show the login/logout links depending on the user's state. It also makes a call to the server to see if the user is logged in when the application loads.

- TeamListCtrl is used for the landing route, and just uses the FifaService to fetch a list of teams when it loads. It then exposes this data for the view to display.

- LoginCtrl has only a function to let the user log in when he fills in his username and password and clicks the login button. If the login is successful, it redirects the user to the home page. In the case of an error, it shows an error message in the UI.

- The TeamDetailsCtrl is the only one that does something unique and interesting, in that it loads a specific team based on the route. Suppose the user navigates to *http://localhost:8000/#/team/ESP*. This triggers the route that loads TeamDetailsCtrl. Now TeamDetailsCtrl has to figure out which team it has been loaded for. It can access this information from a service known as $routeParams. $routeParams has the current team's code set in it at the key code. This is set up via routing, which we will get to in just a bit. It then loads the team details from the server based on this code from the URL.

All server requests happen via $http and return a promise, so we add a .then() function when we care about getting notified about it finishing, or need the result (like loading the teams, an individual team, or the login call).

Let's also quickly take a look at the various HTMLs. These are all *partials*, so they aren't complete HTML documents and don't have html, head, and body tags. First up is the *team_list.html* file:

```
<!-- File: chapter10/routing-example/app/views/teams_list.html -->
<div class="team-list-container">
  <div class="team"
      ng-repeat="team in teamListCtrl.teams | orderBy: 'rank'">
    <div class="team-info row">
      <div class="col-lg-1 rank">
        <span ng-bind="team.rank"></span>
      </div>
      <div class="col-sm-3">
        <img ng-src="{{team.flagUrl}}" class="flag">
      </div>
      <div class="col-lg-6 name">
       <a title="Image Courtesy: Wikipedia"
          ng-href="#/team/{{team.code}}"
          ng-bind="team.name"
          style="color: cadetblue;"></a>
      </div>
    </div>
  </div>
</div>
```

The teams list displays the teams from the controller using an ng-repeat. Each individual name in the list is a link to the details page of the team using the ng-href directive. The images are shown using the ng-src directive.

> The ng-href directive is used whenever we have dynamic URLs. While we can use a statement like href="{{ctrl.myUrl}}", it is *recommended* that we use ng-href instead.
>
> This is because when the application initially loads, there is a small window of time when the href has the value {{ctrl.myUrl}} before AngularJS kicks in and replaces the content. To avoid this, we use ng-href, which initially leaves the href as blank and places the value of ctrl.myUrl in href after AngularJS is up and running.
>
> Similarly, the ng-src directive is used for images that need dynamic URLs. If we use src="{{ctrl.myImg}}" in our HTML, the HTML immediately makes a call to fetch {{ctrl.myImg}} as an image from the server, which will obviously throw an error. Thus, the ng-src directive allows AngularJS to kick in and set the src tag on the img after the value has been calculated. Thus it prevents an extra erroneous request.

Next up is the *login.html* page:

```
<!-- File: chapter10/routing-example/app/views/login.html -->
<div class="login-container"
    ng-controller="LoginCtrl as loginCtrl">
  <div class="alert alert-danger"
      ng-bind="loginCtrl.errorMessage"
```

```
           ng-show="loginCtrl.errorMessage"></div>
      <div class="card login-card">
        <div class="login-form">
          <form name="loginForm"
                ng-submit="loginCtrl.login()"
                class="form-horizontal"
                role="form">
            <div class="form-group">
                <label for="email">Username</label>
                <input type="text"
                       ng-model="loginCtrl.user.username"
                       class="form-control"
                       id="email"
                       placeholder="Enter Username"
                       required="">
            </div>
            <div class="form-group">
                <label for="password">Password</label>
                <input type="password"
                       ng-model="loginCtrl.user.password"
                       class="form-control"
                       id="password"
                       placeholder="Enter Password"
                       required="">
            </div>
            <input type="submit"
                   class="btn btn-success btn-lg"
                   value="Login"
                   ng-disabled="loginForm.$invalid">
        </form>
      </div>
    </div>
  </div>
```

The *login.html* file displays a simple form with two fields for the username and pass
word. It defines the controller using the ng-controller directive directly, and uses the
ng-submit to trigger the login call from the controller. It also has a section that shows
the errorMessage if available.

The last page is the *team_details.html*, which displays all the details of the team in a nice,
orderly fashion:

```
<!-- File: chapter10/routing-example/app/views/team_details.html -->
<div class="team-details-container card">
  <div class="team-logo">
      <img title="Image Courtesy: Wikipedia"
           ng-src="{{teamDetailsCtrl.team.logoUrl}}">
  </div>
  <div class="name">
      <span ng-bind="teamDetailsCtrl.team.name"></span>
      (<span ng-bind="teamDetailsCtrl.team.fifaCode"></span>)
  </div>
```

```
<div class="detail">
  <div class="label">
    <span>Nickname</span>
  </div>
  <div class="title">
    <span ng-bind="teamDetailsCtrl.team.nickname"></span>
  </div>
</div>
<div class="detail">
  <div class="label">
    <span>FIFA Ranking</span>
  </div>
  <div class="title">
    <span ng-bind="teamDetailsCtrl.team.fifaRanking">
    </span>
  </div>
</div>
<div class="detail">
  <div class="label">
    <span>Association</span>
  </div>
  <div class="title">
    <span ng-bind="teamDetailsCtrl.team.association"></span>
  </div>
</div>
<div class="detail">
  <div class="label">
    <span>Head Coach</span>
  </div>
  <div class="title">
    <span ng-bind="teamDetailsCtrl.team.headCoach"></span>
  </div>
</div>
<div class="detail">
  <div class="label">
    <span>Captain</span>
  </div>
  <div class="title">
    <span ng-bind="teamDetailsCtrl.team.captain"></span>
  </div>
</div>
</div>
```

The team details simply displays all the data using ng-bind in the UI, after the controller has fetched the team details for the particular team from the server.

With all this done, let's look at how to set up routing:

```
// File: chapter10/routing-example/app/scripts/app.js
angular.module('fifaApp', ['ngRoute'])
  .config(function($routeProvider) {

    $routeProvider.when('/', {
```

```
      templateUrl: 'views/team_list.html',
      controller: 'TeamListCtrl as teamListCtrl'
    })
    .when('/login', {
      templateUrl: 'views/login.html'
    })
    .when('/team/:code', {
      templateUrl: 'views/team_details.html',
      controller:'TeamDetailsCtrl as teamDetailsCtrl',
      resolve: {
        auth: ['$q', '$location', 'UserService',
          function($q, $location, UserService) {
            return UserService.session().then(
              function(success) {},
              function(err) {
                $location.path('/login');
                $location.replace();
                return $q.reject(err);
              });
          }]
      }
    });
    $routeProvider.otherwise({
      redirectTo: '/'
    });
  });
```

We define our application (and create our module) in the *app.js* file. We define our fifaApp module, and specify that it depends on the ngRoute module so that we can use routing in our application. Let's now dive deep into our routes:

- The / route introduces nothing new, in that it loads a templateUrl and attaches the TeamListCtrl to it when it loads. There are no variables in the URL, nor any access control checks.

- The /login route loads a templateUrl. The reason it doesn't specify a controller in the route configuration is because the HTML defines the controller using the ng-controller syntax. For each route, we can decide to include the controller directly in the HTML or using the controller configuration in the route.

- The largest and most complex of the routes is the Team Detail route. It is defined as /team/:code. This tells AngularJS that as part of the URL, take everything after /team/ and make it available to the controller in case it requires it as the variable code in $routeParams.

- Lastly, there is an otherwise route, which redirects the user to the / route if the user enters a URL that the route configuration doesn't recognize.

Let's dive into the Team Detail route definition a bit more. Here are the key highlights:

- The route itself has the variable code defined in it, which is made available to controllers using $routeParams service. A controller could get the $routeParams service injected, and then access $routeParams.code, as our TeamDetailsCtrl does.

- The controller is defined in the route, and uses the controllerAs syntax to name the instance of the controller teamDetailsCtrl.

- We use a resolve object with one key, auth. This key is arbitrary, but resolve is used as a way of checking with the server to see if the user is currently logged in. The auth key takes a function, using the Dependency Injection syntax, so we can inject any services we need into each individual resolve key.

- The authentication resolve injects UserService into it, and makes a call to User Service.session() (which makes a server call to /api/session). The auth resolve function returns a promise. AngularJS then guarantees the following:

  — AngularJS won't load the page until the promise is successfully fulfilled.

  — AngularJS will prevent the page from loading if the promise fails.

- We also chain the promise and do nothing in the case of success. This ensures that the returned promise succeeds if the server call succeeds.

- We add an error handler in the then of the promise to redirect the user to the login screen, in case the server returns a non-200 response. We also make sure that we *reject the promise* in the case of an error, because we still want the promise to fail. If we don't $q.reject, that tells AngularJS that the error was handled successfully

This ensures that if the user is not logged in when he clicks the link for the details of the team, AngularJS will redirect him to the login page. And because we make a call to the server to authorize the user, if the user logs in from another window or tab, and then clicks it from this screen, he will still proceed to the page without the client prompting for a unneeded login. To check what happens when the user enters the correct username and password, try logging in with "admin" as the username and "admin" as the password.

 Notice that we set the redirection path using $location.path(), as well as call $location.replace(). This prevents the path the user accessed from entering the browser's history.

What this doesn't protect from is the login session expiring while the user is on the page, for which we would use HTTP interceptors. Resolves are great for pre-route checks, but not for checks that need to happen when the user gets to the page.

Additional Configuration

When using AngularJS routing, there are a few other concerns which, while not common, are still important for many Single-Page Applications. In this section, we cover a few of those, including how to have non-# URLs, and how to handle SEO and analytics with AngularJS.

HTML5 Mode

Hash URLs or hashbang URLs are common when working with Single-Page Applications. But it is possible to make an SPA using AngularJS look and behave just like a normal multipage application using something called HTML5 mode and the browser's pushState API. In this mode, when the page initially loads, AngularJS hooks into the browser URL to capture all location changes and handle them within AngularJS without causing a full page reload. That is, a URL like *http://www.myawesomeapp.com/#/first/page* would look like *http://www.myawesomeapp.com/first/page* with HTML5 mode enabled. After the page loads, AngularJS is aware enough to realize which URLs constitute an AngularJS route and which ones it shouldn't override.

To enable HTML5 mode, server-side support is also needed. While AngularJS can handle the initial *index.html* load, and handle all page URLs subsequent to the page load, the server needs to be aware of what URLs AngularJS supports, and what URLs need to be responded by the server. Let's assume that we have an application with two URLs, /*first/page* and /*second/page*. If we navigate to *http://www.myawesomeapp.com/first/page*, assuming that HTML5 mode is enabled, realize that the browser is actually going to make a server request. AngularJS will not have loaded at that point for it to take over and control the browser. Thus it is imperative that the server receives the request for *http://www.myawesomeapp.com/first/page*, and then in turn returns the *index.html* that would have been served for *http://www.myawesomeapp.com*. After that, AngularJS loads with /*first/page* as its route, and handles the routing from there. This is illustrated in Figure 10-2.

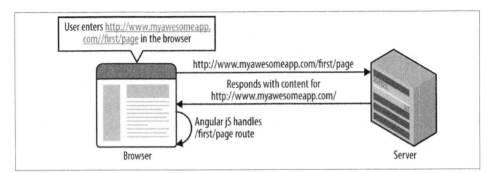

Figure 10-2. How HTML5 mode is handled

Thus to enable HTML5 mode, three things are needed:

- Enable HTML5 mode as part of the application config on the *client side* as follows:

```
angular.module('myHtml5App', ['ngRoute'])
        .config(['$locationProvider', '$routeProvider',
                function($locationProvider, $routeProvider) {

    $locationProvider.html5Mode(true);

    //Optional
    $locationProvider.hashPrefix('!');
    // Route configuration here as normal
    // Route for /first/page
    // Route for /second/page
}]);
```

To set HTML5 mode, we ask for `$locationProvider` as part of the configuration, and call the function `html5Mode` with `true` on it. It's recommended that we also set the `hashPrefix` as ! to easily support SEO, as we will see in the next section. This is all we need to do on the client side for nonhash URLs in AngularJS.

- In *index.html*, we need to add the `<base>` tag with an href attribute to the `<head>` portion. This is to tell the browser where, in relation to the URL, the static resources are served from, so that if the application requests an image or CSS file with a relative path, it doesn't take it from the current URL necessarily.

For example, let us say our base application is served from *http://www.mywebsite.com/app*, and it has HTML5 mode enabled. So when a user navigates to *http://www.mywebsite.com/app/route/15*, our server still serves the *index.html* page, but for the browser, the application path is */app/route/15*. So all relative files will be relative to this URL. Instead, we need something like the following in our HTML:

```
<html>
    <head>
        <base href="/app" />
    </head>
</html>
```

This would ensure that regardless of the URL, all relative paths would be resolved relative to */app* and not to some other URL. If your application is being served from /, then have `<base href="/">` in your `<head>` tag.

- On the *server side*, we need a rule that states that when the server sees a request for */first/page* or */second/page*, it needs to serve the content that it normally serves for the / request, which is usually *index.html*. In NodeJS, it might look something like this:

```
var express = require('express'),
        url = require('url');
```

```
var app = express();

// express configuration here

var INDEX_HTML = fs.readFileSync(
  __dirname + '/index.html', 'utf-8');

var ACCEPTABLE_URLS = ['/first/page', '/second/page'];

app.use(function(req, res, next) {
  var parts = url.parse(req.url);
  for (var i = 0; i < ACCEPTABLE_URLS.length; i++) {
    if (parts.pathname.indexOf(ACCEPTABLE_URLS[i]) === 0) {
      // We found a match to one of our
      // client-side routes
      return res.send(200, INDEX_HTML);
    }
  }
  return next();
});

// Other routes here
```

We have a simple node server that reads and caches the contents of *index.html* into the INDEX_HTML variable. After that, if it sees a request for */first/page* or */second/page*, it returns the contents of INDEX_HTML; otherwise, it continues to the correct response handler by calling next().

SEO with AngularJS

Because Single-Page Applications are heavily dependent on JavaScript executing after the HTML loading to display and render the relevant content, supporting search engine crawlers becomes a little bit more involved and complicated. That said, it is still possible to get search engines to properly crawl our SPA like they would any other normal website.

Google and AJAX App Indexing

Google has plans to start trying to parse and view JavaScript-based pages as the user might see them by actually executing the Java-Script in the page. This is in contrast to the accepted norms up until now, which required just loading the HTML page. The Google Web-master Central (*http://bit.ly/1sKMKvK*) page has more details on it, along with tools (*http://bit.ly/1sKMNHP*) to understand how Google views these pages.

Here are the key things to keep in mind when dealing with search engines:

- Search engines like Google and Bing have defined patterns to work with Single-Page Applications. In particular, to support search engine crawling, it is expected that the SPA will use hashbang URLs instead of pure hash URLs (#! instead of #).

- When search engines crawl, they replace the #! with ?*escaped_fragment*=, and the request is made to the server instead of the client handling it.

At this point, to ensure that the search engine gets the correct content instead of some HTML fragment with {{ }} and no content filled out, we need to ensure that the server recognizes these URLs as coming from the search engine, and handle them differently than the normal user flow. In such a case, there are one of two options:

- Create an HTML snapshot of our entire web application, and serve those HTMLs when the search engine makes a request. This is faster but has the overhead of making sure we keep the HTML snapshots updated. The AngularJS documentation (*http://docs.angularjs.org/api*), which is an AngularJS application, uses this strategy to make sure the AngularJS documentation is searchable on Google.

- Serve live, rendered HTML content when the search engine makes a request. This could be done with something like PhantomJS (*http://phantomjs.org/*), a headless browser, running on the server. When the server sees a request from the search engine, it could get PhantomJS to render the proper page with all JavaScript execution, and then return the fully rendered content to the search engine.

Both of these are involved processes, and if you're looking for a fully packaged solution or pointers on how this might be done, here are a few links and SaaS solutions for SPAs:

- YearOfMoo (*http://www.yearofmoo.com*) has a great in-depth article on enabling SEO for your AngularJS application (*http://bit.ly/1CqIVT6*), which goes into the nitty-gritty details of how you might want to enable it from scratch. It is a recommended read so you understand how it works under the covers.

- The GitHub project angular-seo (*https://github.com/steeve/angular-seo*) is a great starting point for taking YearOfMoo's ideas and implementing them using PhantomJS.

- There are SaaS implementations that take the pain out of indexing your SPA, like BromBone (*http://www.brombone.com/*), Prerender.io (*https://prerender.io/*), and GetSeoJS (*http://www.getseojs.com*), which offer all of these in a single package at a convenient price if you don't want to implement and maintain your own version.

Analytics with AngularJS

Traditional Analytics (like Google Analytics) don't work easily on SPAs, because they add an analytics event for each page load. With an SPA, we need to manually trigger and tell Google Analytics of route changes and other events. Thankfully, the wonderful open source community around AngularJS has already tried multiple approaches and implementations for this. One of the more commonly used options is Angularytics (*https://github.com/mgonto/angularytics*), which provides a great service to manually track events. It comes with a default integration for logging events to the console, or to Google Analytics.

It provides the following out of the box:

- Automated event tracking for page and route changes
- A nice service for manually triggering events at various times from our controllers, services, and directives
- A filter for triggering events from the HTML, such as on the click of a button

Setting it up is as breezy as including the JavaScript source code for Angularytics in our application and then configuring it and instantiating it correctly as part of our app as follows:

```
angular.module('myTrackingApp', ['angularytics'])
    .config(['AngularyticsProvider',
        function(AngularyticsProvider) {
      AngularyticsProvider.setEventHandlers(
        ['GoogleUniversal', 'Console']);
}]).run(['Angularytics', function(Angularytics) {
      Angularytics.init();
}])
```

This code snippet assumes that we have done the following:

- Set up Universal Google Analytics code in our *index.html* file correctly
- Loaded *angular.js* and *angularytics.js*

After that's done, we depend on the Angularytics module and set up the event handlers we want. In the previous example, we add both the `Console` handler and the Google Analytics handler. We also add a `run` method, which executes first in our entire application to ensure that Angularytics is initialized first.

After this is done, we can use this as follows in our HTML:

```
<button ng-click="myCtrl.login() | trackEvent:'Login Page':'clicked login'">
Login</button>
```

The `trackEvent` filter takes the category and type of event that was triggered, and can be appended to any action easily in our HTML.

We can also use it in the controller or service as follows:

```
Angularytics.trackEvent('Create Page', 'Opened');
```

In this line of code, `Angularytics` is a service that we dependency-inject wherever we need it, like a service or controller.

Alternatives: ui-router

The AngularJS router is great and satisfies about 70–80% of our needs with routing. Most SPAs have one general section of the page that responds to URL changes, and shows and displays different content.

But what if we had more complex requirements and wanted to change different parts of our UI differently depending on the URL? Maybe we had a different menu and view for admins versus normal users. Also, we might have sections inside a page that might need to be hidden or shown depending on certain flags and events. With ngRoute, we can use `ng-show` and `ng-hide` directives, or even `ng-switch` to implement these behaviors.

But those can get messy, with extra variables and large files to maintain. It requires rigor and oversight to keep our codebase clean and modular in such a case. Instead, when we have such requirements, we can also use the optional `ui-router` (*https://github.com/angular-ui/ui-router*) for our routing needs, instead of ngRoute. We saw that we can only have one `ng-view` per application. The `ui-router` does away with that restriction. Here are the things to keep in mind when switching to using `ui-router`:

- `ui-router` uses the concepts of states, instead of routes. As part of our configuration, we define the various states in our application and what the `ui-router` should do when it encounters a particular state. The language and syntax for defining states is similar to ngRoute, in that we define our state, followed by a state configuration that includes:
  - `template`
  - `templateUrl`
  - `controller`
  - `resolve`
- Instead of using hrefs and anchors to navigate in our application, the `ui-router` provides a directive called `ui-sref` that allows us to navigate to states. This can be added not only on anchors, but on buttons, images, and any other element on which we need the behavior.
- Instead of using the `$routeProvider` to define our routes, we use the `$statePro vider` to define our states.
- We can have multiple named `ui-views` in our application. We could have, in our *index.html*, a code snippet like the following:

```
<div ui-view="leftNav"></div>
<div ui-view="mainContent"></div>
```

In this example, there are two `ui-views`: one for the left navigation section and another for the main content. Each of these can respond to URL and state changes differently, which allows us to separate and modularize our code even further.

- We can also nest `ui-views` within `ui-views`, unlike `ng-views`. If we have two states, `main` and `main.child`, that means the main state corresponds to the first `ui-view` in *index.html*. This is similar to `ng-view`. When the state transitions to `main.child`, it looks for a `ui-view` directive inside the template of main. If it finds it, it is changed as per the route definition.

There are many more advantages and fine-grained control that we can achieve when we use `ui-router` instead of `ngRoute`. The detailed documentation is available at the UI-Router guide (*http://github.com/angular-ui/ui-router/wiki*).

`ui-router` is highly configurable and modular, but does add some complexity to the codebase. While most of the concepts transfer from `ngRoute` to `ui-router`, there are a few things that don't do it immediately. `ui-router` is state-oriented, and by default does not modify URLs. We need to specify the URL for each state individually.

Adding named and nested views can also be overkill for small or medium projects in terms of complexity, file structure, and loading. We should consider using `ui-router` if our project needs or has the following requirements:

- We need different parts of the page to react differently to URL changes or user interactions.
- We have multiple different (nested) sections of the page that are conditionally shown for various actions and events.
- We don't need the URL to change while the user navigates throughout our application.
- The entire UI layout needs to change completely across different pages.

In such cases, `ui-router` makes sense. If we don't have any of these requirements, the `ngRoute` module should be good enough for our application.

Conclusion

We covered routing in a Single-Page Application, from the simple task of changing templates for each URL change, to a more in-depth example of loading different templates and controllers depending on the route. We also dove into the concept of resolves, which allow us to complete asynchronous tasks before a certain page or route is loaded. This allows us to load data beforehand, as well as do any access control and permission checks we might want to. We then looked at a detailed, in-depth example that brought all of these together into a single application.

After the example, we covered some other common use cases that need to be handled for certain projects, like SEO, analytics, and more. We also took a brief glance at ui-router, which is a more configurable, modular alternative to the AngularJS routing.

In the next chapter, we dive into directives, the AngularJS version of custom components. We look at the basics of creating directives and the various options that allow us to configure how they work.

CHAPTER 11

Directives

Having explored all the other parts of AngularJS, like controllers, services, and filters, we dive deep into directives in this chapter. Directives are the AngularJS way of dealing with DOM manipulation and rendering reusable UI widgets. They can be used for simple things like reusing HTML snippets, to more complex things like modifying the behavior of existing elements (think `ng-show`, `ng-class`, or making elements draggable) or integrating with third-party components like charts and other fancy doodads.

In this chapter, we start with developing a very basic directive, and explore some of the more common options like `template`, `templateUrl`, `link`, and `scopes`. By the end of the chapter, we will have created multiple versions of our simple reusable widgets, each one building on top of the previous, along the way explaining how each directive definition object changes the functioning of our directive.

What Are Directives?

When we hear the word "directives," the very first association that should come to our minds is dealing directly with the UI or the HTML that the user sees. Directives are of two major types in AngularJS (though they can be subclassified further and further):

Behavior modifiers

These types of directives work on existing UI and HTML snippets, and just add or modify the existing behavior of what the UI does. Examples of such directives would be `ng-show` (which hides or shows an existing element based on a condition), or `ng-model` (which adds the AngularJS data-binding hooks to any input to which it is attached).

Reusable components

These types of directives are the more common variety, in which the directive creates a whole new HTML structure. These directives have some *rendering logic* (how and what should it display) and some *business logic* (where should it get the data, what happens when the user interacts with it) attached to it. Some examples of these directives could be a tab widget, a carousel/accordian directive (though HTML5/6/7 might introduce these as a control), and a pie chart directive. These are also the best way to integrate third-party UI components into AngularJS (think jQuery UI or Google Charts).

While directives are the most powerful and complex part of AngularJS, the concepts they are built upon are quite simple. To ensure that we understand how they work, we'll introduce the options one at a time. This chapter focuses on some of the more straight-forward and commonly used options for defining a directive, and the next chapter introduces some of the more complex and less used hooks of a directive.

Alternatives to Custom Directives

Before we jump into directives, let's quickly walk through some other options that might serve us well in the case that we want reusable HTML, or business logic in our HTML. We have two directives, `ng-include` and `ng-switch`, which can help us in extracting HTML into smaller chunks and deciding when to show and hide them in our HTML. In many cases, we can use these two directives instead of writing our custom directives.

ng-include

The `ng-include` directive takes an AngularJS expression (similar to `ng-show` and `ng-click`) and treats its value as the path to an HTML file. It then fetches that HTML file from the server and includes its content as the child (and the only child, replacing all other existing content) of the element that `ng-include` is placed on. Imagine that we extracted a *stock.html* file with the following content:

```
<!-- File: chapter11/ng-include/stock.html -->
<div class="stock-dash">
  Name:
  <span class="stock-name"
        ng-bind="stock.name">
  </span>
  Price:
  <span class="stock-price"
        ng-bind="stock.price | currency">
  </span>
  Percentage Change:
  <span class="stock-change"
        ng-bind="mainCtrl.getChange(stock) + '%'">
  </span>
</div>
```

This HTML is very simple in that it takes a variable called `stock` and displays its `name` and `price` in separate spans. In the last span, it calls a function on `mainCtrl` to calculate and display the percentage change for the current stock. Let's now take a look at *index.html* for this application:

```
<!-- File: chapter11/ng-include/index.html -->
<html>
<head>
  <title>Stock Market App</title>
</head>
<body ng-app="stockMarketApp">

  <div ng-controller="MainCtrl as mainCtrl">
    <h3>List of Stocks</h3>
    <div ng-repeat="stock in mainCtrl.stocks">
      <div ng-include="mainCtrl.stockTemplate">
      </div>
    </div>
  </div>

  <script src="http://code.angularjs.org/1.2.16/angular.js"></script>
  <script src="app.js"></script>
</body>
</html>
```

The main *index.html* file loads AngularJS and our application code, and instantiates ng-app (stockMarketApp). It then loads a controller on the main div, and displays a list of stocks inside of it. We're extracting the content of ng-repeat into *stock.html*, instead of having it inline. We then tell the ng-include to load whatever mainCtrl.stockTemplate points to. Let's now see what the controller is doing:

```
// File: chapter11/ng-include/app.js

angular.module('stockMarketApp', [])
  .controller('MainCtrl', [function() {
    var self = this;
    self.stocks = [
      {name: 'First Stock', price: 100, previous: 220},
      {name: 'Second Stock', price: 140, previous: 120},
      {name: 'Third Stock', price: 110, previous: 110},
      {name: 'Fourth Stock', price: 400, previous: 420}
    ];

    self.stockTemplate = 'stock.html';

    self.getChange = function(stock) {
      return Math.ceil((
        (stock.price - stock.previous) / stock.previous) * 100);
    };
  }]);
```

MainCtrl defines a list of stocks in its controller, each with a name, price, and previous price. It also defines a getChange function, which is used to figure out the percentage change for a particular stock that is passed to it (it also multiplies it by 100, and rounds it off for easier display).

Note that in the previous example, we included the following in *index.html*:

```
<div ng-include="mainCtrl.stockTemplate"></div>
```

This required us to define a variable in the controller and refer to it. Another option is to inline the string directly in the HTML for the ng-include. When we inline it, we have to ensure that AngularJS understands that we have not passed it a variable on our controller, but the actual value itself. We could do that as follows:

```
<div ng-include="'views/stock.html'"></div>
```

Notice the single quotes inside the double quotes. The single quotes tell AngularJS that the value passed to it is a string literal, not a variable. If we don't add the single quotes, AngularJS will look for a variable called views/stock.html (which obviously is an illegal variable name, and doesn't exist), and throw an error saying that it is unable to parse the expression. So don't forget to include the single quotes if you're directly using the filename in the HTML.

Any time we have to serve HTML partials, we need an HTTP server because the browser does not allow serving or requesting files on the *file://* protocol. So to make this application work on our local machine, we have a few options:

- Install Node's http-server by running **sudo npm install -g http-server** (drop sudo if you're on Windows). Then run http-server from the directory that contains *index.html*.

- Python addicts can run **python -m SimpleHTTPServer** from the folder where the *index.html* file is as well.

- Finally, WebStorm can start a built-in server when you ask it to open the *index.html* file in a browser.

At this point if we run this application, we will see an HTML page that displays four stocks, each with its own name, price, and percentage change. ng-include helped us by allowing us to extract the HTML that would otherwise have been in *index.html* (technically, this could be any file that we are working on), and extract it to a smaller, reusable, and easier-to-maintain file.

This is the best feature of ng-include. If we have large HTML files, we can easily extract them out into smaller, easier-to-manage HTML files and make our HTML modular as well.

Limitations of ng-include

While ng-include is great at extracting snippets of HTML into smaller files, it is not without limitations. The *stock.html* file we created has two major limitations if we include it using the ng-include directive in AngularJS:

- The *stock.html* file currently looks for a variable called stock and displays its name, price, and percentage change information. Now, in *index.html*, if we ended up changing the repeater from stock in mainCtrl.stocks to each in mainCtrl.stocks, we would end up showing four empty blocks without the name, price, or change information. This is because although we changed the name of the variable in the main *index.html* file, the *stock.html* file still expects a variable called stock for it to display. Thus, if we are using ng-include, each file that includes *stock.html* must name the variable containing the information stock.

- The *stock.html* file is also currently dependent on being used along with mainCtrl. This is because it expects there to be a mainCtrl.getChange function that it uses to calculate the percentage change of the stock. If *stock.html* is used in some other HTML that either does not have the controller named mainCtrl, or if the controller does not have the function getChange(), then the HTML will not be able to display the percentage change. Thus, the behavior that the extracted HTML depends on will have to be manually included with the right name every time this HTML is used.

In "Creating a Directive" on page 175, we will see how to fix both of these problems using directives that we create.

ng-switch

The ng-switch is another directive that allows us to add some functionality to the UI for selectively displaying certain snippets of HTML. It gives us a way of conditionally including HTML snippets by behaving like a switch case directly in the HTML. Here is how a simple usage of ng-switch might operate:

```
<!-- File: chapter11/ng-switch/index.html -->
<html>
<head>
  <title>Switch App</title>
</head>
<body ng-app="switchApp">

  <div ng-controller="MainCtrl as mainCtrl">
    <h3>Conditional Elements in HTML</h3>
    <button ng-click="mainCtrl.currentTab = 'tab1'">
      Tab 1
    </button>
```

```
    <button ng-click="mainCtrl.currentTab = 'tab2'">
      Tab 2
    </button>
    <button ng-click="mainCtrl.currentTab = 'tab3'">
      Tab 3
    </button>
    <button ng-click="mainCtrl.currentTab = 'something'">
      Trigger Default
    </button>

    <div ng-switch="mainCtrl.currentTab">
      <div ng-switch-when="tab1">
        Tab 1 is selected
      </div>
      <div ng-switch-when="tab2">
        Tab 2 is selected
      </div>
      <div ng-switch-when="tab3">
        Tab 3 is selected
      </div>
      <div ng-switch-default>
        No known tab selected
      </div>
    </div>
  </div>

  <script src="http://code.angularjs.org/1.2.16/angular.js"></script>
  <script type="text/javascript">
    angular.module('switchApp', [])
        .controller('MainCtrl', [function() {
          this.currentTab = 'tab1';
        }]);
  </script>
</body>
</html>
```

This example is a simple application that shows five buttons. Clicking any of the first three buttons opens that tab. The last two buttons set a random value for the current tab. In such a case, the default case is triggered and the last div is shown.

Running this example requires the same steps as the previous example, so get a locally running server started.

It accomplishes this using the ng-switch directive. We add an ng-switch based on the value of mainCtrl.currentTab. Inside the div, we add multiple divs, which are shown selectively. We accomplish this by adding ng-switch-when attributes to the children elements. We add the conditions (like a select statement). Each ng-switch-when takes a string value (for example, "hello"). If this string value matches the value of the expression passed to ng-switch (in this case, the value of the variable mainCtrl.current

Tab), then the element is displayed. If none of the `ng-switch-when` values match the value of the original expression, then the `ng-switch-default` case is triggered.

There are a few things to note about `ng-switch`:

- `ng-switch` loads its content, and then based on the condition, comments out all the `ng-switch-when` conditions that are not satisfied. So even if we use `ng-include` inside `ng-switch-when`, they will not get loaded up front, and will be loaded only when the condition is met.

- `ng-switch-when` is treated as an attribute, and thus the value passed to it is expected to be direct, and not an AngularJS expression. That is, suppose we have `ng-switch="mainCtrl.currentTab"` and then `ng-switch-when="mainCtrl.possibleValue"`. This would expect the value of `currentTab` in the controller to be equal to the string `"mainCtrl.possibleValue"`, and not the value of `mainCtrl.possibleValue`. `ng-switch-when` does not understand AngularJS expressions.

Understanding the Basic Options

We now know how and when to use `ng-include` and `ng-switch`, and understand their shortcomings. Now let's see how we can create a directive to solve some of these problems.

The main intentions of a directive are:

- To make our intention declarative by specifying in the HTML what something is or tries to do.

- To make something reusable so the same functionality can be achieved easily without copying and pasting the code.

- To achieve abstraction in the sense that the user of the directive doesn't need to know or understand how something is performed, but only cares about the end result. The corollary of this is that the underlying implementation can be changed without having to change every single usage.

Let's jump into the options that are available when creating a directive using the example from the `ng-include`, and see how we might convert that into a proper, reusable directive.

Creating a Directive

Creating a directive is just like creating controllers, services, and filters in that the AngularJS module function allows us to create a directive by name. The first argument to the function is the name of the directive, and the second argument is the standard Dependency Injection array syntax, with the last element in the array being our directive function.

Suppose we want to turn the *stock.html* file from the previous example into a reusable directive. Let's start with how we want to use it in our HTML:

```
<div stock-widget></div>
```

If we want to be able to declare that the current div is a stock widget (used as stated previously), we need to declare or create our directive as follows:

```
angular.module('stockMarketApp', [])
  .directive('stockWidget', [function() {
    return {
      // Directive definition will go here
    };
}]);
```

We define the `stockWidget` directive and provide it with a function. This function sets up our directive using what we call a *directive definition object* and returns this definition. AngularJS looks at this definition each time it encounters our directive in the HTML.

By default, when we create a directive this way, we can use it only as an attribute of existing elements in our HTML. That is, by default, we can only use `<div stock-widget>` and not `<stock-widget>`.

Directive and Attribute Naming
One thing to note is the naming of the directive. HTML is case-insensitive by default. To deal with this when translating names of attributes and directives from HTML to JavaScript, AngularJS converts dashes to camelCase. Thus, `stock-widget` (or `STOCK-WIDGET` or even `Stock-Widget`) in HTML becomes `stockWidget` in JavaScript.

Next, let's take a look at some commonly used options when creating directives.

Template/Template URL

The very first thing we can define as part of our directive is whether it has any content that needs to be inserted when the directive is encountered. We do this using the `template` and `templateUrl` keys of the directive definition object (similar to routing).

Let's now achieve the same functionality that we had with the ng-include, but using a directive so that it's more declarative. First, the *app.js* file, which remains unchanged:

```
// This is chapter11/directive-with-template/app.js

angular.module('stockMarketApp', [])
  .controller('MainCtrl', [function() {
    var self = this;
    self.stocks = [
      {name: 'First Stock', price: 100, previous: 220},
      {name: 'Second Stock', price: 140, previous: 120},
      {name: 'Third Stock', price: 110, previous: 110},
      {name: 'Fourth Stock', price: 400, previous: 420}
    ];

    self.getChange = function(stock) {
      return Math.ceil((
        (stock.price - stock.previous) / stock.previous) * 100);
    };
  }]);
```

Similarly, the *stock.html* file also remains unchanged from the previous example:

```
<!-- File: chapter11/directive-with-template/stock.html -->
<div class="stock-dash">
  Name:
  <span class="stock-name"
        ng-bind="stock.name">
  </span>
  Price:
  <span class="stock-price"
        ng-bind="stock.price | currency">
  </span>
  Percentage Change:
  <span class="stock-change"
        ng-bind="mainCtrl.getChange(stock) + '%'">
  </span>
</div>
```

The *index.html* file next changes slightly because it now uses our directive instead of ng-include:

```
<!-- File: chapter11/directive-with-template/index.html -->
<html>
<head>
  <title>Stock Market App</title>
</head>
<body ng-app="stockMarketApp">

  <div ng-controller="MainCtrl as mainCtrl">
    <h3>List of Stocks</h3>
    <div ng-repeat="stock in mainCtrl.stocks">
      <div stock-widget>
```

```
        </div>
      </div>
    </div>

    <script src="http://code.angularjs.org/1.2.16/angular.js"></script>
    <script src="app.js"></script>
    <script src="directive.js"></script>
  </body>
</html>
```

Only the content of ng-repeat has changed; it now states <div stock-widget></div>. Finally, let's see how this directive is defined and created:

```
// File: chapter11/directive-with-template/directive.js
angular.module('stockMarketApp')
  .directive('stockWidget', [function() {
    return {
      templateUrl: 'stock.html'
    };
  }]);
```

In this file, we create a directive with a very simple definition. We tell AngularJS that any time we encounter a directive in our HTML called stock-widget (because we named it stockWidget, which translates to stock-widget in HTML), it should fetch the template *stock.html* from our server and insert it as a child of the element the directive is placed on.

 Note that AngularJS will be smart and fetch the HTML template that's at the templateUrl location only once when the directive is encountered the very first time. After that, it saves the template in its local cache and serves it from there.

If our HTML is small enough, we could possibly look at inlining it directly in our directive using the template key in the directive definition object. Here is how our directive might look if we did away with the *stock.html* file and inlined it in our directive:

```
angular.module('stockMarketApp')
  .directive('stockWidget', [function() {
    return {
      template: '<div class="stock-dash">' +
        'Name: ' +
        '<span class="stock-name"' +
            'ng-bind="stock.name">' +
        '</span>' +
        'Price: ' +
        '<span class="stock-price"' +
            'ng-bind="stock.price | currency">' +
        '</span>' +
        'Change: ' +
```

```
            '<span class="stock-change"' +
                 'ng-bind="mainCtrl.getChange(stock) + '%'">' +
            '</span>' +
            '</div>'
    };
}]);
```

Note that this is a replacement for the directive we created before. Both have the exact same effect in terms of the UI, in that they load an HTML template and place it as a child of the element that the directive is on.

The `template` key makes sense if our HTML snippet is small and easy to maintain. For larger, more complex templates, it almost always makes sense to load them via the `templateUrl` key.

Restrict

The `restrict` keyword defines how someone using the directive in their code might use it. As mentioned previously, the default way of using directives is via attributes of existing elements (we used `<div stock-widget>` for ours).

When we create our directive, we have control in deciding how it's used. The possible values for `restrict` (and thus the ways in which we can use our directive) are:

A

The letter A in the value for `restrict` specifies that the directive can be used as an *attribute* on existing HTML elements (such as `<div stock-widget></div>`). This is the default value.

E

The letter E in the value for `restrict` specifies that the directive can be used as a new HTML *element* (such as `<stock-widget></stock-widget>`).

C

The letter C in the value for `restrict` specifies that the directive can be used as a class name in existing HTML elements (such as `<div class="stock-widget"> </div>`).

M

The letter M in the value for `restrict` specifies that the directive can be used as HTML comments (such as `<!-- directive: stock-widget -→`). This was previously necessary for directives that needed to encompass multiple elements, like multiple rows in tables, etc. The `ng-repeat-start` and `ng-repeat-end` directives were introduced for this sole purpose, so it's preferable to use them instead of comment directives.

Each of these can be used by itself as an argument to the `restrict` key, or could be used in combination with each other. Here's how we might update our `stock-widget` directive to be able to use it as either attributes or elements in our HTML:

```
// File: chapter11/directive-with-restrict/directive.js
angular.module('stockMarketApp')
  .directive('stockWidget', [function() {
    return {
      templateUrl: 'stock.html',
      restrict: 'AE'
    };
  }]);
```

We added a `restrict` key to our directive definition object, and gave it a value of AE. This tells AngularJS that we can use the widget in our HTML as either `<div stock-widget>` or directly as `<stock-widget>`. This also prevents us from using `<div class="stock-widget">`, because we have not allowed it to be used as class names.

Expressions in Class Directives

We have seen four possibilities for the `restrict` key. We will explore in the following sections how to pass values to our directive, but we might wonder how that is possible with the class-based directive. That is, how would `<div my-widget="someExp">` translate to a class-based directive?

Class-based directives translate to `<div class="my-widget: some Exp;">` and AngularJS would treat this as similar to passing a value to an attribute in HTML.

Now that we've explored the various ways in which directives can be used, let's cover some best practices around their usage:

- Internet Explorer 8 and below do not like custom HTML elements. If we plan on using them, we need to manually tell Internet Explorer that we have some new elements by calling `document.createElement('stock-widget')` and so on for each new element. AngularJS, with version 1.3 onwards, has dropped support for (or rather, testing on) Internet Explorer 8.

- Class-based directives are ideal for rendering-related work (like the `ng-cloak` directive that hides and shows elements, or image loading directives).

- Element directives are recommended if we are creating entirely new HTML content.

- Attribute directives are usually preferred for behavior modifiers (like `ng-show`, `ng-class`, and so on).

The link Function

The link keyword in the directive definition object is used to add what we call a "link function" for the directive. The link function does for a directive what a controller does for a view—it defines APIs and functions that are necessary for the directive, in addition to manipulating and working with the DOM.

AngularJS executes the link function for each instance of the directive, so each instance can get its own, fully contained business logic while not affecting any other instance of the directive. The link function gets a standard set of arguments passed to it that remain consistent across directives, which looks something like the following:

```
link: function($scope, $element, $attrs) {}
```

The link function gets passed the scope of the element the directive is working on, the HTML DOM element the directive is operating on, and all the attributes on the element as strings. If we need to add functionality to our instance of the directive, we can add it to the scope of the element we're working with.

Let's take our example from before and move the functionality from mainCtrl into our directive, so the directive doesn't have to depend on there being a MainCtrl with a function called getChange:

```
// File: chapter11/directive-with-link/directive.js
angular.module('stockMarketApp')
  .directive('stockWidget', [function() {
    return {
      templateUrl: 'stock.html',
      restrict: 'AE',
      link: function($scope, $element, $attrs) {
        $scope.getChange = function(stock) {
          return Math.ceil(((stock.price - stock.previous) /
              stock.previous) * 100);
        };
      }
    };
}]);
```

In this code snippet, the directive defines a link function that adds a function called getChange() on its scope. This makes each instance of the directive have a getCh ange() function on its own scope. The function was moved from the controller to the directive, without any other changes. Now let's see how we might use it in *stock.html*:

```
<!-- File: chapter11/directive-with-link/stock.html -->
<div class="stock-dash">
  Name:
  <span class="stock-name"
      ng-bind="stock.name">
  </span>
  Price:
```

```
    <span class="stock-price"
          ng-bind="stock.price | currency">
    </span>
    Percentage Change:
    <span class="stock-change"
          ng-bind="getChange(stock) + '%'">
    </span>
  </div>
```

The *stock.html* file remains largely unchanged, except for the change in the last ng-bind directive. Instead of binding to mainCtrl.getChange(stock), we bind to getChange(stock). This implies that it's looking for a getChange() function on its own scope. Now regardless of which controller we use our directive in, or even if we rename our controller, the stockWidget directive has its own version of the getChange function. It becomes independent.

The link function is also where we can define our own listeners, work directly with the DOM element, and much more. We'll explore more of these in Chapter 13.

What's the Scope?

You might wonder what scope we are adding these functions to. You're right to be worried, and it is something we should always keep in mind when we add functions to the scope in the link function. In the example in this section, ng-repeat in the main *index.html* file creates a scope for each stock in our array, and it is to this scope that we're adding the functions. Because of this, we're not affecting the controller's scope directly, but that is an unintentional side effect of ng-repeat. If we had used our directive outside ng-repeat, we would have ended up modifying the controller's scope directly, which is bad practice.

The default scope given in the link function (unless specified otherwise) is the scope that the parent has. Adding functions to the parent scope should always be frowned upon, because the parent should ideally not be changed from within a child.

We are also still dependent on the variable name stock, which if renamed breaks our UI. We'll see in the next section how to remove this dependency as well.

Scope

By default, each directive inherits its parent's scope, which is passed to it in the link function. This can lead to the following problems:

- Adding variables/functions to the scope modifies the parent as well, which suddenly gets access to more variables and functions.

- The directive might unintentionally override an existing function or variable with the same name.

- The directive can implicitly start using variables and functions from the parent. This might cause issues if we start renaming properties in the parent and forget to do it in the directive.

AngularJS gives us the `scope` key in the directive definition object to have complete control over the scope of the directive element. The `scope` key can take one of three values:

`false`

This is the *default* value, which basically tells AngularJS that the directive scope is the *same* as the parent scope, whichever one it is. So the directive gets access to all the variables and functions that are defined on the parent scope, and any modifications it makes are immediately reflected in the parent as well.

`true`

This tells AngularJS that the directive scope inherits the parent scope, but creates a child scope of its own. The directive thus gets access to all the variables and functions from the parent scope, but any modifications it makes are not available in the parent. This is *recommended* if we need access to the parent's functions and information, but need to make local modifications that are specific to the directive.

object

We can also pass an object with keys and values to the scope. This tells AngularJS to create what we call an *isolated scope*. This scope does *not* inherit anything from the parent, and any data that the parent scope needs to share with this directive needs to be passed in through HTML attributes. This is the *best* option when creating reusable components that should be independent of how and where they are used.

In the object, we can identify what attributes are to be specified in the HTML when the directive is used, and the types of values that will be passed in to the directive. In particular, we can specify three types of values that can be passed in, which AngularJS will directly put on the scope of the directive:

`=`

The = sign specifies that the value of the attribute in HTML is to be treated as a JSON object, which will be bound to the scope of the directive so that any changes done in the parent scope will be automatically available in the directive.

`@`

The @ sign specifies that the value of the attribute in HTML is to be treated as a string, which may or may not have AngularJS binding expressions ({{ }}). The value is to be calculated and the final value is to be assigned to the directive's scope. Any changes in the value will also be available in the directive.

&

The & sign specifies that the value of the attribute in HTML is a function in some controller whose reference needs to be available to the directive. The directive can then trigger the function whenever it needs to.

To make our directive fully contained and reusable, we can now pass the stock object to our widget. This way, if the variable is renamed outside, the new variable can be passed to our directive, making it independent of the name. This can be done using the = binding with the scope object, and we can reassign the value to a consistent name on the directive's isolated scope. Let's first see how we might want to change the usage of the directive in the *index.html* file:

```html
<!-- File: chapter11/directive-with-scope/index.html -->
<html>
<head>
  <title>Stock Market App</title>
</head>
<body ng-app="stockMarketApp">

  <div ng-controller="MainCtrl as mainCtrl">
    <h3>List of Stocks</h3>
    <div ng-repeat="s in mainCtrl.stocks">
      <div stock-widget stock-data="s">
      </div>
    </div>
  </div>

  <script src="http://code.angularjs.org/1.2.16/angular.js"></script>
  <script src="app.js"></script>
  <script src="directive.js"></script>
</body>
</html>
```

The entire *index.html* file remains mostly the same except for a slight change in ng-repeat and the way we use our directive. We renamed the repeater from stock in mainCtrl.stocks to s in mainCtrl.stocks. Our directive now says stock-data="s", which is basically a way for us to pass the value we care about to our directive in a consistent way. Now whether stock is named stock, s, or xyz, we pass it to our widget using the stock-data key.

Let's see how this is implemented in our directive:

```javascript
// File: chapter11/directive-with-scope/directive.js
angular.module('stockMarketApp')
  .directive('stockWidget', [function() {
    return {
      templateUrl: 'stock.html',
```

```
        restrict: 'A',
        scope: {
          stockData: '='
        },
        link: function($scope, $element, $attrs) {
          $scope.getChange = function(stock) {
            return Math.ceil(((stock.price - stock.previous) /
                stock.previous) * 100);
          };
        }
      };
    }]);
```

We define an isolated scope in this code snippet by passing an object to the scope key of the directive definition object. Inside the object, we define a stockData key whose value is =. This has the following effects:

- It creates a variable called stockData on the directive's isolated scope.

- In the HTML, the value of stockData can be set by using the attribute stock-data.

- The value of stockData is *bound* to the object that the HTML attribute stock-data points to. Any change in the controller's value is immediately relected in the stockData variable in the directive's scope as well.

Let's see how *stock.html* changes now:

```
<!-- File: chapter11/directive-with-scope/stock.html -->
<div class="stock-dash">
  Name:
  <span class="stock-name"
        ng-bind="stockData.name">
  </span>
  Price:
  <span class="stock-price"
        ng-bind="stockData.price | currency">
  </span>
  Percentage Change:
  <span class="stock-change"
        ng-bind="getChange(stockData) + '%'">
  </span>
</div>
```

In the HTML, all references to the parent's stock variable have been replaced with the directive's own instance, stockData.

At this point, the HTML and the directive are no longer dependent on the context in which they are used, because all the data and logic that the directive needs are either contained (using the link function) or passed to it (using the isolated scope).

If at this point we had left the original variable in ng-repeat as stock (instead of s), and our HTML referred to stock instead of stockData, we would see an empty value. This is because the moment we isolate the scope, the directive can no longer access anything from its parent scope because it is removed from the traditional scope heirarchy.

Whenever we pass data using object binding to directives, it is done by reference. AngularJS uses this fact to ensure that any changes done to the variable in the controller are reflected inside the directive. But this also means that if the reference to the variable gets reassigned in the directive, then the data-binding breaks in AngularJS.

Let's take an example to see this in action. First, we add a method in our controller to create all new stock objects called changeAllStocks, and a method called changeFirst Stock to change the name of the first stock only:

```
// File: chapter11/directive-broken-reference/app.js

angular.module('stockMarketApp', [])
  .controller('MainCtrl', [function() {
    var self = this;
    self.stocks = [
      {name: 'First Stock', price: 100, previous: 220},
      {name: 'Second Stock', price: 140, previous: 120},
      {name: 'Third Stock', price: 110, previous: 110},
      {name: 'Fourth Stock', price: 400, previous: 420}
    ];
    self.changeAllStocks = function() {
      for (var i = 0; i < 4; i++) {
        self.stocks[i] = {
          name: 'Controller Stock',
          price: 200,
          previous: 250
        };
      }
    };

    self.changeFirstStock = function() {
      self.stocks[0].name = 'Changed First Stock';
    };
  }]);
```

The *index.html* file adds two buttons that trigger these functions:

```
<!-- File: chapter11/directive-broken-reference/index.html -->
<html>
<head>
  <title>Stock Market App</title>
</head>
<body ng-app="stockMarketApp">

  <div ng-controller="MainCtrl as mainCtrl">
```

```
    <h3>List of Stocks</h3>
    <div ng-repeat="s in mainCtrl.stocks">
      <div stock-widget stock-data="s">
      </div>
    </div>

    <button ng-click="mainCtrl.changeAllStocks()">
      Change All Stock From Controller
    </button>
    <button ng-click="mainCtrl.changeFirstStock()">
      Change First Stock From Controller
    </button>
  </div>

  <script src="https://ajax.googleapis.com/ajax/libs/angularjs/1.2.19/angular.js">
  </script>
  <script src="app.js"></script>
  <script src="directive.js"></script>
</body>
</html>
```

Our directive also adds a similar function that changes the current stock, called change Stock:

```
// File: chapter11/directive-broken-reference/directive.js
angular.module('stockMarketApp')
  .directive('stockWidget', [function() {
    return {
      templateUrl: 'stock.html',
      restrict: 'A',
      scope: {
        stockData: '='
      },
      link: function($scope, $element, $attrs) {
        $scope.getChange = function(stock) {
          return Math.ceil(((stock.price - stock.previous) /
              stock.previous) * 100);
        };

        $scope.changeStock = function() {
          $scope.stockData = {
            name: 'Directive Stock',
            price: 500,
            previous: 200
          };
        };
      }
    };
  }]);
```

The *stock.html* file adds a button that triggers the directive's changeStock function:

```
<!-- File: chapter11/directive-broken-reference/stock.html -->
<div class="stock-dash">
  Name:
  <span class="stock-name"
        ng-bind="stockData.name">
  </span>
  Price:
  <span class="stock-price"
        ng-bind="stockData.price | currency">
  </span>
  Percentage Change:
  <span class="stock-change"
        ng-bind="getChange(stockData) + '%'">
  </span>

  <button ng-click="changeStock()">
    Change Stock in Directive
  </button>
</div>
```

Now when we run this, we'll try out a few flows in the UI:

1. First, we click either of the two buttons in the main HTML (change all stocks, or change first stock). After we click either of these, we click any of the individual (or just the first, if the first stock name button in the controller was clicked) buttons on a stock. When we do this, the UI first updates when we click the button in the controller, and then updates when we click one of the individual buttons. The UI updates as we would expect.

2. Next, we click the button on the first stock, followed by "Change First Stock from Controller." When we click the first button, the stock updates its values. But the controller button now has no effect. This is because while previously an update from the controller trickled down into the directive, a reference change (we reassigned $scope.stockData) in the directive ensures that any changes in the directive are no longer visible in the controller. Think of it this way: if the controller referred to reference R1, then the directive initially also pointed to R1. But now that we included $scope.stockData = something, the directive refers to R2. So a change in R1 now has no effect in R2, which is why the stock-widget still shows old data even though we change it in the controller.

3. Finally, we can try clicking the button on an individual stock first. Then we click "Change All Stock from Controller." This updates the individual stock first, and then updates all the stocks to the same name. The reason this works, whereas it didn't before, is because we have the list of stocks in an ng-repeat. When we change the reference from the controller, ng-repeat triggers again and creates new directive instances with the correct reference. This is why this flow works and the previous doesn't.

Now let's expand our directive such that we can use the other two types of attributes on the scope. We want to pass a string from our controller and get a hook from our directive to trigger a function in our controller any time the user clicks a button inside the directive instance. Let's do this step by step. First, let's look at our controller:

```
// File: chapter11/directive-with-scope-advanced/app.js

angular.module('stockMarketApp', [])
  .controller('MainCtrl', [function() {
    var self = this;
    self.stocks = [
      {name: 'First Stock', price: 100, previous: 220},
      {name: 'Second Stock', price: 140, previous: 120},
      {name: 'Third Stock', price: 110, previous: 110},
      {name: 'Fourth Stock', price: 400, previous: 420}
    ];

    self.onStockSelect = function(price, name) {
      console.log('Selected Price ', price, 'Name ', name);
    };
  }]);
```

We modify our controller to add a function to be triggered whenever a stock is selected. This function is called with the price and name of the stock that was selected, and just logs it to the console. We already removed the getChange function from this controller when we moved it into the link function of the directive:

```
<!-- File: chapter11/directive-with-scope-advanced/index.html -->
<html>
<head>
  <title>Stock Market App</title>
</head>
<body ng-app="stockMarketApp">

  <div ng-controller="MainCtrl as mainCtrl">
    <h3>List of Stocks</h3>
    <div ng-repeat="s in mainCtrl.stocks">
      <div stock-widget
           stock-data="s"
           stock-title="Stock {{$index}}. {{s.name}}"
           when-select="mainCtrl.onStockSelect(stockPrice, stockName)">
      </div>
    </div>
  </div>

  <script src="http://code.angularjs.org/1.2.16/angular.js"></script>
  <script src="app.js"></script>
  <script src="directive.js"></script>
</body>
</html>
```

Our main *index.html* file has changed how we use our `stock-widget`. In addition to the stock data, we now pass it a title as well as a function to call when the stock is selected. The `stock-title` attribute takes a string value, which also allows for string interpolations (or handling the {{ }} syntax), so we can pass it a combination of hardcoded text and variable values. `when-select` takes the reference of the function it calls, along with the parameter names for the function. We define it as `stockPrice` and `stockName`, and these keys are important as we'll see when we define them in our HTML. Do note that unlike an `ng-bind` or `ng-show` in which saying `mainCtrl.onStockSelect()` would actually call this function, the `when-select` only makes a reference of this function available to our directive, and it's up to us to decide when this function is actually triggered:

```html
<!-- File: chapter11/directive-with-scope-advanced/stock.html -->
<div class="stock-dash">
  Name:
  <span class="stock-name"
        ng-bind="stockTitle">
  </span>
  Price:
  <span class="stock-price"
        ng-bind="stockData.price | currency">
  </span>
  Percentage Change:
  <span class="stock-change"
        ng-bind="getChange(stockData) + '%'">
  </span>
  <button ng-click="onSelect()">Select me</button>
</div>
```

Our directive's template has also slightly changed. Instead of displaying the `stock.name` for the name of the stock, we now display the passed-in `stockTitle`. This variable is coming directly from the HTML attribute that was passed in to the `stock-widget` directive. We also added a button to allow users to click to simulate the user selecting a stock. Now let's see how the directive has changed to get all of this to work:

```javascript
// File: chapter11/directive-with-scope-advanced/directive.js
angular.module('stockMarketApp')
  .directive('stockWidget', [function() {
    return {
      templateUrl: 'stock.html',
      restrict: 'A',
      scope: {
        stockData: '=',
        stockTitle: '@',
        whenSelect: '&'
      },
      link: function($scope, $element, $attrs) {
        $scope.getChange = function(stock) {
          return Math.ceil(((stock.price - stock.previous) /
              stock.previous) * 100);
```

```
        };

        $scope.onSelect = function() {
          $scope.whenSelect({
            stockName: $scope.stockData.name,
            stockPrice: $scope.stockData.price,
            stockPrevious: $scope.stockData.previous
          });
        };
      }
    };
  }]);
```

There are three things of note that changed in our *directive.js* file:

- Our scope key now has two additional attributes. The first is stockTitle (again, stockTitle in JavaScript becomes stock-title in HTML), and its value is set to @. This allows us to pass in strings to our directive, which can also have AngularJS bindings (using the {{ }} syntax).

- We also added a whenSelect key with a value set to &. This makes the function that was specified in our HTML available to the directive on its scope as whenSelect.

- Finally, we added an onSelect function to the scope that gets triggered on click of the button in *stock.html*. This function ensures that the controller's function gets called whenever the user clicks the button in the directive.

The stockTitle binding takes the value of the interpolated string and sets it to $scope.stockTitle automatically. We can then access it from the link function using $scope.stockTitle, or directly from our HTML as we did in ng-bind for the name.

The whenSelect binding parses the function mentioned in the HTML and makes it available on $scope.whenSelect. The difference is in how this function is triggered. With function bindings, AngularJS tries to make passing in a function as generic and customizable as possible. Let's consider a simple example to demonstrate this.

Suppose the directive allows us to pass in a function that can take up to three parameters: the stock price, the stock name, and the stock's previous price. Now assume that the directive always calls the function that's passed in with these three parameters, in the order specified before. That means that if a controller cares only about the stock's previous price, it has to take all three parameters and access only the third one. If a controller only cares about the price and the previous price, again, it has to list all three parameters and use only the first and third. What if there are more than three parameters? Then it gets even more messy to use.

AngularJS tries to relieve this by making the following changes:

- Each directive, when triggering a function passed to it by the & key on its scope, can define the various parameters that it makes available to the controller.

- Each controller can then decide which of these parameters it cares about (by using the key related to the parameter in the HTML).

- The controller can decide the order and the number of parameters it wants from the directive.

Thus, if a controller only cares about the price and the previous keys on the stock object, it can just ask for those particular ones. This way, each controller is allowed to ask for whatever it wants, in the order it wants.

The directive accomplishes this by passing an object to the function passed to it. In this object, each key dictates one parameter that the controller can ask for, and the value assigned to that key is the value the controller receives when it asks for that particular key. In our previous example, the whenSelect function is called with an object with three keys:

- stockName

- stockPrice

- stockPrevious

And its values correspond to the individual directive's stock values. Our controller decides that it only cares about stockPrice and stockName in that order (by specifying it in the HTML in that order, with those keys). Do note that the key names specified in the HTML (in our *index.html*) have to exactly match those provided by our directive. AngularJS will then inject those values in the order the controller asks for. Our controller decided to ignore stockPrevious, while another controller could have just asked for stockPrevious, ignoring the rest.

We can thus define a set of parameters that each controller can ask for as part of the function it's passing to a directive.

Replace

The last attribute of the directive we look at in this chapter is replace. In all the previous examples, when AngularJS encounters our directive, it fetches the HTML for the directive and inserts it as a child of the element the directive is encountered on. In some cases, we might not want the original element to remain and instead be completely replaced with new HTML.

For such cases, AngularJS offers the replace key as part of the directive definition object. The replace key takes a Boolean, and it defaults to false. If we specify it to true, AngularJS removes the element that the directive is declared on, and replaces it with the HTML template from the directive definition object (or the contents from templateUrl). Any existing attributes and classes on the HTML element that the directive is on are migrated from the old element to the new one.

If we run our existing directive without the replace attribute or after setting replace to false, the generated HTML for each individual instance of the directive would look something like the following:

```
<div stock-widget stock-data="s" stock-title="XYZ">
    <div class="stock-dash">
      Name:
      <span class="stock-name"
            ng-bind="stockTitle">
      </span>
      Price:
      <span class="stock-price"
            ng-bind="stockData.price | currency">
      </span>
      Percentage Change:
      <span class="stock-change"
            ng-bind="getChange(stockData) + '%'">
      </span>
      <button ng-click="onSelect()">Select me</button>
    </div>
</div>
```

If we add replace: true to our directive definition object, the generated HTML for each instance of the directive would change to the following:

```
<div stock-widget stock-data="s" stock-title="XYZ" class="stock-dash">
    Name:
    <span class="stock-name"
          ng-bind="stockTitle">
    </span>
    Price:
    <span class="stock-price"
          ng-bind="stockData.price | currency">
    </span>
    Percentage Change:
    <span class="stock-change"
          ng-bind="getChange(stockData) + '%'">
    </span>
    <button ng-click="onSelect()">Select me</button>
</div>
```

We would lose the wrapper div, and all the attributes (stock-widget, stock-data, etc.) would be migrated to the main div element of the HTML template of the directive.

In simple terms, the replace key decides whether the template of the directive replaces the current element or the contents of the current element.

replace Is Deprecated

With AngularJS version 1.3 forward, the `replace` keyword in the directive definition object has been deprecated. The next release of AngularJS plans to remove it completely, so be careful and avoid using the `replace` keyword if at all possible.

Conclusion

We looked at how simple it is to migrate snippets of our HTML along with functionality, in a step-by-step manner, to its own directive. We first looked at directives like `ng-include` and `ng-switch`, which allow us to split our HTML into smaller, more manageable chunks. We then created our own directive using the directive definition object.

We added a template to our directive using the `templateUrl` key, its own functionality and business logic using the `link` function, and made it fully contained and reusable by passing it any data it needed using an isolated scope. We explored the various options and ways in which we can pass data to isolated scope, including objects, strings, and functions. Finally, we looked at the `replace` option of the directive.

In Chapter 12, we dig into unit testing of directives. We explore how to create simple directive instances in our unit test, as well as considerations to keep in mind when writing unit tests for directives.

Unit Testing Directives

In Chapter 11, we saw how to create simple, reusable components using directives. We explored basic configuration of directives like `template` and `templateUrl`, the `link` function, `scope`, and `restrict`. We have also seen in previous chapters how we can unit test controllers and services. Both controllers and services are pure JavaScript functions at the end of the day, and thus we could easily instantiate them and test them in our unit tests. Directives, on the other hand, are directly associated with the DOM, because they create HTML elements or modify their behavior.

In this chapter, we deal with the distinctions that we have to keep in mind while unit testing directives. We see how we can instantiate instances of a directive in a unit test, and learn how AngularJS works under the covers at the same time. By the end of this chapter, we will have written a comprehensive unit test for our stock widget from the previous chapter, while still making sure it is stable and runs fast.

Steps Involved in Testing a Directive

At its core, there are a few key steps (some of which parallel the unit tests for our controllers) that you can use as a checklist when writing unit tests for a directive:

1. Get the `$compile` service injected into the unit test.
2. Create the HTML element that will trigger the directive you have created.
3. Create the `scope` against which you want the directive to be tested again.
4. Remember that there is no server in the unit test. If the directive loads a template using the `templateUrl` key, add an expectation on `$httpBackend` for loading the `templateUrl` and designate the HTML that's to be used instead of the template in the test.

5. Compile the HTML element using the $compile service with the scope you've created.

6. Write expectations on how the directive should be rendered and on the functions that are defined in the link function.

The first five tests are going to be standard for any unit test we write for a directive. Only the last two—where we start testing the rendering and business logic encapsulated in a directive—change from one directive to another.

The Stock Widget Directive

To quickly recap what our directive definition was, let's look at our stock directive definition:

```
// File: chapter12/stockDirective.js
angular.module('stockMarketApp', [])
  .directive('stockWidget', [function() {
    return {
      templateUrl: 'stock.html',
      restrict: 'A',
      scope: {
        stockData: '=',
        stockTitle: '@',
        whenSelect: '&'
      },
      link: function($scope, $element, $attrs) {
        $scope.getChange = function(stock) {
          return Math.ceil(((stock.price - stock.previous) /
              stock.previous) * 100);
        };
        $scope.onSelect = function() {
          $scope.whenSelect({
            stockName: $scope.stockData.name,
            stockPrice: $scope.stockData.price,
            stockPrevious: $scope.stockData.previous
          });
        };
      }
    };
  }]);
```

In this example, we removed all the other controllers from the module, so we define a new module that has only the stockWidget directive. We defined our directive with the following key points:

- The rendering logic of the directive is encapsulated in *stock.html*, which is loaded using templateUrl.

- The directive is restricted to attributes and cannot be used as elements or a class name.

- It has an isolated `scope` with the `stockData` and the `stockTitle` passed in along with `whenSelect`, the function to be called when the user selects a stock.

- The `link` function defines a function to calculate the percentage change as well as a function for the UI to call when a button is clicked.

Setting Up Our Directive Unit Test

In this section, we explore how to set up our unit test to a point where we can start testing the functionality of our directive. To recap, the steps we need to accomplish are:

1. Get the `$compile` service injected into our test.

2. Set up our directive instance HTML.

3. Create and set up our scope with the necessary variables.

4. Determine the template to load because our server is mocked out.

5. Instantiate an instance of our directive using the `$compile` service.

6. Write our expectations for rendering and behavior.

 In these examples, we are using the *karma.conf.js* file that we used previously. The examples were run against AngularJS version 1.2.19 with Karma version 0.12.16. Because of the way we set up Karma, we must make sure that the *karma.conf.js* file is in the same folder as the tests and source code.

Let's take a look at our unit test setup:

```
// File: chapter12/stockDirectiveRenderSpec.js
describe('Stock Widget Directive Rendering', function() {

  beforeEach(module('stockMarketApp'));

  var compile, mockBackend, rootScope;

  // Step 1
  beforeEach(inject(function($compile, $httpBackend, $rootScope) {
    compile = $compile;
    mockBackend = $httpBackend;
    rootScope = $rootScope;
  }));

  it('should render HTML based on scope correctly', function() {
```

```
// Step 2
var scope = rootScope.$new();
scope.myStock = {
  name: 'Best Stock',
  price: 100,
  previous: 200
};
scope.title = 'the best';

// Step 3
mockBackend.expectGET('stock.html').respond(
  '<div ng-bind="stockTitle"></div>' +
  '<div ng-bind="stockData.price"></div>');

// Step 4
var element = compile('<div stock-widget' +
  ' stock-data="myStock"' +
  ' stock-title="This is {{title}}"></div>')(scope);

// Step 5
scope.$digest();
mockBackend.flush();

// Step 6
expect(element.html()).toEqual(
  '<div ng-bind="stockTitle" class="ng-binding">' +
    'This is the best' +
  '</div>' +
  '<div ng-bind="stockData.price" class="ng-binding">' +
    '100' +
  '</div>');
  });
});
```

Let's walk through the preceding example step by step to see how we test the rendering of our directive:

Step 1

> The very first thing we do is inject all the necessary services to create and test our directive in beforeEach. This includes $compile, which is necessary to create instances of our directive; $rootScope to be able to create scopes to test our directives against; and the $httpBackend, to simulate and handle the server call to load the template.

Step 2

> We set up scope against which we will create our directive instance. This is similar to the controller, which will have our data. We create the stock instance myStock as well as a title variable on this scope.

Step 3

Because our directive loads the template by URL, and because there is no server in a unit test, we have to set expectations in `$httpBackend` on what server template will be loaded and what its content will be. Because it is a unit test, we just give it some dummy HTML that can be used to test element rendering and data accuracy.

Step 4

We create an instance of the directive. We first compile the HTML that triggered our directive. This returns a compiled function, which we then call with `scope` to compile it against.

Step 5

We `digest` the scope and `flush` the server requests. This is done to tell AngularJS to update all the bindings in the HTML and ensures that the HTML that we specified in the `$httpBackend` call gets loaded and rendered to write the rest of our test. We dig into the `$digest` cycle in more detail in "The Digest Cycle" on page 206.

Step 6

At this point, we have a fully instantiated version of our directive. Here, we write the expectations and tests for rendering to see if the data was picked up from the scope correctly and that the HTML attributes were correctly passing along the data.

To run these tests, execute `karma start` from the folder containing the directive and the unit test. The *karma.conf.js* file remains the same as before.

Next, let's see how we might test the business logic and behavior of a directive. We use the same setup and naming convention from before, but focus our tests on the functions added to the scope instead of the HTML:

```
// File: chapter12/stockDirectiveBehaviorSpec.js
describe('Stock Widget Directive Behavior', function() {

  beforeEach(module('stockMarketApp'));

  var compile, mockBackend, rootScope;

  // Step 1
  beforeEach(inject(function($compile, $httpBackend, $rootScope) {
    compile = $compile;
    mockBackend = $httpBackend;
    rootScope = $rootScope;
  }));

  it('should have functions and data on scope correctly',
      function() {
    // Step 2
    var scope = rootScope.$new();
    var scopeClickCalled = '';
    scope.myStock = {
```

```
      name: 'Best Stock',
      price: 100,
      previous: 200
    };
    scope.title = 'the best';
    scope.userClick = function(stockPrice,
                                stockPrevious,
                                stockName) {
      scopeClickCalled = stockPrice +
        ';' + stockPrevious +
        ';' + stockName;
    };

    // Step 3
    mockBackend.expectGET('stock.html').respond(
        '<div ng-bind="stockTitle"></div>' +
        '<div ng-bind="stockData.price"></div>');

    // Step 4
    var element = compile(
        '<div stock-widget' +
        ' stock-data="myStock"' +
        ' stock-title="This is {{title}}"' +
        ' when-select="userClick(stockPrice, ' +
            'stockPrevious, stockName)">' +
        '</div>'
    )(scope);

    // Step 5
    scope.$digest();
    mockBackend.flush();

    // Step 6
    var compiledElementScope = element.isolateScope();

    expect(compiledElementScope.stockData)
        .toEqual(scope.myStock);
    expect(compiledElementScope.getChange(
      compiledElementScope.stockData)).toEqual(-50);


    // Step 7
    expect(scopeClickCalled).toEqual('');

    compiledElementScope.onSelect();

    expect(scopeClickCalled).toEqual('100;200;Best Stock');
  });
});
```

In this example, Steps 1 through 5 are exactly the same as the previous example. What changes are Step 6 and the newly added Step 7 (which is really just an extended Step 6, because it adds more expectations on the functionality):

Step 6

We ask for the isolated scope of the element we're working with. This is different from `element.scope()`, which would give us the parent scope if called on an element with a directive. We then check if the directive has the correct stock data on its own scope. We also check if the `getChange` function defined in the directive works as expected.

Step 7

The last thing we test is the function callback. We have a variable defined in our test, which is initially set to empty. We use this as a log of what happened in the test. We then trigger the directive's `onSelect` function (we could have also triggered it through the UI, if our rendered HTML had a button). This should trigger the scope `userClick` function, which sets the string variable. We then check if it is called with the right values after the function is triggered.

In this way, we can test the behavior of our directive, and ensure that it is performing the correct things given the right inputs and conditions.

Other Considerations

Some things to keep in mind when we're unit testing directives:

How do we test the real HTML rendering?

If we use `templateUrl` while defining our directive, we can't load the actual HTML in a unit test because we don't have a server. We have a few options at this point. We can test our directive with a dummy template, which we've done previously in our example. Another option would be to use `template` instead of `templateUrl`, which ensures that the `template` is loaded as part of the directive. But this can get quite messy. One final option is to use something like Grunt-HTML2JS (*https://github.com/karlgoldstein/grunt-html2js*), which takes HTML templates and converts them into AngularJS services and factories. This way, we can load our templates as services and make them available in our unit test.

What about dependent AngularJS services?

If our directive depends on an AngularJS service or factory, we can go about testing it the very same way as we did earlier. AngularJS will figure out the dependencies and inject them automatically. We can also get the services injected into our unit tests like we did in Chapter 7.

The AngularJS bindings don't work

Because we are manually creating the HTML and compiling it, the AngularJS life cycle that takes care of updating the HTML with the latest and greatest data from the scope is not running. So we have to manually trigger it to let AngularJS know, by calling `scope.$digest()`. We dive into this in detail in "The Digest Cycle" on page 206. This is critical in a unit test.

Conclusion

In this chapter, we covered the last and most complex of unit test cases, which is unit testing a directive. We took our `stockWidget` directive from Chapter 11 and created a scaffolding to be able to unit test it. We then tested the rendering behavior, followed by the functionality and business logic encapsulated in the directive.

In Chapter 13, we dig further into AngularJS directives. In particular, we cover the other directive options we didn't touch upon in Chapter 11, like `controller`, `transclude`, and `compile`.

Advanced Directives

We covered creating simple, reusable components in Chapter 11, and saw how to unit test them in Chapter 12. We dug into some common options, like `template` and `tem plateUrl`, `scope`, `restrict`, and `replace`, and saw how to pass data to our directive to make it fully self-contained. These cover 70–80% of the general use cases. The topics we cover in this chapter address the other 20%, which deal with getting a deeper understanding of the AngularJS life cycle.

In this chapter, we first review the AngularJS life cycle in detail. We then go over the remaining options of the directive definition object, including `transclude`, `compile`, `controller`, and `require`, as well as when to use them. With all that covered, we dig into the common use case of extending `ng-model` with either creating new input directives or creating our own custom validators. Finally, we see how we can integrate with third-pary UI components like graphs and charts.

Life Cycles in AngularJS

Before we jump into any of the advanced directive definition options, it helps to get a better understanding of how AngularJS goes about instantiating a directive and using the directive definition object. And any talk about the directive life cycle is not complete without understanding how AngularJS accomplishes much of its magic underneath the covers.

AngularJS Life Cycle

When an AngularJS application is loaded in our browser window, the following events are executed in order:

1. The HTML page is loaded:

   a. The HTML page loads the AngularJS source code (with jQuery optionally loaded before).

   b. The HTML page loads the application's JavaScript code.

2. The HTML page finishes loading.

3. When the document ready event is fired, AngularJS bootstraps and searches for any and all instances of the ng-app attribute in the HTML:

   a. If AngularJS is bootstrapped manually, this needs to be triggered by the code we write.

4. Within the context of each (there could be more than one) ng-app, AngularJS starts its magic by running the HTML content inside ng-app through what is known as the compile step:

   a. The compile step goes through each line of HTML and looks for AngularJS directives.

   b. For each directive, it executes the necessary code as defined by that directive's definition object. In case the directive creates or loads new HTML, it recursively descends into HTML until all directives are recognized by the compiler.

   c. At the end of the compile step, a link function is generated for each directive that has a handle on all the elements and attributes that need to be controlled by AngularJS.

5. AngularJS takes the link function and combines it with scope. The scope has the variables and contents that need to be displayed in the UI. This combination generates the *live view* that the user sees and interacts with:

   a. AngularJS will take the variables in scope, and display them in the UI if the HTML refers to a scope variable.

   b. Each controller and subcontroller is instantiated with its own scope that will be used to display data in the UI.

   c. AngularJS also adds watchers and listeners for all the directives and bindings to ensure it knows which fields it needs to track and which data field to bind with.

6. At the end of this, we have a live, interactive view with the content filled in for the user.

This entire flow is demonstrated in Figure 13-1.

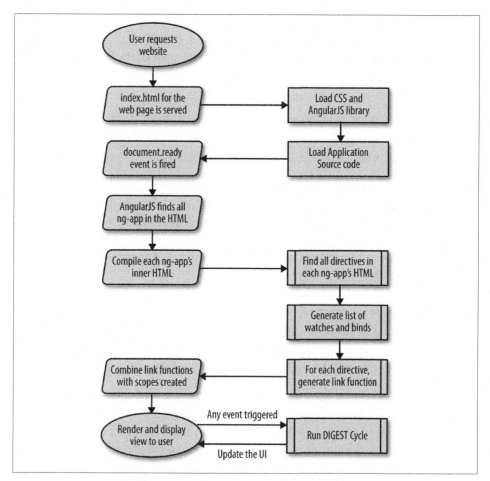

Figure 13-1. The AngularJS initial life cycle

At this point, as we mentioned, the first view that the user sees and interacts with has been generated, with the content dynamically being retrieved from the controller and scopes. Now how and when should the UI be updated? Think about the ng-bind and ng-model directives that change the state and the UI based on the state. When would the values from it need to be updated in the HTML?

- The first inclination might be to periodically check if any of the variables have changed, and then update the UI if they have. This requires a polling function that checks every 1 second, for example. But this is suboptimal and would result in the entire framework slowing to a crawl for a medium-sized application. So clearly this is a bad idea.

- The second, better approach (and the one AngularJS uses) is to be smart about updating the UI. If we think about it, the model that is driving the application cannot randomly change. It can change only in response to one of the following events:
  - The user makes a modification (types in, checks a checkbox, clicks a button, etc.) in a form or input element.
  - A server request is made and its response comes back (XHR or asynchronous request returning).
  - A `$timeout` or `$interval` is used to execute something asynchronously.

Outside of these events, the data cannot change randomly on its own. So AngularJS adds watchers for all its bindings and `ng-model`. And whenever one of the aforementioned events happens, AngularJS checks its watchers and bindings to see if anything has changed. If nothing has changed, AngularJS proceeds without doing anything. But if AngularJS finds that one of the fields it's controlling has changed underneath, it triggers an update of the UI.

The Digest Cycle

The update cycle that we mentioned earlier has a name in AngularJS: *the digest cycle*. The digest cycle in AngularJS is responsible for keeping the UI up to date in an AngularJS application. The AngularJS UI update cycle happens as follows:

1. When the application loads, or when any HTML is loaded within AngularJS, AngularJS runs its compilations step, and keeps track of all the watchers and listeners that are needed for the HTML (these would be from `ng-bind`, `ng-class`, and so on). When linked with the scope, we get the actual current values that are then displayed in the UI.
2. AngularJS also keeps track of all the elements that are bound to the HTML for each scope.
3. When one of the events mentioned in the previous section (such as a user click) happens, AngularJS triggers the digest cycle.
4. In the digest cycle, AngularJS starts from `$rootScope` and checks each watcher in the scope to see if the current value differs from the value it's displaying in the UI.
5. If nothing has changed, it recurses to all the parent scopes and so on until all the scopes are verified.
6. If AngularJS finds a watcher at any scope that reports a change in state, AngularJS stops right there, and *reruns the digest cycle*.
7. The digest cycle is rerun because a change in a watcher might have an implication on a watcher that was already evaluated beforehand. To ensure that no data change is missed, the digest cycle is rerun.

8. AngularJS reruns the digest cycle every time it encounters a change until the digest cycle stabilizes. On average, this takes two to three cycles for a normal AngularJS application.

    a. To prevent AngularJS from getting into an infinite loop where one watcher updates another model and vice versa, AngularJS caps the digest cycle reruns to 10 by default.

9. When the digest stabilizes, AngularJS accumulates all the UI updates and triggers them at once.

This entire flow is represented in Figure 13-2.

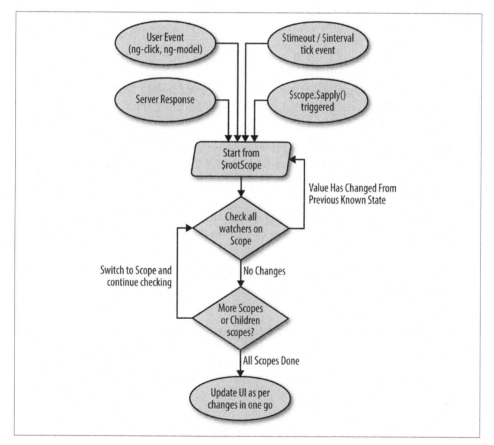

Figure 13-2. AngularJS digest life cycle

Lightweight Watchers

Because watchers and listeners can be executed multiple times by AngularJS for a single update, it's recommended that any watch that we add execute really fast. Thus it is almost always a bad idea to do time- and CPU-intensive tasks within watchers.

The general rule of thumb is that no individual watcher function take more than 20 microseconds, and no more than 2,000 variables be tracked or watched at any one point in time.

Directive Life Cycle

An individual directive has its own life cycle that follows a similar structure to the life cycle we saw before, but with a few key additions and differences. Here are the key steps in a directive's life:

1. When the application loads, the directive definition object is triggered. This happens only once, so anything declared or expressed before returning the directive definition object can be treated as the constructor for the directive, and will be executed once the very first time the application loads.

2. Next, when the directive is encountered in the HTML the very first time, the template for the directive is loaded (either asynchronously from the server or directly as a template from the definition). In either case, the template is cached and reused in further instances of the directive.

3. This template is then compiled and AngularJS handles the other directives present in the HTML. This generates a `link` function that can be used to link the directive to a scope.

4. The scope for the directive instance is created or acquired. This could be the parent scope, a child of the parent scope, or an isolated scope as the case might be (as discussed in Chapter 11).

5. The `link` function (and the controller) execute for the directive. This is where we add functionality that is specific to each instance of the directive.

We will now see how the other directive definition keys help us in creating more advanced directives.

Transclusions

AngularJS directives have a concept of transclusions to allow us to create reusable directives where each implementation might need to render a certain section of the UI differently. To understand how this works, we will first take the stock widget directive from Chapter 11 and then modify it to use transclusions. The following code snippets are mostly unchanged stock widget directives and related HTML and controller code from Chapter 11.

First up is the directive declaration:

```
// File: chapter13/directive-no-transclusion/directive.js
angular.module('stockMarketApp')
  .directive('stockWidget', [function() {
    return {
      templateUrl: 'stock.html',
      restrict: 'A',
      scope: {
        stockData: '='
      },
      link: function($scope, $element, $attrs) {
        $scope.getChange = function(stock) {
          return Math.ceil(((stock.price - stock.previous) /
            stock.previous) * 100);
        };
      }
    };
  }]);
```

This is mostly unchanged, and uses the simpler version (instead of the one with function binding that was used in later examples in Chapter 11). The HTML for the directive also remains largely unchanged:

```
<!-- File: chapter13/directive-no-transclusion/stock.html -->
<div class="stock-dash">
  Name:
  <span class="stock-name"
        ng-bind="stockData.name">
  </span>
  Price:
  <span class="stock-price"
        ng-bind="stockData.price | currency">
  </span>
  Percentage Change
  <span class="stock-change"
        ng-bind="getChange(stockData) + '%'">
  </span>
</div>
```

The controller also remains unchanged from the example in Chapter 11:

```
// File: chapter13/directive-no-transclusion/app.js

angular.module('stockMarketApp', [])
  .controller('MainCtrl', [function() {
    var self = this;
    self.stocks = [
      {name: 'First Stock', price: 100, previous: 220},
      {name: 'Second Stock', price: 140, previous: 120},
```

```
          {name: 'Third Stock', price: 110, previous: 110},
          {name: 'Fourth Stock', price: 400, previous: 420}
      ];
   }]);
```

The main *index.html* file is the only file that gets a minor change, but only in how we use the directive we created:

```
<!-- File: chapter13/directive-no-transclusion/index.html -->
<html>
<head>
  <title>Stock Market App</title>
</head>
<body ng-app="stockMarketApp">

  <div ng-controller="MainCtrl as mainCtrl">
    <h3>List of Stocks</h3>
    <div ng-repeat="s in mainCtrl.stocks">
      <div stock-widget stock-data="s">
        This content will be blown away
      </div>
    </div>
  </div>

  <script src="https://ajax.googleapis.com/ajax/libs/angularjs/1.2.19/angular.js">
  </script>
  <script src="app.js"></script>
  <script src="directive.js"></script>
</body>
</html>
```

In *index.html*, we added some content inside the stock-widget directive by trying to provide some custom rendering data that we want included as part of our rendering.

Now when we run this application (remember to *start a local server first*, as we saw in previous chapters), we see that the content we added as a child of our directive in *index.html* is ignored, and only the contents of template are loaded. This is the *default* behavior of any AngularJS directive, in that if it has a template or templateUrl, it will remove the content of the element where the directive is found and replace it with the template specified in the directive definition object.

This is fine for a majority of cases, but when we need custom HTML to be added as part of our directive (think accordions or tab widgets), this is not what we want. In these cases, where we want AngularJS to respect both the inner contents where the directive is used, as well as the original template of the directive, we use the concept of *transclusion*.

Basic Transclusion

Basic transclusion can be thought of as a two-step process:

1. First, we tell the directive that we are going to use transclusion as part of this directive. This tells AngularJS that whenever the directive is encountered in the HTML, to make a copy of its content and store it so that it's not lost when AngularJS replaces it with the directive's template. This is accomplished by setting the key `transclude` to `true` as part of the directive definition object.

2. Second, we need to tell AngularJS where to put the content that was stored in the template. This is accomplished by using the `ng-transclude` directive, which ensures that the content that was captured is made a child of the element in the directive template.

Let's take a look at how we might modify the preceding example to use transclusions. The controller and the *index.html* file remain unchanged from before, so we won't repeat it. The first change we make is to the directive definition:

```
// File: chapter13/directive-transclusion/directive.js
angular.module('stockMarketApp')
  .directive('stockWidget', [function() {
    return {
      templateUrl: 'stock.html',
      restrict: 'A',
      transclude: true,
      scope: {
        stockData: '='
      },
      link: function($scope, $element, $attrs) {
        $scope.getChange = function(stock) {
          return Math.ceil(((stock.price - stock.previous) /
              stock.previous) * 100);
        };
      }
    };
  }]);
```

In the directive definition, we added the key `transclude` and set its value to `true`. There is no other change in the definition.

Next we take a look at the *stock.html* file to see how it changes:

```
<!-- File: chapter13/directive-transclusion/stock.html -->
<div class="stock-dash">
  <span ng-transclude></span>

  Price:
  <span class="stock-price"
```

```
        ng-bind="stockData.price | currency">
    </span>
    Percentage Change:
    <span class="stock-change"
        ng-bind="getChange(stockData) + '%'">
    </span>
</div>
```

We removed the name and the binding for stockData.name and replaced it with a span, and added the ng-transclude directive on it. The end effect of this change is as follows:

- When AngularJS encounters the stock-widget directive in *index.html*, it grabs its inner content (Recommended Stock : {{s.name}}) and stores it for later use.

- When it includes the directive's template in the instance, it looks for the ng-transclude directive, and places the content that it stored in step 1 as a child in the element with ng-transclude.

- Thus, when the UI renders for each stock in the stocks array, we get the Recommended Stock text followed by each stock's name.

Scope of an ng-transclude

You might be wondering how ng-transclude works, especially because we isolated the scope for our directive, whereas the ng-transclude content explicitly refers to something that is available in the scope of ng-repeat, but not inside the directive's scope.

When AngularJS encounters transclude, it clones the HTML before replacing it with the template or templateUrl contents. Then, when it encounters ng-transclude, it compiles the transcluded content, but links it to the parent scope instead of the isolated scope of the directive. Thus, the transcluded content still has access to the parent controller and its content, while the directive HTML has an isolated scope (or a new scope, as the case might be).

Thus, the transcluded content and the directive content form a sibling relationship but do not share the same scope. This is because the transcluded content is not expected to know the inner workings of the directive, but is instead expected to be dependent on the usage and context in which it is used.

Advanced Transclusion

In the previous example, we covered the case where we have some content specific to the usage of the directive that we need placed inside our directive at a certain location. We accomplished this using the transclude keyword along with the ng-transclude directive inside our directive.

Another common use case with dynamic user-dependent content is to have multiple copies of the template made and used as and when we need it. For example, instead of displaying the content of our directive once, we might need to show it multiple times inside a carousel. This is also what happens with the ng-repeat directive, where we define a template that needs to be repeated, and then for each instance we create the template and insert it in our directive dynamically.

Let's see how we can accomplish this use case using the transclude property of our directive definition object. In our next example, we try to create a trivial replacement for the ng-repeat that will pick up some variables from our outer scope, and add some variables for each instance. We won't make it auto-update, but will instead focus on how to use transclusion to render multiple instances of our template.

First up, the *app.js* file, which doesn't change:

```
// File: chapter13/directive-advanced-transclusion/app.js

angular.module('stockMarketApp', [])
  .controller('MainCtrl', [function() {
    var self = this;
    self.stocks = [
      {name: 'First Stock', price: 100, previous: 220},
      {name: 'Second Stock', price: 140, previous: 120},
      {name: 'Third Stock', price: 110, previous: 110},
      {name: 'Fourth Stock', price: 400, previous: 420}
    ];
  }]);
```

This remains exactly the same. Next up is the main *index.html* file, which also gives us a peek into how we want to use this directive:

```
<!-- File: chapter13/directive-advanced-transclusion/index.html -->
<html>
<head>
  <title>Stock Market App</title>
</head>
<body ng-app="stockMarketApp">

  <div ng-controller="MainCtrl as mainCtrl">
    <h3>List of Stocks</h3>
    <div simple-stock-repeat="mainCtrl.stocks">
      We found {{stock.name}} at {{currentIndex}}
    </div>
  </div>

  <script src="https://ajax.googleapis.com/ajax/libs/angularjs/1.2.19/angular.js">
  </script>
  <script src="app.js"></script>
  <script src="directive.js"></script>
</body>
</html>
```

We replaced the usage of our stock-widget directive. We replaced ng-repeat with our new directive, called simple-stock-repeat. This directive takes any array from our controller and uses the content of the directive as a template to create one for each instance in our array. The directive exposes the current item as the variable stock, and also exposes additional information like the index of the item in the variable curren tIndex. When we run the previous HTML, we expect that the "We found…" statement be repeated four times, once for each stock, each one with its index in the array.

Now let's see how we accomplish this in the directive definition:

```javascript
// File: chapter13/directive-advanced-transclusion/directive.js
angular.module('stockMarketApp').directive('simpleStockRepeat',
    [function() {
  return {
    restrict: 'A',
    // Capture and replace the entire element
    // instead of just its content
    transclude: 'element',
    // A $transclude is passed in as the fifth
    // argument to the link function
    link: function($scope, $element, $attrs, ctrl, $transclude) {
      var myArray = $scope.$eval($attrs.simpleStockRepeat);

      var container = angular.element(
        '<div class="container"></div>');
      for (var i = 0; i < myArray.length; i++) {
        // Create an element instance with a new child
        // scope using the clone linking function
        var instance = $transclude($scope.$new(),
            function(clonedElement, newScope) {
          // Expose custom variables for the instance
          newScope.currentIndex = i;
          newScope.stock = myArray[i];
        });
        // Add it to our container
        container.append(instance);
      }

      // With transclude: 'element', the element gets replaced
      // with a comment. Add our generated content
      // after the comment
      $element.after(container);
    }
  };
}]);
```

We introduced quite a few new things in this directive, so let's walk through each one individually:

- The first change is in the `transclude` key of the directive definition object. In the previous example, we had set it to `true`, which tells AngularJS to pick up the content of the element on which the directive is applied and retain it. When we specify `transclude` to `element`, it notifies AngularJS to copy the entire element, along with any directives that might be present on it for transclusion.

- The `link` function, as we saw in Chapter 11, takes three arguments by default: the scope of the directive, the element on which the directive is present, and the attributes on the element. In addition, we can pass directive controllers to the directive as the fourth argument. But the fifth argument is what we care about, which is a transclusion function that is generated only when we use the `transclude` key in the directive definition object.

  This `transclude` function is a constructor that allows us to create new instances of our template as many times as needed depending on our use case. The function takes an optional scope (if a new scope is needed for the element; otherwise, it inherits the directive's scope) and a mandatory clone linking function as the second argument.

- In the very first line, we evaluate the variable mentioned in the HTML along with the directive to get a handle on the array that we want to repeat on. This is accomplished by calling `$eval` on the scope with a string that contains the JavaScript we want to evaluate in the context of the scope.

- Because `transclude` *element* copies the entire element, it also removes the element from the HTML. So we create a container element within which to put all our instances that we create.

- We then run a `for` loop for each instance in our array, and call the `transclude` function that is passed to the linking function. This returns a new HTML element that is a fully compiled and linked version of our template that can then be inserted into our main body.

- As mentioned previously, the first argument to the `transclude` function is an optional scope. In our example, we create a new child scope. This is so that any modification made to the scope does not get reflected in the parent scope. This is always a *good practice* to make sure no global states step on each other.

- The second argument that we pass to the `transclude` function is a linking function for the cloned element. This is where we add any behavior or variable that is specific to this instance of the template (like `currentIndex` and `stock` for us).

- We then add the created instance of our template to the container element, and then finally add the container element after our directive instance (which at this point is just a comment node in the HTML). Without this step, we would have fully compiled, working AngularJS-ready DOM elements that wouldn't appear in the rendered UI.

In general, we can use the transclude concept any time we need a component whose templating and UI changes depend on its usage and context. We can decide whether or not we need `transclude` as follows:

- Does each user of the directive need to specify his own template or rendering logic? If so, then use `transclude`.
- Is only the content of the directive important, or is the element on which the directive is applied necessary as well? Use `transclude: true` in the former, and `transclude: element` in the latter.
- If it's a simple matter of displaying the transcluded content as is, use the `ng-transclude` directive directly in your directive template.
- Do we need to generate multiple copies of the template or add behavior, variables, and business logic to the scope on which the transclusion is done? If so, inject the transcluding function into our `link` function.
- Call the transclusion function with an optional new scope (this is recommended) and linking function for that instance. Within the linking function, add the functions and variables that the template needs.

When creating directives for tasks such as carousels and infinite scrolling, you can consider using transclusions to make your life easier.

Directive Controllers and require

In Chapter 11, we introduced the concept of the `link` function for directives, which we mentioned is the ideal place to add behavior and business logic to your directives. But if you peruse the AngularJS source code, or go through the AngularJS documentation on directives (*https://docs.angularjs.org/guide/directive*), you will notice that directives also allow you to define controllers.

The reason we use the `link` function and not controllers to define our directive-specific behavior is that directive controllers are present for a completely different use case. Directive controllers are used in AngularJS for inter-directive communication, while `link` functions are fully contained and specific to the directive instance. By inter-directive communication, we mean when one directive on an element wants to communicate with another directive on its parent or on the same element. This encompasses sharing state or variables, or even functions.

Let's see how we might create and use directive controllers to create a `tabs` directive. Now instead of letting the top-level `tabs` directive recursively create tabs inside of it, we will also create a tab directive for each individual tab in the set of tabs. Now obviously, the tab directive can only be used in the context of the set of tabs. It also needs to be able to let the parent know it was selected so the tab set can decide to hide and show content accordingly. Let's see how we can accomplish this using directive controllers:

```
// File: chapter13/directive-controllers/app.js

angular.module('stockMarketApp', [])
  .controller('MainCtrl', [function() {
    var self = this;

    self.startedTime = new Date().getTime();
    self.stocks = [
      {name: 'First Stock', price: 100, previous: 220},
      {name: 'Second Stock', price: 140, previous: 120},
      {name: 'Third Stock', price: 110, previous: 110},
      {name: 'Fourth Stock', price: 400, previous: 420}
    ];
  }]);
```

The *app.js* file that defines our controller has not changed much. It still defines a list of stocks, and adds a variable called startedTime. Each of these variables will be shown in separate tabs in our final UI. Next, let's take a look at how we use the tabs and tab directives we're building in the *index.html* file:

```
<!-- File: chapter13/directive-controllers/index.html -->
<html>
<head>
  <title>Stock Market App</title>
  <link rel="stylesheet" href="main.css">
</head>
<body ng-app="stockMarketApp">

  <div ng-controller="MainCtrl as mainCtrl">
    <tabs>
      <tab title="First Tab">
        This is the first tab.
        The app started at {{mainCtrl.startedTime | date}}
      </tab>
      <tab title="Second Tab">
        This is the second tab
        <div ng-repeat="stock in mainCtrl.stocks">
          Stock Name: {{stock.name}}
        </div>
      </tab>
    </tabs>
  </div>

  <script src="https://ajax.googleapis.com/ajax/libs/angularjs/1.2.19/angular.js">
  </script>
  <script src="app.js"></script>
  <script src="tabs.js"></script>
```

```
      <script src="tab.js"></script>
   </body>
   </html>
```

We define a div that's controlled by MainCtrl, inside of which we want to display two tabs. The first tab has the title "First Tab", and when the tab is selected, displays the date and time on which the application was opened. This content comes from MainCtrl. The second tab as the title "Second Tab", and displays the names of each stock in the stocks array in MainCtrl.

With the usage out of the way, we can now take a look at how the directive is created. Let's first look at the tabs directive, which acts as the container for a set of tabs:

```
// File: chapter13/directive-controllers/tabs.js
angular.module('stockMarketApp')
  .directive('tabs', [function() {
    return {
      restrict: 'E',
      transclude: true,
      scope: true,
      template: '<div class="tab-headers">' +
        '  <div ng-repeat="tab in tabs"' +
        '       ng-click="selectTab($index)"' +
        '       ng-class="{selected: isSelectedTab($index)}">' +
        '    <span ng-bind="tab.title"></span>' +
        '  </div>' +
        '</div>' +
        '<div ng-transclude></div> ',
      controller: function($scope) {
        var currentIndex = 0;
        $scope.tabs = [];
        this.registerTab = function(title, scope) {
          if ($scope.tabs.length === 0) {
            scope.selected = true;
          } else {
            scope.selected = false;
          }
          $scope.tabs.push({title: title, scope: scope});
        };

        $scope.selectTab = function(index) {
          currentIndex = index;
          for (var i = 0; i < $scope.tabs.length; i++) {
            $scope.tabs[i].scope.selected = currentIndex === i;
          }
        };

        $scope.isSelectedTab = function(index) {
          return currentIndex === index;
        };
      }
```

```
    };
  }]);
```

The `tabs` directive leverages the transclusion concept from before, as well as defines a controller. Let's take a more detailed look at the most interesting parts of the `tabs` directive:

- The directive uses `transclusion` (not element-level transclusion, though) to pick up the individual tabs and add the tab titles above them.

- The `tabs` directive also defines its own `scope`, because it needs to add certain functions to the scope, and we don't want to collide or override any properties or functions on the parent.

- The directive `template` defines a section to repeat over individual tabs (stored in a tabs array on the scope) and display them. The template also handles clicking an individual tab as well as highlighting the selected tab using functions on the scope of the directive.

- The `tabs` directive `template` defines a div in the template where the contents are translcuded into using `ng-transclude`. This is where the entire content of the `tabs` directive in the HTML (each individual `tab`) gets placed during runtime.

- Next, instead of defining a `link` function, we define a directive `controller`. The reason we do this is because we want children directives of the `tabs` directive to be able to access certain functionality from the `tabs` directive. Whenever we need to communicate between child and parent directives, or between sibling directives, we should consider using directive controllers.

- A directive `controller` is a function that gets the scope and element injected in. This is similar to the `link` function that we've been using so far, but the difference is that functions we define in the controller on `this` can be accessed by child or sibling controllers (we'll see how in just a bit). Thus, the `controller` can define functions that are specific to the directive instance by defining them on $scope as we have been doing so far, and define the API or accessible functions and variables by defining them on `this` or the controller's instance.

- In this case, we define the `tabs` variable on the `scope`, as well as `selectTab` and `isSelected` on it, which are used by the directive template for selecting tabs and highlighting the selected tab. Both of these functions set or unset a selected variable on the scope of an individual tab to handle showing and hiding tabs.

- We also define a function named `registerTab` on the controller's instance. This function, because it is not defined on the scope, will not be accessible from the directive's HTML. This function adds a `title` and `scope` object to an array. This array is used to display the list of tabs at the top.

Now, let's look at the tab directive to see how it hooks into the tabs directive and leverages the controller we defined:

```
// File: chapter13/directive-controllers/tab.js
angular.module('stockMarketApp')
  .directive('tab', [function() {
    return {
      restrict: 'E',
      transclude: true,
      template: '<div ng-show="selected" ng-transclude></div>',
      require: '^tabs',
      scope: true,
      link: function($scope, $element, $attr, tabCtrl) {
        tabCtrl.registerTab($attr.title, $scope);
      }
    };
  }]);
```

The tab directive is much simpler:

1. The first thing the tab directive does is set up transclusion, because it defines a template of its own.

2. In the template, we use the ng-transclude to add the content inside a div, and add a condition to selectively hide and show the div based on a selected variable on the scope.

3. We add a new key, require, and use the value ^tabs (we'll see what the ^ symbol means in "require Options" on page 221). This tells AngularJS that for the tab directive to work, it requires that one of the parent elements in the HTML be the tabs directive, and we want its controller to be made available to the tab directive.

4. We define a new scope for this directive so that local variables don't override anything in the parent scope.

5. In the link function, we get the controller we required as the fourth argument (after scope, element, and attributes). This is an instance of the controller we defined in the tabs directive, and is dynamically injected based on what AngularJS finds.

6. Inside the link function, we register the tab with the parent tabs directive function that we defined earlier.

Now the flow in the application is as follows:

1. When the tabs directive (the parent one) is found in the HTML, the content is transcluded and a space for the tabs is preserved in the HTML (using ng-repeat). The actual tabs are inserted below it.

2. Each individual tab registers with the parent, so that the parent tabs controller can decide which tab is currently selected, and highlight and hide/show the other tabs as needed.

3. Each tab again uses transclusion on its content to wrap it in a container so that it can be hidden and shown as needed.

4. On registration, the tabs controller sets the very first tab as selected (using a scope variable on the scope passed up to the tabs controller).

5. After that, the ng-click handles hiding and showing of the individual tabs using the functions defined on the scope of the tabs directive.

require Options

The require keyword in the directive definition object either takes a string or an array of strings, each of which is the name of the directive that must be used in conjunction with the current directive.

For example:

```
require: 'tabs'
```

tells AngularJS to look for a directive called tabs, which exposes a controller on the same element the directive is on. Similarly:

```
require: ['tabs', 'ngModel']
```

tells AngularJS that both the tabs and ng-model directives must be present on the element our directive is used on. When used as an array, the link function gets an array of controllers as the fourth argument, instead of just one controller.

Now, each individual string can take some prefixes, which define how AngularJS should behave when finding these directives. For example:

```
require: 'tabs'
```

implies that AngularJS should locate the directive tabs on the same element, and throw an error if it's not found:

```
require: '?tabs'
```

This implies that AngularJS should try to locate the directive tabs on the same element, but pass null as the fourth argument to the link function if it isn't found. That is, prefixing ? tells AngularJS to treat the directive as an optional dependency.

Furthermore, we can also tell AngularJS to look for a directive not on itself, but on its parent chain. This can be done as:

```
require: '^tabs'
```

This is what we used in our previous example, which tells AngularJS that the `tabs` directive must be present on one of the parent elements (not necessarily the immediate parent).

We can also mix and match these prefixes. For example:

```
require: '?^tabs'
```

implies that a parent element of our directive may or may not have the `tabs` directive, but if it is present, it should be injected into our directive `link` function.

Input Directives with ng-model

We saw in the previous section how we can create directive controllers and use them to communicate between directives and to shared state. In this section, we leverage this concept, extend the already existing `ng-model` directive, and integrate with third-party input widgets. The thought behind this is that `ng-model` is already good at what it does, which is the two-way data-binding. If we introduce a new input widget in our AngularJS application, we want it to behave the same way, in that we add the widget in out HTML, add an `ng-model` to it, and be done with it.

We'll look at how easy it is to accomplish this by incorporating a third-party input slider into our application. For the purpose of this example, we use the awesome jQuery-based `noUiSlider` (*http://refreshless.com/nouislider/*) and wrap it inside a reusable directive. We start with the main *index.html* file, which demonstrates how we want to use this directive:

```html
<!-- File: chapter13/directive-slider/index.html -->
<html>
<head>
  <title>Slider App</title>
  <link rel="stylesheet" href="jquery.nouislider.css">
  <style type="text/css">
    .slider {
      display: block;
      height: 20px;
      margin: 20px;
    }
  </style>
</head>
<body ng-app="sliderApp">

  <div ng-controller="MainCtrl as mainCtrl">

    <div>
      The current value of the slider is {{mainCtrl.selectedValue}}
    </div>

    <no-ui-slider class="slider"
```

```
              ng-model="mainCtrl.selectedValue"
              range-min="500"
              range-max="5000">

  </no-ui-slider>

  <div>
    <input type="number"
           ng-model="mainCtrl.textValue"
           min="500"
           max="5000"
           placeholder="Set a value">
    <button ng-click="mainCtrl.setSelectedValue()">
      Set slider value
    </button>
  </div>
</div>

<script src="http://code.jquery.com/jquery-1.11.1.js"></script>
<script src="jquery.nouislider.min.js"></script>
<script src="https://ajax.googleapis.com/ajax/libs/angularjs/1.2.19/angular.js">
</script>
<script src="app.js"></script>
<script src="noui-slider.js"></script>
</body>
</html>
```

The HTML is mostly straightforward. We included the CSS for noUiSlider in the HEAD tag, and at the end, added a dependency on jQuery first, and then the noUiSlid er JavaScript file before adding our standard AngularJS dependencies.

As part of the main div controlling the application, we first display the current value of the selectedValue variable from the controller. We then use our no-ui-slider directive and bind it to the same selectedValue variable that we print before using ng-model. We also give it a fixed range using the range-min and range-max attributes on it.

We then have another section that holds a text box bound to a different variable (text Value) and a button. Clicking the button should set the value of the slider to the value in the text box.

Let's look at the controller driving this application:

```
// File: chapter13/directive-slider/app.js

angular.module('sliderApp', [])
  .controller('MainCtrl', [function() {
    var self = this;

    self.selectedValue = 2000;
```

```
        self.textValue = 4000;

        self.setSelectedValue = function() {
          self.selectedValue = self.textValue;
        };
    }]);
```

The controller for our slider application is really tiny. It's just a bunch of model variables (selectedValue and textValue), and a function to take the value of textValue and set it on selectedValue. The aim is that when the setSelectedValue function is triggered, the slider takes the value that is present in the text box. Both variables have some initial value so that the the UI is slightly more interesting.

Now we can finally see how the noUiSlider directive accomplishes this:

```
// File: chapter13/directive-slider/noui-slider.js
angular.module('sliderApp')
  .directive('noUiSlider', [function() {
    return {
      restrict: 'E',
      require: 'ngModel',
      link: function($scope, $element, $attr, ngModelCtrl) {

        $element.noUiSlider({
          // We might not have the initial value in ngModelCtrl yet
          start: 0,
          range: {
            // $attrs by default gives us string values
            // nouiSlider expects numbers, so convert
            min: Number($attr.rangeMin),
            max: Number($attr.rangeMax)
          }
        });

        // When data changes inside AngularJS
        // Notify the third party directive of the change
        ngModelCtrl.$render = function() {
          $element.val(ngModelCtrl.$viewValue);
        };

        // When data changes outside of AngularJS
        $element.on('set', function(args) {
          // Also tell AngularJS that it needs to update the UI
          $scope.$apply(function() {
            // Set the data within AngularJS
            ngModelCtrl.$setViewValue($element.val());
          });
        });
      }
    };
  }]);
```

How do we accomplish creating the slider directive? Let's take a look, step by step, at the directive we created:

1. We created an element directive, which requires that the ngModel directive be used on the same element as the noUiSlider directive that we're creating.

2. In the link function, we first create the noUiSlider by calling its constructor with the appropriate parameters. We use the attributes from the HTML, but make sure that we convert them from strings to numbers.

3. Because noUiSlider is a jQuery plugin, and we load jQuery before we load AngularJS in *index.html*, we get to directly call the noUiSlider function on our element, because jQuery seamlessly integrates into AngularJS.

4. Then, to finish integrating ngModel into our third-party input integration, we need to accomplish two steps:

   a. When the data changes within AngularJS, we need to update the third-party UI component. We do this by overriding the $render method on the ngModelCtrl, and setting the value in the third-party component inside of it. The latest and greatest value that's currently set in the variable referred to by ngModel is available in the ngModelCtrl in the $viewValue variable. AngularJS calls the $render method whenever the model value changes inside AngularJS (for example, when it is initialized to a value in our controller).

   b. When the data changes outside AngularJS, we need to update AngularJS with the new value. We do this by calling the $setViewValue function on the ngModelCtrl with the latest and greatest value inside the set listener.

5. Also, as mentioned in the AngularJS life cyle, AngularJS updates the UI whenever it knows that things within its control have changed. A third-party UI component is outside the AngularJS life cycle, so we need to manually call $scope.$apply() to ensure that AngularJS updates the UI. The $scope.$apply() call takes an optional function as an argument and ensures that the AngularJS digest cycle that's responsible for updating the UI with the latest values is triggered.

When we integrate any third-party UI component that needs to act as an input widget, it always makes sense to integrate it and leverage the ngModel directive so that it works seamlessly like any other input widget. When we do this, we need to take care of the two-way data-binding:

- When the data inside AngularJS changes, we need to update the third-party component data with the latest and greatest values (handled by overriding the ngModelCtrl.$render function).

- When the data outside AngularJS changes (through an event outside AngularJS), we need to capture it and update AngularJS's model (by calling `ngModelCtrl.$set ViewValue` with the updated value).

Because the only listeners we add are on the element, when the element is destroyed, those listeners are removed. If we add another listener, then we're responsible for cleaning them up as well.

Custom Validators

Now that we understand directive controllers as well as how to leverage `ngModel` to create our own input directives, we can create our own custom validators. As we saw in Chapter 2, AngularJS has a lot of built-in directives for form and input validation, like `required`, `ng-required`, `ng-minlength`, and so on. Between them, they give us a strong base of validators to start using in our application.

But after a certain point, each user needs certain validation that they find themselves repeating across multiple use cases. In such a case, it would be better for us to create our own custom validators using AngularJS.

Let's take a slightly contrived example where we want to ensure that the text the user enters in a text box is a valid US zip code, which is one of the three following forms:

- 12345
- 12345 1234
- 12345-1234

Let's look at *index.html* for this, which demonstrates the usage of our new validator directive:

```
<!-- File: chapter13/directive-custom-validator/index.html -->
<html>
<head>
  <title>Stock Market App</title>
  <style>
    input.ng-invalid {
      background: pink;
    }
  </style>
</head>
<body ng-app="stockMarketApp">

  <div ng-controller="MainCtrl as mainCtrl">
    <h3>Zip Code Input</h3>
    <h5>Zips are allowed in one of the following formats</h5>
    <ul>
      <li>12345</li>
```

```
    <li>12345 1234</li>
    <li>12345-1234</li>
  </ul>
  <form novalidate="">
    Enter valid zip code:
    <input type="text"
           ng-model="mainCtrl.zip"
           valid-zip>

  </form>
</div>

<script src="https://ajax.googleapis.com/ajax/libs/angularjs/1.2.19/angular.js">
</script>
<script src="app.js"></script>
<script src="directive.js"></script>
</body>
</html>
```

The only interesting part of the HTML is the form, which houses an input with ng-model on it. We want to ensure that the user types valid US zip codes into it, which is why we add the valid-zip validator directive on it. The *app.js* file is very trivial and simple:

```
// File: chapter13/directive-custom-validator/app.js

angular.module('stockMarketApp', [])
  .controller('MainCtrl', [function() {
    this.zip = '1234';
  }]);
```

app.js creates a controller and adds a default, invalid value to the zip field on the constructor. Finally, let's look at the directive that creates our custom validator:

```
// File: chapter13/directive-custom-validator/directive.js
angular.module('stockMarketApp')
  .directive('validZip', [function() {
    var zipCodeRegex = /^\d{5}(?:[-\s]\d{4})?$/g;
    return {
      restrict: 'A',
      require: 'ngModel',
      link: function($scope, $element, $attrs, ngModelCtrl) {
        // Handle DOM update --> Model update
        ngModelCtrl.$parsers.unshift(function(value) {
          var valid = zipCodeRegex.test(value);
          ngModelCtrl.$setValidity('validZip', valid);
          return valid ? value : undefined;
        });

        // Handle Model Update --> DOM
        ngModelCtrl.$formatters.unshift(function(value) {
          ngModelCtrl.$setValidity('validZip',
```

```
                    zipCodeRegex.test(value));
                  return value;
              });
            }
          };
        }]);
```

Our zipCode directive defines a regular expression that we can use to validate whether or not a given string is a valid US zip code. Our directive itself depends on and leverages the ngModel controller by requiring it as part of the directive definition. Finally, we get to the link function, and here again, similar to the previous input directive, we have to handle both ways of data flow in the application.

When the data changes in the DOM, AngularJS goes through each parser, and the parser gets to check the validity of the data before passing it along in the chain. We add our own parser to the chain of parsers, and perform our validity check here using the regular expression. In either case, we set the validity of our directive on the ngModel controller. The parser function has to return the correct value (if the data is valid) or undefined (in case the data isn't).

We also need to handle the case where the model is updated (due to a server response, say). In this case, AngularJS runs the data through a formatting step to ensure that it's taking the correct API. We again check for validity here and return the value.

In both of these cases, we set the validity of the element using the name of the directive on the ngModel controller.

Now, we could very well do asynchronous validation in either of these cases by making a server call through $http. So email or username availability checks could be wrapped in their own validators. Your imagination is the only limit with these validators!

Compile

In the directive life cycle, we mentioned that a directive goes through two distinct phases: a compile step and a link step. We explored the link step in detail; now we dig into the compile step.

By the time we get to the link step of the directive, the directive's HTML has already been parsed and all the relevant directives within it have been picked up by the AngularJS compiler and attached to the correct scope. At this point, if we dynamically add any directives to the HTML or do large-scale DOM manipulation that involves integration with existing AngularJS directives, it won't work correctly.

The compile step in a directive is the correct place to do any sort of HTML template manipulation and DOM transformation. We *never use the link and compile functions together*, because when we use the compile key, we have to return a linking function from within it instead. Let's take an example of a `form-element` directive to see how it works in practice:

```html
<!-- File: chapter13/directive-compile/index.html -->
<html>
<head>
  <title>Dynamic Form App</title>
</head>
<body ng-app="dynamicFormApp">

  <div ng-controller="MainCtrl as mainCtrl">
    <form novalidate="" name="mainForm">
      <form-element type="text"
                    name="uname"
                    bind-to="mainCtrl.username"
                    label="Username"
                    required
                    ng-minlength="5">
        <validation key="required">
          Please enter a username
        </validation>
        <validation key="minlength">
          Username must be at least 5 characters
        </validation>
      </form-element>

      Username is {{mainCtrl.username}}

      <form-element type="password"
                    name="pwd"
                    bind-to="mainCtrl.password"
                    label="Password"
                    required
                    ng-pattern="/^[a-zA-Z0-9]+$/">
        <validation key="required">
          Please enter a password
        </validation>
        <validation key="pattern">
          Password must only be alphanumeric characters
        </validation>
      </form-element>
      Password is {{mainCtrl.password}}

      <button>Submit</button>
    </form>

  </div>

  <script src="http://code.angularjs.org/1.2.16/angular.js"></script>
  <script src="app.js"></script>
  <script src="directive.js"></script>
```

```
  </body>
</html>
```

In this HTML, we want to define a form with a bunch of labels and input fields. Each field has its own validation logic and different error messages that we need to display for each particular field. Instead of writing complex HTML using what we saw in Chapter 4, we instead want to abstract some of that using the `form-element` directive, on which we specify the validation and binding rules. The `form-element` directive also allows us to define validation messages to show on different error conditions. These validation messages would then be shown and hidden under the right conditions automatically without the need for any extra code. One requirement for our new directive is that it must be used inside a form in the HTML.

Here are the fields we support with our `form-element` directive:

- The type of input field (text, password, and so on)
- The name of the input field to be able to find errors for it correctly
- The `ngModel` variable to bind to
- The label to be shown beside the form field
- Any `ngModel`-based validation, like `required`, `ngMinlength`, `ngPattern`, and so on

The controller for this is pretty trivial, and is as follows:

```
// File: chapter13/directive-compile/app.js

angular.module('dynamicFormApp', [])
  .controller('MainCtrl', [function() {
    var self = this;
    self.username = '';
    self.password = '';
}]);
```

The controller defines some variables for the HTML to bind to, and nothing else. We don't implement an `onClick` function for the form, because we are not focusing on that particular flow.

Now our directive needs to look at the HTML, and do the following:

- Generate the right input tag with the correct `ng-model`, and the validation rules.
- Generate the template for all the error messages and ensure they are shown on the correct condition.
- Ignore any attributes that are not known or handled by the directive correctly.
- Add functions to the scope to show the error messages correctly.

Let's see how we can accomplish this using our directive:

```
// File: chapter13/directive-compile/directive.js
angular.module('dynamicFormApp')
  .directive('formElement', [function() {

    return {
      restrict: 'E',
      require: '^form',
      scope: true,
      compile: function($element, $attrs) {
        var expectedInputAttrs = {
          'required': 'required',
          'ng-minlength': 'ngMinlength',
          'ng-pattern': 'ngPattern'
          // More here to be implemented
        };

        // Start extracting content from the HTML
        var validationKeys = $element.find('validation');
        var presentValidationKeys = {};
        var inputName = $attrs.name;
        angular.forEach(validationKeys, function(validationKey) {
          validationKey = angular.element(validationKey);
          presentValidationKeys[validationKey.attr('key')] =
            validationKey.text();
        });

        // Start generating final element HTML
        var elementHtml = '<div>' +
          '<label>' + $attrs.label + '</label>';
        elementHtml += '<input type="' + $attrs.type +
                          '" name="' + inputName +
                          '" ng-model="' + $attrs.bindTo + '"';

        $element.removeAttr('type');
        $element.removeAttr('name');
        for (var i in expectedInputAttrs) {
          if ($attrs[expectedInputAttrs[i]] !== undefined) {
            elementHtml += ' ' + i + '="' +
              $attrs[expectedInputAttrs[i]] + '"';
          }
          $element.removeAttr(i);
        }
        elementHtml += '>';

        elementHtml +=
          '<span ng-repeat="(key, text) in validators" ' +
            ' ng-show="hasError(key)"' +
            ' ng-bind="text"></span>';

        elementHtml += '</div>';
        $element.html(elementHtml);
```

```
            return function($scope, $element, $attrs, formCtrl) {
              $scope.validators = angular.copy(presentValidationKeys);
              $scope.hasError = function(key) {
                return !!formCtrl[inputName]['$error'][key];
              };
            };
          }
        };
      }]);
```

The following are the points of interest in the formElement directive that we previously defined:

1. We add require to ensure the formElement directive is used as a subchild of any form, and give it a new child scope so that any functions we add are restricted and do not override any global variables or functions.

2. We give it a compile function, which gets called with the element and the attributes. The compile function executes before the scope is available, so it does not get the scope injected in.

3. We start extracting and parsing the existing form-element tag from the HTML, and picking out the validation rules, messages, and existing attributes that we care about.

4. After that, we start generating the new HTML that will be used for the directive. Because we will be adding AngularJS directives dynamically, we are doing this in the compile. If we do this in the link step, AngularJS won't detect these directives and our application won't work.

5. We add the input tag with the name ng-model and all the validations that were present in the HTML.

6. We then replace the existing content of the directive with this newly generated content.

7. Finally, we return a postLink function (we *cannot* have a link keyword along with compile; we need to return the link function from within compile instead), which adds the validators array and a hasError function to show each of the validation messages under the correct conditions. This uses the form controller, which was required by the directive as per the standards defined in Chapter 4.

AngularJS Convenience Functions

You might have noticed that we called a function named angular.forEach as part of the formElement directive compile function. AngularJS exposes a bunch of global

---

functions that we can use when writing our application to perform common tasks that are not part of the basic JavaScript API. These include the following functions:

angular.forEach
> Iterator over objects and arrays, to help you write code in a functional manner.

angular.fromJson *and* angular.toJson
> Convenience methods to convert from a string to a JSON object and back from a JSON object to a string.

angular.copy
> Performs a deep copy of a given object and returns the newly created copy.

angular.equals
> Determines if two objects, regular expressions, arrays, or values are equal. Does deep comparison in the case of objects or arrays.

angular.isObject, angular.isArray, *and* angular.isFunction
> Convenience methods to quickly check if a given variable is an object, array, or function.

angular.isString, angular.isNumber, *and* angular.isDate
> Convenience methods to check if a given variable is a string, number, or date object.

There are many more. Check out all the functions in the official AngularJS docs (*https://docs.angularjs.org/api/ng/function*).

When we execute this application, we will see a form with two input fields and the error messages for required immediately. As we type in, we will see the required message switch with another validation message before finally showing the valid form.

As mentioned before, compile is only used in the rarest of cases, where you need to do major DOM transformations at runtime. In a majority of cases, you might be able to accomplish the same with transclusion, or pure link function. But it does give you that extra flexibility when you need it.

Pre- and Post-Linking

The link function we generally write (and even return from the compile function) is what is known as a post-link function. When a post-link function executes, all children directives have been compiled and linked at this point. DOM transformations (not adding new AngularJS directives, but creating a chart, for example) are safe at this point as well.

But in case we needed a hook to execute something before the children are linked, we can add what is called `pre-link` function. At this point, the children directives aren't linked, and DOM transformations are not safe and can have weird effects.

The way to have a pre- and post-`link` function is to define it as an object instead of just having a function. That is, instead of:

```
{
  link: function($scope, $element, $attrs) {}
}
```

You can have:

```
{
  link: {
    pre: function($scope, $element, $attrs) {},
    post: function($scope, $element, $attrs) {}
  }
}
```

This is true for the return from the compile function as well, where instead of returning the `post-link` function, we can return an object with a pre- and post-key.

Priority and Terminal

The last two options we look at when creating directives are `priority` and `terminal`. `priority` is used to decide the order in which directives are evaluated when there are multiple directives used on the same element. For example, when we use the `ngModel` directive along with `ngPattern` or `ngMinlength`, we need to ensure that `ngPattern` or `ngMinlength` executes only after `ngModel` has had a chance to execute. Thus, we can give `ngPattern` a lower priority than `ngModel` to ensure it executes afterwards.

By default, any directive we create has a priority of 0. The larger the number, the higher the priority, and higher priority directives are compiled and linked before lower priority ones.

The `terminal` keyword in a directive is used to ensure that no other directives are compiled or linked on an element after the current priority directives are finished. Also, children directives will not be touched or compiled when `terminal` is set to `true`. By default, it is set to `false`. Any directives on an element at the same priority will execute, because the order of execution of directives at the same priority is not defined.

Third-Party Integration

By now we have covered all the important features of the directive definition object, as well as created some complex directives. In this section, we will explore common steps that are involved in integrating or bringing in display-oriented third-party directives. These could be things like charts and graphs, or any other integration where instead of an input, we deal with data display.

In the case of a simple HTML display of data (like our stockWidget directive), we can simply use the AngularJS data-binding directives to accomplish the task. But when it comes to third-party components, we need to take care of the data-binding ourselves.

In these kinds of directives, as directive creators, we have a few tasks we need to accomplish:

1. Depending on the library, wait for the library to load before starting our directive.
2. Take in the data from a controller, and convert it into a format suitable for our third-party component.
3. Display the data using the third-party component.
4. Whenever the data changes inside AngularJS, update the third-party component.
5. Listen for events from the third-party component and pass them to the relevant controller through function bindings.

We will now integrate Google Charts, which uses an asynchronous loader to load its API, and create a pieChart directive for easy use. Most directives will not be as complex, but regardless, the following example should give you a framework within which you can integrate any and every type of display directive you might need.

As always, we start with the main *index.html* file, to take a look at the setup and usage before we dig into the implementation:

```
<!-- File: chapter13/directive-google-chart/index.html -->
<html>
<head>
  <title>Google Chart App</title>
</head>
<body ng-app="googleChartApp">

  <div ng-controller="MainCtrl as mainCtrl">
    <div>
      <button ng-click="mainCtrl.changeData()">
        Change Pie Chart Data
      </button>
    </div>
    <div pie-chart
        chart-data="mainCtrl.pieChartData"
        chart-config="mainCtrl.pieChartConfig">
    </div>
  </div>

  <script src="http://www.google.com/jsapi"></script>
```

```
      <script src="http://code.angularjs.org/1.2.16/angular.js"></script>
      <script src="app.js"></script>
      <script src="googleChartLoader.js"></script>
      <script src="pieChart.js"></script>
  </body>
  </html>
```

The HTML that's using pieChart is quite straightforward. We use the pie chart as an attribute directive, and pass it some configuration as well as the data it needs in order to display as arguments to the directive. This allows us to make it reusable instead of tying it down to a specific service or the same configuration object every time. We also have a button that's used to change the data that's driving the pie chart.

In terms of script dependencies, we also load the Google Charts asynchronous API loader (*http://www.google.com/jsapi*), which provides the API to load the Google Charts API. We will see how to leverage AngularJS promises to wait for this API to load before starting to draw our charts.

Next, let's look at our main controller for the application, which defines the data and the configuration for the pie chart:

```
// File: chapter13/directive-google-chart/app.js

angular.module('googleChartApp', [])
  .controller('MainCtrl', [function() {
    var self = this;
    self.pieChartData = [
      {label: 'First', value: 25},
      {label: 'Second', value: 54},
      {label: 'Third', value: 75}
    ];

    self.pieChartConfig = {
      title: 'One Two Three Chart',
      firstColumnHeader: 'Counter',
      secondColumnHeader: 'Actual Value'
    };

    self.changeData = function() {
      self.pieChartData[1].value = 25;
    };
  }]);
```

The *app.js* file declares the pieChartData variable, which is an array of keys and values in its own format. This is hardcoded here, but could be retrieved from a server call using $http as well. We also have some hardcoded configuration that dictates the name of the chart, and the columns for the chart. Finally, we have a very simple function (change Date()) that changes the value of one element of the data to see if the pie chart updates itself automatically as a result.

The next part we dig into is the asynchronous loader, which ensures that the pie Chart directive doesn't try drawing the chart before our API is loaded:

```
// File: chapter13/directive-google-chart/googleChartLoader.js
angular.module('googleChartApp')
  .factory('googleChartLoaderPromise',
    ['$q', '$rootScope', '$window',
    function($q, $rootScope, $window) {
    // Create a Deferred Object
    var deferred = $q.defer();

    // Load Google Charts API asynchronously
    $window.google.load('visualization', '1',
      {
        packages: ['corechart'],
        callback: function() {
          // When loaded, trigger the resolve,
          // but inside an $apply as the event happens
          // outside of AngularJS life cycle
          $rootScope.$apply(function() {
            deferred.resolve();
          });
        }
      });

    // Return the promise object for the directive
    // to chain onto.
    return deferred.promise;
  }]);
```

The googleChartLoaderPromise factory loads the visualization library once at load, and returns a promise that can be chained on to know when the load is complete. It does so using the $q service (refer to "The $q Service" on page 94 for a quick refresher on $q) in AngularJS, which we also saw previously in Chapter 10 for handling re solve in a route. In addition to being able to reject the current promise using $q.re ject(data), the $q service also allows us to create and work with our own promises, which is what we use here.

We create a deferred object, which represents an asynchronous task that will be fulfilled in the future. We create it by calling $q.defer(). We then return deferred.promise, on which users of the API can add .then() to be notified when this asynchronous task will be fulfilled (or rejected). We then call the Google API with the appropriate arguments to load the visualization library and give it a callback to be notified when this asynchronous task is completed.

Inside the callback, we resolve the deferred object we created, which is the trigger for all the .then to execute. But because this callback is called outside the life cycle of AngularJS, we need to wrap it in a $rootScope.$apply function to ensure AngularJS knows to redraw the UI and run a complete digest cycle as needed.

Finally, we can look at the `pieChart` directive to see how it integrates with the `google ChartsLoaderPromise` service as well as Google Charts:

```
// File: chapter13/directive-google-chart/pieChart.js
angular.module('googleChartApp')
  .directive('pieChart', ['googleChartLoaderPromise',
      function(googleChartLoaderPromise) {
    var convertToPieChartDataTableFormat =
        function(firstColumnName, secondColumnName, data) {
      var pieChartArray = [[firstColumnName, secondColumnName]];
      for (var i = 0; i < data.length; i++) {
        pieChartArray.push([data[i].label, data[i].value]);
      }
      return google.visualization.arrayToDataTable(
          pieChartArray);
    };

    return {
      restrict: 'A',
      scope: {
        chartData: '=',
        chartConfig: '='
      },
      link: function($scope, $element) {

        googleChartLoaderPromise.then(function() {
          var chart = new google.visualization.PieChart(
            $element[0]);

          $scope.$watch('chartData', function(newVal, oldVal) {
            var config = $scope.chartConfig;
            if (newVal) {
              chart.draw(
                convertToPieChartDataTableFormat(
                  config.firstColumnHeader,
                  config.secondColumnHeader,
                  newVal),
                {title: $scope.chartConfig.title});
            }
          }, true);
        });
      }
    };
}]);
```

Our actual `pieChart` directive is quite simple if you ignore the Google Chart–specific API calls and look at it at a conceptual level. Here's what is happening:

1. Our `pieChart` directive depends on the service we defined previously, and injects it in.

2. We define a function `convertToPieChartDataTableFormat`, which takes the data that we have in our controller and converts it into a format that we can pass to the Google Charts API.

3. We define a pretty standard directive with an isolated scope that defines the attributes that need to be passed to it.

4. In our `link` function, we use the promise returned from the service, and do our work in the success handler inside the `then` of the promise. This ensures that we don't try calling a Google Charts API unless and until the Google Charts API has successfully finished loading as per our service.

5. Inside the success handler of the promise, we create an instance of a Google Pie Chart, using the element that we are currently on as the target. This ensures that we don't go looking for a random element in our body, or use ID-based selectors, each of which would make our directive hard to reuse.

6. We then add a watch on the `chartData` field on the scope, and give it a function to call as the second argument, and the Boolean `true` as the third argument. This tells AngularJS to do what we call a deep watch on `$scope.chartData`, and whenever it (or any element inside of it) changes, call the function.

7. The `change` function is called with both the old and the new value. When we get a valid new value, we draw the chart after converting the data from the format passed to the directive to a format that Google Charts understands.

8. Whenever the data in AngularJS changes (either because of a user change or newer data from the server), this function is automatically called, so we don't have to manually do any other work to ensure that our chart is updated.

Now, when you open up the *index.html* file in your browser, you will see a chart rendered with the initial data. When we click the button in the page, the data gets updated in the controller. Because the data is passed to the directive by reference, the directive gets the latest data as well and the watch function is triggered. This updates the chart with the latest values and we get an automatically updating UI with no additional work.

If we wanted to only add a data point, or be restrictive on how and when we want to update the chart, we can add that logic inside the watch as needed. The following same concepts apply to almost any display-oriented directives you might want to build, and thus these building blocks go a long way for any application you're working on:

- Waiting for the API to load.
- Passing in the data to a reusable directive.
- Converting the data to the necessary format and doing the initial draw.
- Watching the data, and updating the UI as necessary.

Best Practices

Now that we know how to create pretty much any type of directive of any complexity, we'll cover some things to keep in mind to ensure that the directives we create behave cleanly and are fast under all conditions.

Scopes

If in your directive, you find yourself adding variables and functions to the scope in the `link` or the `controller`, then it is recommended that either you set the `scope` key in the directive definition object to `true`, or you create an isolated scope for the directive.

For example, say our controller has a Boolean variable called `selected` to decide whether or not a certain checkbox is selected. If our `tabs` and `tab` directive do not create a new scope or use an isolated scope, then the directive is going to override the `selected` variable on the controller and cause all kinds of unintended effects.

If our directive needs access to functions and variables from the parent scope, we have one of two options:

- Create a child scope, and add any variables and functions to the child scope. This can be accomplished by setting `scope: true` in the directive definition object. But if the parent scope has any functions or variables, those would still be accessible in the directive.
- Create an isolated scope, and pass in any variables and functions using data- and function-binding. This is the ideal pattern, because this removes any possibility that the directive might need a certain variable or function in the parent scope for the directive to work successfully. Directives with isolated scopes are the most reusable directives.

Clean Up and Destroy

AngularJS adds listeners and watchers to keep its UI updated when we use bindings and other directives. To ensure that none of them leak or stay around past their need, AngularJS removes them when their scopes and elements are destroyed.

When we create directives in AngularJS with their own scope (child or isolated), any watchers we add on the scope and any listeners we add on the element passed to the directive are automatically cleaned up when that directive is destroyed in the UI.

That said, AngularJS cannot clean up event listeners we add on elements outside of the scope and HTML of the directive. When we add these listeners or watchers, it becomes our responsibility to clean up when the directive gets destroyed. We can listen for the destruction of a directive in two possible ways:

Listen for the $destroy *event on the scope*

As we saw previously, we can add event listeners on the scope itself. Each scope broadcasts an event called $destroy, which is a notification that the scope is about to be destroyed and cleaned up. Any controller or directive can listen for it and do additional clean-up when this event is triggered. Any listeners that we manually add or intervals or timeouts that are currently executing need to be cleaned up in the $destroy event handler. A sample handler would be as follows:

```
$scope.$on('$destroy', function() {
    // Do clean up here
});
```

Listen for the $destroy *event on the element*

If the scope is inherited (not a new scope or an isolated scope), but we still need to do clean-up when the directive is destroyed, the other alternative is to listen for the $destroy event on the element itself. This is a jQuery event that is fired by AngularJS when the element is about to be removed from the DOM. A sample handler for this would be as follows:

```
$element.$on('$destroy', function() {
    // Do clean-up here
});
```

Watchers

AngularJS allows us to add our own event listeners (or watchers, in AngularJS terminology) on scope variables and functions. These basically get triggered by AngularJS whenever the variable under watch changes, and we get access to both the new and the old value in such a case.

There are a few kinds of watches we can add, and it helps to be aware of the implications of each:

$watch

The most standard watch, which takes:

- A string, which is the name of a variable on the scope
- A function, whose return value is evaluated

In either case, whenever the value changes (a straightforward shallow check), then the function passed to it as the second argument is triggered with the old and new value.

Deep $watch

The same as the standard watch, but takes a Boolean true as the third argument. This forces AngularJS to recursively check each object and key inside the object or variable and use angular.equals to check for equality for all objects. Obviously, it catches all changes, but also consumes more CPU cycles. So be careful that you don't abuse deep watches across your application. Instead, it's preferable to have a Boolean that signals if something internally has changed and watch that.

$watchCollection

Slightly optimized version of the watch aimed at arrays. Similar arguments as the $watch, but expects that the value is an array. The function is triggered any time an item is added, removed, or moved in the array. It *does not* watch for changes to individual properties in an item in the array.

$apply (and $digest)

The most common mistake or error that happens when integrating with a third-party component is that we hook everything up correctly and then stare at our screen wondering why the UI is not getting updated. And the root cause more often than not is a missing $apply() call, or triggering the digest cycle manually by calling $digest().

Whenever you're working with third-party components, remember that there are two distinct life cycles at play. The first is the AngularJS life cycle that is responsible for the keeping the UI updated and the second is a third-party component's life cycle. When the two meet, developers are responsible for letting AngularJS know that something outside its life cycle has changed and that it needs to update its UI. And this is done by triggering $scope.$apply(), which starts a digest cycle on the $rootScope.

Sometimes, another event in AngularJS will automatically trigger and take care of this, but in any case if you are updating any scope variables in response to an external event, make sure you manually trigger the $scope.$apply() or $scope.$digest().

Conclusion

In this chapter, we dove deep into the most complex parts of AngularJS and covered some of the rarer, but very powerful features of directives. We created a stock widget that could take in custom templates and thus could be customized for each usage as per the need using simple template transclusion. We also created a very dumb and simple equivalent of a one-time repeater using advanced transclusion and transclusion functions. We also saw how to communicate across the tabs and tab directives using directive controllers, and how to leverage existing controllers of directives like ngModel to create input directives like sliders and custom validators. The last directive definition object configuration we covered was how to create a declarative form-element directive and generate custom dynamic templates using the compile step of directives.

We then saw how simple it was to create a pie chart directive using Google Charts while exploring the concepts and fundamentals of creating any display component and the simple steps for integrating third-party UI widgets. Finally, we saw some best practices to keep in mind when creating directives to ensure that we have don't suffer any performance issues or strange bugs.

With this, we have covered all of the major parts of the core AngularJS codebase. In the next chapter, we see how to write end-to-end scenario tests for AngularJS using the Protractor test runner.

CHAPTER 14

End-to-End Testing

By now, we have covered all the moving parts that comprise an AngularJS application, including controllers, views, services, filters, and directives. We also talked about the importance of unit testing, and saw how we can individually test each part and component of AngularJS. A great set of unit tests can save an amazing amount of time for developers, from debugging to preventing bugs to catching regressions.

But unit tests are only great up to a certain point. They can test whether your application works correctly, *assuming* that the server behaves in a certain way. We saw this with the unit tests for services and XHRs in Chapter 7, in which we mocked out the server using the $httpBackend service in the unit test. This allowed us to write rapid unit tests that were reliable, stable, and super fast. These tests will catch the logic of your controllers and service, but what if the server changes its return value? Or what if the server URLs themselves have changed? What about formatting and display of the HTML, especially if we have made a typo in an ng-bind expression?

To catch these, we need to write end-to-end tests, which open the browser, navigate to a live running version of our web application, and click around using the application as a real-world user would. To accomplish this, we use Protractor (*https://github.com/angular/protractor*).

In this chapter, we see how to set up a very simple end-to-end test for a demo application using Protractor. We create a Protractor config, write an end-to-end test, and see it in action. We also go over the initial setup and requirements needed to run these tests as well as best practices when working with them. By the end of the chapter, you should be familiar with Protractor and tests using Protractor.

The Need for Protractor

So why Protractor? Why yet another testing tool? With AngularJS, the very first attempt at making it easy to write end-to-end scenario tests was something known as AngularJS

Scenario Runner (*http://code.angularjs.org/1.2.16/docs/guide/e2e-testing*). This used to be a full end-to-end runner that was AngularJS-aware so that tests would be more stable and deterministic.

We realized that simulating user actions like clicks and typing through JavaScript was not ideal, and did not replicate the real user flow. So with Protractor, the aim was to build on top of something like Selenium WebDriver (*http://docs.seleniumhq.org/projects/webdriver/*), which actually works at the OS level to work with the browser and perform actual clicks and keystrokes.

But at the same time, we still want to avoid one of the major issues with end-to-end tests of AJAX applications, primarily, waiting for the page to load. With a normal web page, we can figure out when a page is loaded, and then when the user clicks a link, the entire page reloads. Thus, we can know exactly when a page is loaded to continue testing.

With a Single-Page Application, there is only one page load. And data can be fetched asynchronously (and usually is) even after the page load is completed. So how do we know in our end-to-end test when to check if a particular data item is shown or not? We have a couple options:

- We wait for an arbitrary amount of time after a page loads or a link is clicked—about five seconds.
- We wait for a certain element on the page to be shown before performing our checks.

Both of these, though, are very nondeterministic. All it takes is for a certain server call to take 5.1 seconds instead of 5 and our test breaks. Over time, we start waiting for another test run, even if a test fails to catch these nondeterministic failures. And finally, we just stop relying on end-to-end tests.

With Protractor, the need to wait an arbitrary time for arbitrary events disappears. Protractor is built on top of WebDriver, but is AngularJS-aware. Thus, when a button is clicked and a server call is made, Protractor knows to wait for the server call to return before proceeding with the rest of the test. Thus, as developers, we can focus on writing the test and expect it to execute similar to how a user would see it, without having conditions and timeouts for certain elements to load or disappear.

Initial Setup

Protractor is a NodeJS package, and so can be installed using npm (make sure you have node installed first) by running:

```
sudo npm install -g protractor
```

This installs Protractor along with all its dependencies as a global package for use across projects.

We also need WebDriver to actually start and control the browsers on which we run unit tests. When we install Protractor, it gives us the necessary scripts to download and install WebDriver locally as well. We can install WebDriver by running:

```
sudo webdriver-manager update
```

At this point, we have all the necessary tools installed to run our Protractor tests. Running the tests is as simple as executing:

```
protractor path/to/protractor.conf.js
```

What does this *protractor.conf.js* file look like? We dive into this next.

Protractor Configuration

The Protractor configuration file is a JavaScript file that basically holds all the configuration elements that Protractor needs to be able to run the end-to-end tests. These include configuration options like:

- Where is the server running?
- Where is the Selenium WebDriver on which to run the tests?
- What tests should be executed?
- What browsers should the tests be run on?

And much more. Let's take a look at a sample configuration with the most commonly used options, which is what we will be using for the tests in this chapter:

```
// File: chapter14/protractor.conf.js
exports.config = {
  // The address of a running Selenium server
  seleniumAddress: 'http://localhost:4444/wd/hub',

  // The URL where the server we are testing is running
  baseUrl: 'http://localhost:8000/',

  // Capabilities to be passed to the WebDriver instance
  capabilities: {
    'browserName': 'chrome'
  },

  // Spec patterns are relative to the location of the
  // spec file. They may include glob patterns.
  specs: ['*Spec*.js'],

  // Options to be passed to Jasmine-node
  jasmineNodeOpts: {
    showColors: true // Use colors in the command-line report
  }
};
```

This configuration file is the simplest Protractor configuration file we could use. It has the following things of note:

- Specifies that the Selenium server is running locally on port 4444.
- Specifies that the server is running at *http://localhost:8000/*.
- Specifies that the browser to automatically run is Chrome.
- Points out the *spec.js* file that holds the end-to-end test code.
- Some configuration options for Jasmine to show colors in the command line.

More detail about the configuration options that Protractor supports is available in the Reference Configuration (*http://bit.ly/1CqK9h6*) file on GitHub.

Now what do we need to do before we can run this test? From the *chapter14* folder on GitHub, do the following:

1. Start Selenium locally (this can be done with `webdriver-manager start`).
2. Start the server locally (`node server.js` in our example).
3. Start Protractor (`protractor test/e2e/protractor.conf.js`).

Before we do this, let's see how an end-to-end test looks.

An End-to-End Test

Protractor tests use the same Jasmine scaffolding syntax we've been using for our unit tests, so we have the same `describe` blocks for a set of tests, and individual `it` blocks for each test. In addition to these, Protractor exposes some global variables that are needed for writing end-to-end tests, namely:

`browser`
>   This is a wrapper around WebDriver that allows us to interact with the browser directly. We use this object to navigate to different pages and page-level information.

`element`
>   The `element` object is a helper function to find and interact with HTML elements. It takes a strategy to find the elements as the argument, and then gives you back an element that you can interact with by clicking and sending keystrokes to it.

`by`
>   The `by` is an object with a collection of element-finding strategies. We can find elements by `id` or `CSS` classes, which are built-in strategies of WebDriver. Protractor adds a few strategies on top of that to find elements by `model`, `binding`, and `repeater` as well, which are AngularJS-specific ways to find certain elements on the page.

Without further ado, let's take a look at how a test for the routing application we wrote in Chapter 10 would work (the code for the app is available at GitHub in the *chapter14* folder (*http://bit.ly/1CqJQmD*)). Start the app by first installing the dependent packages using **npm install** followed by **node server.js**:

```
// File: chapter14/simpleRoutingSpec.js

describe('Routing Test', function() {

  it('should show teams on the first page', function() {
    // Open the list of teams page
    browser.get('/');

    // Check whether there are 5 rows in the repeater
    var rows = element.all(
        by.repeater('team in teamListCtrl.teams'));
    expect(rows.count()).toEqual(5);

    // Check the first row details
    var firstRowRank = element(
      by.repeater('team in teamListCtrl.teams')
        .row(0).column('team.rank'));
    var firstRowName = element(
      by.repeater('team in teamListCtrl.teams')
        .row(0).column('team.name'));
    expect(firstRowRank.getText()).toEqual('1');
    expect(firstRowName.getText()).toEqual('Spain');

    // Check the last row details
    var lastRowRank = element(
      by.repeater('team in teamListCtrl.teams')
        .row(4).column('team.rank'));
    var lastRowName = element(
      by.repeater('team in teamListCtrl.teams')
        .row(4).column('team.name'));
    expect(lastRowRank.getText()).toEqual('5');
    expect(lastRowName.getText()).toEqual('Uruguay');

    // Check that login link is shown and
    // logout link is hidden
    expect(element(by.css('.login-link')).isDisplayed())
        .toBe(true);
    expect(element(by.css('.logout-link')).isDisplayed())
        .toBe(false);
  });

  it('should allow logging in', function() {
    // Navigate to the login page
    browser.get('#/login');

    var username = element(
      by.model('loginCtrl.user.username'));
```

```
var password = element(
  by.model('loginCtrl.user.password'));

// Type in the username and password
username.sendKeys('admin');
password.sendKeys('admin');

// Click on the login button
element(by.css('.btn.btn-success')).click();

// Ensure that the user was redirected
expect(browser.getCurrentUrl())
    .toEqual('http://localhost:8000/#/');

// Check that login link is hidden and
// logout link is shown
expect(element(by.css('.login-link')).isDisplayed())
    .toBe(false);
expect(element(by.css('.logout-link')).isDisplayed())
    .toBe(true);

  });
});
```

We have two tests in this example. The first test:

- Opens up the main page of the teams application.
- Fetches all the rows by using the repeater, and then checks whether there are five rows present on the main page.
- Fetches the name and rank of the first row and asserts that they are as expected.
- Fetches the name and rank of the last row and asserts that they are as expected.
- Checks that the login link is shown and the logout link is hidden.

Thus, the first test purely deals with rendering and logic to ensure that the application is correctly hooked up to the server and is capable of fetching and displaying the content correctly.

The second test deals with user interaction by:

- Opening up the login page.
- Entering the username and password to the correct model.
- Clicking the login button by CSS selector.
- Ensuring that the login is successful by checking the URL of the redirected page.
- Checking that the login link is hidden and the logout link is shown.

Notice that we didn't add any wait conditions in either of the tests. We wrote the tests as if a user would be interacting with the application, and let AngularJS and Protractor worry about when to proceed with the tests.

To execute these tests, execute the following in order:

1. If the server is not running, run **node server.js** from the *appUnderTest* folder. You might need to run **npm install** from that folder first.

2. If Selenium is not up and running, run **webdriver-manager start**.

3. Run **protractor protractor.conf.js** from the folder containing the config file and the specs.

We will see Protractor open the Chrome browser through Selenium, navigate to the main page of our locally running application, and click through and run our tests as we have defined them. At the end, it should print out whether they were successful, or the reason for failure in case they failed.

Considerations

There are a few things we have to keep in mind, as well as some best practices that should be followed, when working with and writing end-to-end tests in AngularJS. Let's go over them one by one:

Location of ng-app
> When you write a simple Protractor test for AngularJS, and point it at any URL that hosts an AngularJS application, Protractor's default behavior is to look at the body element of the HTML to find ng-app. It then kicks in and does its magic. But in case ng-app is not on the body tag, but on a subelement, we need to manually tell Protractor how to find it. This is done through the rootElement option of the Protractor configuration, which takes a CSS selector to the element using ng-app. For example, if ng-app was on the following element inside our body tag:

> ```
> <div class="angular-app" ng-app="myApp"></div>
> ```

> then we'd have to specify the following line in our Protractor configuration file:

> ```
> rootElement: ".angular-app"
> ```

> This would tell Protractor to find the element with the CSS class angular-app. This is not needed if you have the ng-app on the body element.

Polling
> If you have any kind of polling logic in your code, where you have to keep fetching some information or doing some calculations every few seconds, make sure you're not using the $timeout service AngularJS provides for that. Protractor has issues

figuring out when AngularJS is done with its work. If you need polling, and need to write end-to-end tests for it, make sure you use the $interval service instead. Protractor understands and deals with the $interval service, and behaves like you would expect it to.

Manual bootstrapping

Protractor currently does not support working with AngularJS applications that are manually bootstrapped. Thus, if you need to write end-to-end tests for such an application, you might have to work with the underlying WebDriver (by using browser.driver.get instead of browser.get, and so on), and add wait conditions to ensure that all the things are loaded before proceeding with the test. You would not be able to leverage any of the benefits that Protractor offers.

Future execution

WebDriver commands that we write in our tests don't return the actual values, but rather promises that will execute later in the browser (in various browsers even). Thus, console.log won't actually print the values because it doesn't have them at the point the code is executed.

Debugging

Protractor has great built-in support for debugging, because it leverages the Web-Driver debugging. To debug any test, we can just add the following line at the point where we want to start debugging:

```
browser.debugger();
```

This could be after any of the lines in the test. Then we run our tests using the following command:

```
protractor debug path/to/conf.js
```

This opens up the Node debugger, which allows us to step through the various breakpoints in our test. We now need to type "c" and click Enter, to tell Protractor to continue running the tests. Protractor will run the tests like normal in the browser up until the point it hits the debugger statement. At that point, it stops and waits for further instructions to resume the test. This is a real, live application in the browser that you can interact with and debug to see exactly what the Protractor runner is seeing. You can actually click around and change the state of the test to make it fail as well. When you are done debugging, you can type "c" and click Enter to continue running the test until the next debug point or the end of the test, whichever comes first.

The last thing to consider is how to organize your tests in such a way that makes them easy to maintain and reuse. In the test that we wrote in the previous section, we used element and by to find elements in the page and interact with it by clicking, entering keys, and asserting the state of the UI. But when we write our tests, we want to create an API that allows us to easily understand the intent of the test. This is useful because it becomes easier to understand the test, as well as allow anyone to quickly build a set of larger, more encompassing tests using the same API. To accomplish this, we use the concept of PageObjects.

Let's rewrite the Teams List page test to use PageObjects instead of directly working with the WebDriver APIs at a test level:

```
// File: chapter14/routingSpecWithPageObjects.js

// The PageObjects are ideally in separate files
// to allow for reuse across all the tests,
// but are listed here together for ease of understanding

function TeamsListPage() {
  this.open = function() {
    browser.get('/');
  };

  this.getTeamsListRows = function() {
    return element.all(by.repeater('team in teamListCtrl.teams'));
  };

  this.getRankForRow = function(row) {
    return element(
      by.repeater('team in teamListCtrl.teams')
        .row(row).column('team.rank'));
  };

  this.getNameForRow = function(row) {
    return element(
      by.repeater('team in teamListCtrl.teams')
        .row(row).column('team.name'));
  };

  this.isLoginLinkVisible = function() {
    return element(by.css('.login-link')).isDisplayed();
  };

  this.isLogoutLinkVisible = function() {
    return element(by.css('.logout-link')).isDisplayed();
  };
}

describe('Routing Test With PageObjects', function() {

  it('should show teams on the first page', function() {
    var teamsListPage = new TeamsListPage();

    teamsListPage.open();

    expect(teamsListPage.getTeamsListRows().count()).toEqual(5);
```

```
    expect(teamsListPage.getRankForRow(0).getText())
      .toEqual('1');
    expect(teamsListPage.getNameForRow(0).getText())
      .toEqual('Spain');

    expect(teamsListPage.getRankForRow(4).getText())
      .toEqual('5');
    expect(teamsListPage.getNameForRow(4).getText())
      .toEqual('Uruguay');

    // Check that login link is shown and
    // logout link is hidden
    expect(teamsListPage.isLoginLinkVisible()).toBe(true);
    expect(teamsListPage.isLogoutLinkVisible()).toBe(false);
  });
});
```

We created a JavaScript class called `TeamsListPage`, which exposes some APIs to open the page, get all the rows, and get the individual name and rank for a given row. Then in our test, we can work with an instance of the `TeamsListPage` object, which makes the test much easier to read than before. We can do something similar for the Login Page test as well.

PageObjects encapsulate abstractions on how to access certain elements and how to interact with them in a single place, thus allowing for simple reuse as well as handling change in a single place rather than making the change in multiple places.

Conclusion

We installed Protractor and set up our configuration for a very simple end-to-end test. We then wrote our first two end-to-end tests, one of which checked the rendering and display logic of the main page, and the other which tried the login flow in our application. We also covered some considerations that should be kept in mind when writing these tests.

With a suite of such tests (and Protractor allows you to define multiple suites for various needs), you can quickly and confidently ensure that the application you're developing is working correctly without having to manually and repeatedly test each individual flow. For a large-scale application, a smoke set of end-to-end tests is a must.

Now that we've covered and touched upon almost every single aspect of AngularJS, the next chapter brings them all together and covers best practices and guidelines that should be followed for any AngularJS project. We also cover some tools and applications that can make your AngularJS development easier.

CHAPTER 15

Guidelines and Best Practices

We covered a whole lot of stuff about AngularJS, and dove deep into almost every part of the AngularJS framework. We haven't started scratching the surface of how deep and complex AngularJS can be, but we do have a strong base on the moving parts to start considering the bigger picture. In this chapter, our aim is to take a step back from AngularJS and consider it in the larger picture of your end-to-end web-based application. To that extent, we look at:

- Testing
- File and directory structure
- Best practices
- Building your application
- Tools and libraries

We'll talk about how to efficiently accomplish each one, and consider a way to perform them such as to ensure long-term maintainability and project health without reducing the velocity of development.

Testing

The first and foremost rule of web application development is that testing happens *before* the application development starts, *while* you are developing the application, and *after* you've finished development. We've tried to imbibe that mentality into this book by bringing up unit testing and end-to-end testing whenever applicable.

Test-Driven Development

Writing your unit tests and specifications up front is by far the best approach to building any large-scale, maintainable application using AngularJS. We covered some of the major reasons why you should unit test in AngularJS in Chapter 3. In this section, we cover some of the best practices and thoughts to keep in mind when approaching testing for your own projects.

Variety of Tests

There are schools of thought that say if you perform test-driven development (TDD), you will never have a bug. Of course, in practice, TDD is great for hammering out the nitty-gritty implementation details, but when it comes to a large project with complex integrations, your unit tests are never going to catch all possible bugs and breakages. This is why it's essential to have a proper set of unit tests, integration tests, and scenario tests to have any level of confidence in your application:

Unit tests

A unit test is concise and focused on testing only one piece (a controller, service, filter, etc.) and in that, one function. We test (using Karma, which we first saw in Chapter 3) whether given the right inputs and the right state, does it produce the right output, or generate the right side effects? If at all possible, we mock out dependencies to ensure that we are testing a piece in isolation. For example, a controller unit test could mock out the service completely and assume it works correctly.

With a unit test, that is the foremost thought. We ask *if* all the other pieces are working correctly, does the part being tested work correctly? We are systematically guaranteeing each individual piece's correctness so that when we're tracking down a hard-to-find bug, we can immediately discount the parts that we know are fully tested.

Integration tests

Unit tests are great, fast, and tiny—but they have a limitation. They make certain assumptions about the other integration points for our controllers and services. They assume they behave in a certain way or return a certain output. More often than not, the assumptions might not be true. Integration tests (again, written using Karma and Jasmine in AngularJS) are the ones that test whether the different parts of your application are correctly configured and hooked up. These might check whether the controller communicates with the service, and whether the service has the right side effects and returns the correct values. We did something like this in "Integration-Level Unit Tests" on page 118 where we tested the integration of our controller with a service and ensured that the service made the right call and returned the right values.

In an integration test, you can test the controller-service interaction, and whether interceptors are correctly configured. You can also test complex interactions by checking what happens when two functions are called one after the other, or if a polling feature is correctly fetching the data every few seconds.

Integration tests are still mocking out the XHR calls though, so any tests we write will not communicate with our server. Even trying to load a template for a directive (like we saw in Chapter 12) will also be mocked out. Thus, even with an integration test, while we can be assured that our frontend application logic might be correctly hooked up and working, we're still depending on the fact that our server responds in a certain way, which is not tested.

Scenario tests

The final kinds of tests we should consider having for our application are end-to-end, scenario tests. These, as described in Chapter 14, entail opening a browser, loading our frontend application, and clicking through the various pages as a user would. These are the truest level of user tests, and are testing the end-to-end flow of our application. Still, we recommend writing a few of these, and not replacing all your tests with scenario tests because:

- You need an exponential number of tests to cover all the cases that you can otherwise split and catch with unit and integration tests.

- A scenario test failing still doesn't give you the necessary information about what's broken, just that something is broken.

A good set of scenario tests will be small, stable, deterministic, and try to catch most of the integration points. The aim of scenario tests is to ensure that, at the very least, your most basic features and flows in your application are correctly hooked up and working.

A common, accepted breakdown, in terms of the quantities of between the preceding three types of tests in your application is 70:20:10, where 70% of your tests are unit tests, 20% are integration level tests, and 10% are end-to-end, scenario tests. That is the golden ratio to shoot for.

When to Run Tests

You've written these amazing set of tests that are rock solid, and capture and prevent every possible bug that you could have in your application. Now what? When do you run these? Here are a few possible places where you should ideally be running them:

On every save

At the very least, your unit tests and integration tests should be run on every save. Your scenario tests might be a bit too much, but both unit and integration tests are *ridiculously fast* (if they are not, you are doing something wrong!). Karma has this feature called `autoWatch`, which if enabled, automatically runs the tests in case a source file changes. We will look at WebStorm as an IDE in a bit, which also has Karma integrated into it and can automatically run tests every time you save. The advantage of this is that it gives you instant feedback; when something goes wrong you can just undo it to get back to a clean state.

Before pushing

If you're not using a version control system, then stop and do so immediately. Any significantly sized project (basically, anything that is not a throwaway) should be hosted in a version control repository (like Git (*http://git-scm.com/*) or Mercurial (*http://mercurial.selenic.com/*)). Once you do that, you want to ensure that any code getting pushed or commited to your repository is valid, and that nothing is broken. Most of these systems give you hooks (Git Hooks (*http://git-scm.com/book/en/ Customizing-Git-Git-Hooks*), for example) to allow you to execute certain scripts and commands when a certain acitivity happens. In an ideal setup, you want to execute your unit, integration, and scenario tests as a pre-commit or pre-push hook to ensure that any code checked in to your codebase is valid and working.

Continuous integration

Continuous integration is the concept of a build machine picking up the changes from your version control system and running a build and tests on the latest code, whenever new code is checked in. This ensures that any breakages and failures are caught immediately when something bad is checked in, versus only at the time of releasing a version with a bunch of changes together. It allows us to trace a problem to an exact change in the system. Both Karma and Protractor integrate easily with most open source continuous integration systems like Jenkins (*http://jenkins-ci.org/*) and Travis (*https://travis-ci.org/*), so if you have a build system, make sure that it's running all your AngularJS tests.

All these are action items that you need to do once and get it set up. Then it runs happily in the background, and enforces code quality for your project. So do it up front, and reap the benefits later.

Project Structure

One of the most important and often asked questions in an AngularJS project is how to structure your project in terms of files and folders. This is both in terms of your own code as well as importing third-party libraries, managing templates and partials, and getting the build structure in place. In this section, we deal with some general best practices before diving into directory structure and third-party library strategies and finally finishing with some good starting points where you can get your project up and running quickly.

Best Practices

We will keep this section short and concise and expand on it in the following sections. Use this as a quick guide and refresher when you have any doubts or decision making to do:

- Have one controller, service, directive, or filter per file. Don't club them into large single files.

- Don't have one giant module. Break up your applications into smaller modules. Let your main application be composed of multiple smaller, reusable modules.

- Prefer to create modules and directories by functionality (authorization, admin-services, search, etc.), over type (controllers, services, directives). This makes your code more reusable.

- Use the recommended syntax of using the module functions (`angular.module('so meModule').controller…`, etc.) over any other syntax you might see online or any-where else.

- Use namespaces. Namespace your modules, controllers, services, directives, and filters. Have *mycompany*-chart for directives, *myProject*AuthService, and so on. That way, anyone coming in can quickly distinguish your own code from third-party and core AngularJS code.

- Most of all, be consistent. This is not AngularJS-specific, but don't change the way you name files, folders, directives, or controllers from one place in your application to another.

Directory Structure

When we talk about directory structure in this section, we are only talking about the frontend application and not your server application. The AngularJS application would just be a folder that would typically be statically served from your server. At the highest level of your frontend application, you might have the following folders:

app
> The *app* folder houses all the JavaScript code that you develop. We'll talk about this in more detail next.

tests
> Houses all your unit tests and possibly the end-to-end scenario tests as well.

data
> Any data that is common but not dynamic in your application can be stored here.

scripts
> Build scripts and other common utility scripts can be stored in this folder.

Other files
> The *package.json*, *bower.json*, and other files that don't really need a directory can be in the main folder.

Before we jump into what the *app* folder or the *tests* folder looks like, let's get some high-level concepts out of the way:

Group by functionality or component

A lot of examples and starter projects for AngularJS suggest a folder structure where there is a folder for all the controllers, a folder for all the services, and so on. We've seen this as a major bottleneck when a project starts growing. So instead, we suggest that you group your code into folders based on components or functionality. So login, authorization, and search could all be components that could have individual folders. Your views or subsections of the app could similarly be grouped into folders, like *admin* and *view*, within which there could be subfolders for *search*, *list*, and so on.

Components and app sections

There are two concepts that we like to use when structuring our application. The first one is called components, which are basically reusable widgets in your application that are not tied down to a certain page or section of the UI. These are things like a datepicker directive or an authorization service—common across your application. The *components* directory contains folders that contain:

- Related services, directives, and related files.
- Dependent data like CSS, images, and others can be located here, or separately, depending on the need.
- Each folder could be further divided into subfolders if the component is complex.

The second is app sections, which reflect your application structure and can be routes, pages (like search, listing, admin, view, etc.), or even small subsections of the page (like a dashboard). The sections folders generally:

- Reflect views that are shown to the user.
- Contain only the template HTML (and CSS), and the controller that works with it.

A component or a section (or a subcomponent or subsection) could have a module definition of its own. The decision of whether a component or section needs a module definition comes down to whether the module can be reused or selectively included in different applications.

Tests should mirror the app

The *tests* folder would mostly contain the protractor-based, end-to-end, *scenario tests*. The structure inside the *tests* folder would mimic your application and its views. In that sense, each view or section of the page under test in the live running application could have a subfolder with its own tests. The folder structure here should reflect how your application is structured and flows through it, rather than try to fit inside the existing directory structure.

The *unit tests*, on the other hand, are colocated with your application code, in each subfolder inside the *app* folder. Thus each controller, service, directive, or filter has its unit test right alongside it in the same folder. This makes it easier to find and manage, while giving the build tools the responsibility to ensure that tests don't get included in your application bundle.

Naming conventions

The Google JavaScript Style Guide (*http://bit.ly/1oOEfQ7*) is a great place to start, and we build on top of that with a few AngularJS-specific recommendations. In particular:

- When it comes to filenames, the filename should be descriptive enough to be able to figure out which section or component it's in and what type of AngularJS object it is. For example, if we have a section called adminsearch in our application, then the folder could be called *adminsection*, and the controller inside it would be called `adminsection-controller.js`.

- Ideally, a controller file should end with *-controller.js*, a service with *-service.js*, a directive with *-directive.js*, and a filter with *-filter.js*.

- Test files should have the filename, followed by *test.js*. Thus, a datepicker directive might have the filename *datepicker-directive.js* and the test named *datepicker-directive_test.js*.

- Prefer to use lowercase when naming your files, instead of camelCase or each word starting with uppercase.

With these thoughts and concepts in mind, let's see how this might apply to an actual project. Here we demonstrate how a simple CRUD application might look:

- app
  - *app.css*
  - *app.js*
  - *index.html*
  - components // *Reusable common components*
    - datepicker
      - *datepicker-directive.js*
      - *datepicker-directive_test.js*
    - authorization
      - *authorization.js*

— *authorization-service.js*

— *authorization-service_test.js*

— ui-widgets

    — *ui-widgets.js*

    — grid

       — *grid.html*

       — *grid-directive.js*

       — *grid-directive_test.js*

    — dialog

       — *dialog-service.js*

       — *dialog-service_test.js*

— list

  — *list.html*

  — *list.css*

  — *list-controller.js*

  — *list-controller_test.js*

— login

  — *login.html*

  — *login-controller.js*

— search

  — *search.html*

  — *search.css*

  — *search-controller.js*

  — *search-controller_test.js*

— detail

  — *detail.html*

  — *detail-controller.js*

  — *detail-controller_test.js*

— admin

  — create

    — *create.html*

    — *create-controller.js*

　　　　　　　— *create-controller_test.js*

　　　　— update

　　　　　　　— *update.html*

　　　　　　　— *update-controller.js*

　　　　　　　— *update-controller_test.js*

- vendors *// third-party dependencies go here*

　　　— underscore

　　　— jquery

　　　— bootstrap

- e2e *// end-to-end scenario tests*

　　　— *runner.html*

　　　— *login_scenario.js*

　　　— *list_scenario.js*

　　　— *search_scenario.js*

　　　— *detail_scenario.js*

　　　— admin

　　　　　　— *admin_create_scenario.js*

　　　　　　— *admin_update_scenario.js*

Third-Party Libraries

We saw how your own application and its source code might be structured, but what about the third-party dependencies and libraries that you can't do without? We do provide for a general vendors folder in the main application folder to host all the third-party dependencies, but that is just one part of the story.

To make managing, updating, and versioning of your third-party dependencies easy and manageable, we suggest you use something like Bower (*http://www.bower.io*), which is a package management tool for web dependencies. Almost any and every third-party dependency you use in an AngularJS project more than likely has a Bower package you can depend on.

Using Bower is a simple, three-step procedure:

1. Install Bower (Bower is a NodeJS Package, so you can simply install it by running `npm install bower`).

2. List your dependencies in a Bower package definition file (usually stored as *bower.json*). This lists all your dependent libraries, and the version you depend on.

3. Run bower install in any project (or bower update) to get the latest and greatest dependencies cloned right into your project folder with the correct versioning automatically taken care of.

Bower helps by:

- Removing the necessity to check third-party libraries into your codebase.
- Easily knowing, managing, and upgrading the version of any third-party library by just changing it in a single JSON file.
- Making it easy for anyone starting on your project to quickly figure out what third-party libraries you are using in your project.

In short, it makes it seamless to quickly integrate third-party libraries into your project. AngularJS itself is available as a Bower package. So definitely give it a whirl in the next project you start!

Starting Point

We covered a lot, and provided our opinion on how you should approach an AngularJS project from the file and directory structure, naming conventions, and some general good practices. But you don't need to do this all from scratch. The AngularJS community is awesome, and they have a lot of helpful tools and libraries to get you a starter project from which you can start working. Some options for you to take a look at when starting your project include:

Yeoman

Yeoman is a workflow management tool that automates a lot of the routine, chore-like tasks that are necessary in any project. It is not an AngularJS-specific tool, but has plugins for AngularJS. AngularJS automates a lot of the boilerplate code you might write, but the task of creating a route, adding the HTML and the controller, creating the skeleton for the unit test, and so on still need to be done by you. Yeoman goes one step further and automates these tasks for you. So you can write a command such as yo angular:route myNewRoute, which generates *route.html*, adds a controller skeleton, adds the test skeleton, adds the JavaScript to *index.html*, and so on for you. And there are multiple AngularJS generators with slightly different syntax and folder structures for you to find something that suits you and your needs. Yeoman also gives you the build scripts and grunt tasks that you would need for any medium to large project.

Angular seed projects

There are multiple seed projects for AngularJS that again, give you a starting base set of directory structures, application skeleton, and build scripts. Some of the more commonly used and well-known projects are `ng-boilerplate` and `angular-seed`. Both of these give you the initial project structure and grunt tasks that you need to get started.

Mean.io

Finally, if you are in the market for an end-to-end solution, and are open to using NodeJS for your application server needs, then do take a look at Mean.IO (*http://www.mean.io*). The MEAN stack, which has become famous in the past few years, stands for MongoDB, Express, AngularJS, and NodeJS. Mean.IO provides a ready starting point for any project using this stack, with all the necessary folder structure, build scripts, and more. While it imposes its own structure and paradigm as well, it is well thought out and worth a try.

Build

We talked about folder structure, naming conventions, and even bootstrapping our AngularJS project. Some of the bootstrapping mechanisms come with build scripts and grunt tasks already, but it is still essential that we understand what building our AngularJS project entails, and the components and key things to keep in mind when we create one.

Grunt

Grunt is the de facto standard when it comes to build scripts for JavaScript-based projects. Grunt is a task runner based on JavaScript and NodeJS, and comes with a whole set of plugins to automate certain build step tasks, like:

- Concatenating files
- Copying/moving files
- Renaming files
- Minifying CSS
- Minifying JavaScript
- Running tests or shell scripts

With Grunt, we define a JavaScript file that imports all the necessary Grunt plugins, and then we can use JavaScript to define our own tasks as well as the actions to perform when a certain grunt task is executed. For example, we might define a build task in Grunt, which does the following:

- Runs the Karma- and Protractor-based tests to validate the state of our application
- Globs the JavaScript files into a single JavaScript file
- Runs a JavaScript Compiler to remove spaces and reduce the size of our JavaScript
- Compiles the CSS into one small file
- Moves the HTML, JavaScript, and CSS into a separate directory for deployment

We could have another task to run all the unit and integration tests using Karma only and so on. Grunt is extremely customizable and allows you to set up the tasks and flows as you need for your application.

Serve a Single JavaScript File

With Grunt (or some other similar build tool in place), we need to keep track of a few things and make sure they're accomplished during our build process. First and foremost is handling the JavaScript files (rather, the number of JavaScript files) we serve to *index.html* (or any other HTML file really). When we are developing an AngularJS application, it makes it easier for us to develop and maintain when we have multiple files and folders so that things are easy to read and debug. But serving 250 JavaScript files to the production application is a sureshot recipe for a slow-loading website.

The browser usually has a restriction on the number of parallel GET requests it can make to the same domain. So say a browser can only fetch 8 files at a time, then the 250 files will get broken down into chunks of 8 files and fetched, which will take forever on any user's computer.

The recommended way to serve JavaScript files in production is to glob (or combine) all your JavaScript files into one single JavaScript file for production. This way, when your application requests your application-specific JavaScript files, it is one request and not 250 or even 50 separate requests.

If your application is being served on an intranet, or all the JavaScript files (including your third-party dependencies) will be served only by your application, you can consider combining your third-party JavaScript libraries into a single file and serving it as well.

But with third-party dependencies, it often makes sense to rely on Content Delivery Neworks (CDNs) and get the file from those instead of serving your own version. That way, if a user has previously loaded BootStrap from a CDN for another website, he gets to avoid loading it again for your website and can use it directly from his cached copy. Two great CDNs for JavaScript libraries are Google's AJAX CDN (*http://bit.ly/ NFMLTw*) and CDNJS (*http://cdnjs.com/*). Between the two of them, you should be able to find most core third-party dependencies.

By the way, globbing or combining files into a single file is applicable not just for Java-Script, but also for any CSS files you might have. The aim when you load your application is that it should not make more than 3–5 parallel requests at any given time, to prevent any browser from blocking and serializing the requests.

Minification

While globbing or combining JavaScript files reduces the number of parallel requests that are made, it still doesn't reduce the total size or data that is transferred over the wire. To ensure a fast, zippy application, you need to tackle both.

It is always good sense to both glob or combine your JavaScript (and CSS), as well as run it through a minifier like UglifyJS (*https://github.com/mishoo/UglifyJS*) or the Google Closure JavaScript Compiler (*https://developers.google.com/closure/compiler/*). These JavaScript compilers go through your JavaScript, removing unnecessary things like spaces and comments to reduce the size of the JavaScript files. In addition, in certain modes of the compiler, it can also rename variables and functions to smaller names, because the browser doesn't care what a function is named when it is executing it.

Don't forget that you should be using the safe style of Dependency Injection before you run your minification step. Otherwise, you might be left with a broken application. You can also evaluate using ng-annotate (*https://github.com/olov/ng-annotate*), which is an open source library that converts your nonminification-safe code into minification-safe code.

Similarly, CSS compilers also remove spaces and comments and can sometimes recognize optimal ways of rewriting CSS for it to be efficient.

Ensure that you do include minification as a build step for any application you create.

ng-templates

A grunt task that is available for online use is ng-templates (*https://github.com/eric clemmons/grunt-angular-templates*), which allows you to preload all the HTML templates that you use in your application instead of making an XHR request for them when it is needed. The ng-templates grunt task reads all the HTML, and generates an AngularJS JavaScript file that inlines all the HTML into AngularJS's templateCache when the app loads.

The ng-templates build task is great if you have a small number of templates, or are willing to preload all your templates to speed up your runtime. But if you have a large number of templates, you can consider preloading the most common templates and views in your application, and let the others load asynchronously as needed.

Best Practices

With folder structure and build practices out of the way, let's focus on some AngularJS best practices. These are things you should do, or avoid religiously so that you aren't caught unawares at the worst possible time. Some of these might be pure common sense, and others really specific, but all of them are worth keeping in mind.

General

The following are some high-level things to keep in mind when writing your AngularJS application:

- Prefer small files to large files. They are much easier to maintain, debug, and understand than large files. An arbitrary rule of thumb for a large file is over 100 lines.

- Use the AngularJS version of setTimeout, which is the $timeout service, and the AngularJS version of setInterval, which is the $interval service. You can easily mock them out and write unit tests where you don't actually have to wait for an interval to finish to test your functionality. You can even control how many times an interval function should be called from your tests. So use the AngularJS versions instead.

- Any controller or directive, if it adds $timeout or $interval, should remember to clean it up or cancel it when it is destroyed, to prevent it from unnecessarily executing in the background.

- If you are adding listeners outside of AngularJS, ensure that it is cleaned up correctly. AngularJS manages its own scopes and listeners, but anything you manually add might need to be managed and cleaned up. You can do this when the scope is destroyed by adding a $scope.$on('$destroy', function() {}) listener.

- Try to avoid doing deep watches ($scope.$watch, with the third argument as true). It is expensive, and overusing it can cause performance issues in your application. Instead, prefer to have a simple Boolean that reflects when an object has changed, and watch that instead.

- Try to follow the AngularJS paradigm of model-driven programming. Let the model and data drive the UI, and if you need to update the UI, all you should have to do is update the model. The UI should update itself automatically.

- Use HttpInterceptors when you have common tasks you need to do every time the server returns an authorization error, or a "404 not found." Let the services and controllers take care of specific error handling only.

Services

Services are useful for common APIs and application-level stores. Here are some good tips to get the most out of your services:

- Services are singletons for your application. Leverage this—use it as a service API, as a data store, as a cache. Services are great for it.
- If you need to share state across the application, think of a service.
- There is no performance difference between using service, factory, or provider. All are implemented the same way. Use whichever one suits your coding style and needs, and stick with it.
- Services are the only place where adding event listeners on the $rootScope is acceptable. This is because services don't have their own scope.
- Multilayered, composite services are great. Instead of having one giant service that does everything, split it into smaller services. Then have one larger service that uses each of the individual ones.
- XHR calls should be done in services using $http. This gives you one single place to look at all your API calls, and change URLs in one single place. The service should return a promise to ensure a consistent API.
- Integrations with third-party service libraries (think third-party non-UI libraries, like SocketIO) should be done as a service. This allows you to integrate and replace it seamlessly at any given point, as well as mock it out for unit testing.

Controllers

Here are some guidelines to keep in mind when creating your controllers:

- Prefer to use the newer syntax when working with controllers, or defining variables and functions on the controller's this. That is, use the controllerAs syntax and avoid using the $scope syntax whenever possible. The newer syntax is more concise and easier to understand.
- Watch out for using the this variable. Prefer to assign it to a local variable (like self), and then use it.
- Controllers should not reference the DOM or reach out into the DOM. Do not use jQuery directly in your controllers.
- Controllers should ideally just have the presentation logic of what data to fetch, how to show it, and how to handle user interactions. And most of these should pass through to a service when possible.

- Only put the variables and functions that need to be accessed from the HTML on the controller's this. Anything that the HTML does not need can and should be local variables inside the controller. The exception, of course, are functions that you want to unit test.

- If a controller is for a specific route that needs to be accessible via a URL, then ensure that the controller loads all the data it needs when it is instantiated.

- If a controller needs to store some state for the entire application, it should be stored in a service, and not $rootScope. Never $rootScope.

- Controllers can $broadcast or $emit events on their own scope, or inject the $rootScope and fire events on $rootScope. But a controller should never add a listener on $rootScope. This is because a controller and its scope can get destroyed, but the $rootScope remains across the application, along with its listeners, which will keep triggering even if the controller is not present.

Directives

Directives are some of the most powerful parts of AngularJS. Here's how you can ensure you get the most out of your directives:

- If you're bringing in a third-party UI component, bring it in as an AngularJS directive.

- Try to isolate the scope if you want reusable components, because this ensures that you don't modify the parent scope, or depend on anything from any parent scope.

- Don't forget to $scope.$apply() in case you're responding to an event or callback that is external to AngularJS and updating the AngularJS model. Otherwise, your UI won't get updated at the correct moment.

- If you add any event listeners on elements external to the directive, or any polling functions, ensure that you clean it up when the directive gets destroyed.

- You should do your cleanup on the $scope $destroy event if you are creating a new child scope or an isolated scope. But in case you're inheriting the parent scope, prefer to do your cleanup on the $element $destroy event.

- If a controller needs to share state with a directive, it should:
  — Pass in the state using HTML attributes (and the isolated scope) if the component is not specific to your project and can be reusable.
  — Pass in the state using a service if it is a specific component.

- Pass in an object using the = binding on the scope, and add a $scope.$watch on it if you need to perform an operation whenever the object changes.

- *Never reassign* the reference of any object passed in through the scope. That is, if the scope.firstObject is passed in via = binding, you should never set or overwrite the value of scope.firstObject in your directive. Updating a key on firstObject is fine, but the firstObject itself should never be reassigned.

Filters

Filters are great for the last step formatting that we need to do, or data manipulation. Here are two things to keep in mind:

- Every filter used in the HTML gets evaluated in every digest cycle. If you know the data is not going to change that often, you can optimize by using and applying the filter directly in your controller as shown in Chapter 8.
- Filters should be fast, because each filter is expected to execute multiple times during the life of an application. So don't do any heavy processing, and definitely don't do any DOM manipulation inside your filter.

Tools and Libraries

In this final section, we'll look at some tools and libraries that can make your life as an AngularJS developer easier. These could be developer tools, or existing component libraries and modules for common requirements in your projects.

Batarang

First and foremost, if you are working on AngularJS, you owe it to yourself to go get Batarang (*http://bit.ly/1sKlEVk*), a Chrome extension to help debug and work with AngularJS projects. When installed, it adds an AngularJS tab to the Developer Tools in Chrome as shown in Figure 15-1.

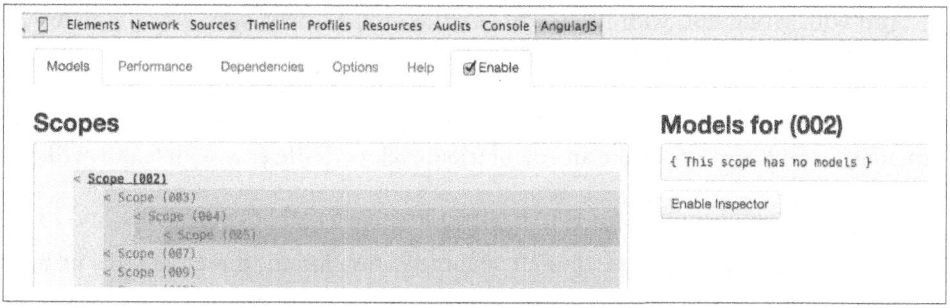

Figure 15-1. Batarang extension in Chrome Developer Tools

The Batarang extension adds three very interesting and useful tabs to the Chrome Developer Tools:

Models

The Models tab contains a live view into the scope hierarchy of your AngularJS application. The Models tab shows you all the scopes that are currently present in your view, and allows you to click any scope to see the variables and functions that are present and their current values. For any scope, you can click the < icon to jump to the HTML element that the scope is present on, to see where in your HTML a particular scope is. As you navigate around in your page, the scope values also get updated.

Performance

The Performance tabs gives you a live view of the performance of your AngularJS application. It gives you a sorted list of the watchers triggered in a digest cycle, and the time taken in milliseconds and as a percentage of the digest cycle. With this information, if you are optimizing your application or figuring out your bottlenecks, you have an immediate action list of things you need to tackle. You can also export the performance as JSON so that you can compare it after you have made your changes and fixes to see how it stacks up.

Dependencies

The last tab gives you a visualization of the dependency structure of your application. It lists all the services that your application provides and creates, as well as ones it depends on. It then tells you visually which services depend on which other services, and so on. A great starting point for anyone new to the application, or trying to figure out the core, most important, and used services in an application.

When Batarang is installed, you can actually dig into any live AngularJS application by just opening the Chrome Developer Tools and enabling Batarang for the website.

WebStorm

An IDE, or lack thereof, can make a huge difference in the productivity of a developer. And with JavaScript, with its lack of compiler, type safety, and dynamic nature, it becomes essential to have a solid working environment. WebStorm (*http://www.jetbrains.com/webstorm/*), a JavaScript IDE from Jetbrains, is one of the most solid IDEs out there currently for JavaScript. And the best part? It is superbly integrated with AngularJS and Karma, to make an AngularJS developer's life easy with features like:

- AngularJS autocomplete for HTML attributes like `ng-click`, `ng-class`, and so on.
- Ability to jump to external (online) documentation for any directive while using it.
- Control- (or Command-) click any directive, function, or controller in your HTML to jump to its definition.

- Refactoring support, from renaming of variables and properties, to even directives.
- Live templates to create skeletons for common tasks like controller and directive definitions.
- Karma integration, to run Karma unit tests right from within WebStorm.

And much more. We highly recommend WebStorm for AngularJS development, so give the 30-day free trial a whirl. You can't go wrong with it.

Optional Modules

Finally, we will quickly cover some of the other optional modules that AngularJS core provides, and when you would need to or want to use them:

ngCookies

Traditionally, cookies have been string-based for years on end. The ngCookies module gives you a service to interact with browser cookies in an object form. You can directly save objects with keys, and retrieve them as objects, instead of dealing with strings and parsing them. A very useful module in case you are working with cookies in your application.

ngSanitize

If you have the need to work with user-generated content, and need to display it in the UI, you can possibly expose yourself to Cross Site Scripting (XSS) attacks, especially if the user enters JavaScript and HTML where he should be entering text. The ngSanitize module gives you APIs and directives to declare which inputs are validated, and how to render them. You can opt to render some content as entered, or render it as HTML, or even as HTML with JavaScript and CSS execution allowed. A must-have module in case you are dealing with content that the user can enter and manipulate.

ngResource

The $http library is a low-level resource, needing us as developers to be specific in the URL we hit, the arguments, the method of the request, and so on. But to ensure reusability and separation of concerns, we would wrap the $http service in our own service, and provide methods like save, query, and update. If we have a RESTful server, on the other hand, we can use the ngResource module and the $resource service. The $resource service takes a URL regex, and knows how to automatically translate that into RESTful calls. For example, if our server has a REST API for projects at the following URL: */api/project/:pId*, and we define a service called project that returns $resource('/api/project/:pId'), then it creates a service that allows us to make calls like Project.query() or Project.save({pId: 15}, data), and have AngularJS automatically translate the URLs to GET */api/project* or POST to */api/project/15* with data without us manually having to define the query and save functions. The `ngResource` is a great module if you have RESTful APIs on your server side.

ngTouch

AngularJS plays great on mobile as well, with its small footprint and minimal dependencies. The `ngTouch` module is a great add-on that adds directives like `ng-swipeleft` and `ng-swiperight` for dealing with touch interfaces. In addition, it also handles something called `fastclick`, which is necessary to ensure your mobile web application responds instantly to touch events.

ngAnimate

Finally, a new introduction with AngularJS 1.2 is the `ngAnimate` module. This completely optional module allows you define animations for common transitions in AngularJS. With the `ngAnimate` module, you can animate items hiding and showing using `ng-show` and `ng-hide`, even complete views and addition and removal of classes. When the `ngAnimate` module is included, most AngularJS directives give you CSS-class based hooks to animate or transition different elements that you can define your own animations on. Want your UI to slide in from the right? Want to have an element in the repeater displace the other elements and then fade in? You can do all this and more using `ngAnimate`.

Conclusion

In this final chapter, we covered testing at a high level and the best ways to get the most out of your unit and integration tests in a project, including the best times to run them. We then covered one of the most asked about questions in AngularJS, which is how to structure your project and folders. We talked about some concepts to keep in mind and saw how it might apply to a straightforward CRUD application.

We then jumped into the aspect after your application is done, which is building and deploying it. We covered Grunt and how it could be integrated, along with some additional things to keep in mind when deploying AngularJS projects. Our next topic was best practices in AngularJS, both from a general standpoint, as well as specific to controllers, directives, services, and filters. Finally, we looked at tools and libraries like Batarang and WebStorm, as well as the optional modules that AngularJS includes.

This brings us to the end of our journey together with this book. We tried to cover all the various parts at a reasonable depth in an order that made sense. There is nowhere near enough space or time for this book to cover each and every part of AngularJS, but this gives you a very strong base on which to rapidly build amazing, sleek, and performant web applications. Keep trying new things, and join us in the journey of making AngularJS a great framework!

Index

We'd like to hear your suggestions for improving our indexes. Send email to index@oreilly.com.

About the Authors

Shyam Seshadri is the owner/CEO of Fundoo Solutions (*http://www.befundoo.com*), where he splits his time between working on innovative and exciting new products for the Indian markets, and consulting about and running workshops on AngularJS. Prior to Fundoo Solutions, Shyam completed his MBA from the prestigious Indian School of Business in Hyderabad. Shyam's first job out of college was with Google, where he worked on multiple projects, including Google Feedback (AngularJS's first customer!), and various internal tools and projects. Shyam currently operates from his office in Navi Mumbai, India.

Brad Green works at Google as an engineering manager. In addition to the AngularJS project, Brad also directs Accessibility and Support Engineering. Prior to Google, Brad worked on the early mobile web at AvantGo, founded and sold startups, and spent a few hard years toiling as a caterer. Brad's first job out of school was as lackey to Steve Jobs at NeXT Computer writing demo software and designing his slide presentations. Brad lives in Mountain View, CA, with his wife and two children.

Colophon

The animal on the cover of *AngularJS: Up and Running* is a thornback cowfish (*Lactoria fornasini*). This fish of many names—thornback, thornback cow, backspine cowfish, shortspined cowfish, blue-spotted cowfish—is usually found on rocky reefs or sandy slopes in a tangle of sponge and weeds in the Western Indo-Pacific region. They feed primarily on worms and other invertebrates.

These boxfish can grow up to 15 centimeters long and anywhere between 3 to 50 centimeters wide. Members of the boxfish family are recognizable by the hexagonal pattern on their skin. Their bodies are shaped like a boxy triangle from which their fins, tail, eyes, and mouth protrude, allowing them to swim with a rowing motion. As they age, their shapes change from more rounded to more square-shaped, and their brighter colors dim.

The thornback cowfish protects itself by secreting cationic surfactants through their skin, a reaction triggered by stress. The toxins, usually secreted in the form of a mucus, dissolve into the environment and irritate fish in the surrounding area.

Many of the animals on O'Reilly covers are endangered; all of them are important to the world. To learn more about how you can help, go to *animals.oreilly.com*.

The cover image is from *Johnson's Natural History*. The cover fonts are URW Typewriter and Guardian Sans. The text font is Adobe Minion Pro; the heading font is Adobe Myriad Condensed; and the code font is Dalton Maag's Ubuntu Mono.

Have it your way.

O'Reilly eBooks

- Lifetime access to the book when you buy through oreilly.com
- Provided in up to four, DRM-free file formats, for use on the devices of your choice: PDF, .epub, Kindle-compatible .mobi, and Android .apk
- Fully searchable, with copy-and-paste, and print functionality
- We also alert you when we've updated the files with corrections and additions.

oreilly.com/ebooks/

Safari Books Online

- Access the contents and quickly search over 7000 books on technology, business, and certification guides
- Learn from expert video tutorials, and explore thousands of hours of video on technology and design topics
- Download whole books or chapters in PDF format, at no extra cost, to print or read on the go
- Early access to books as they're being written
- Interact directly with authors of upcoming books
- Save up to 35% on O'Reilly print books

See the complete Safari Library at safaribooksonline.com

O'REILLY®

©2014 O'Reilly Media, Inc. O'Reilly logo is a registered trademark of O'Reilly Media, Inc. 14373

Get even more for your money.

Join the O'Reilly Community, and register the O'Reilly books you own. It's free, and you'll get:

- $4.99 ebook upgrade offer
- 40% upgrade offer on O'Reilly print books
- Membership discounts on books and events
- Free lifetime updates to ebooks and videos
- Multiple ebook formats, DRM FREE
- Participation in the O'Reilly community
- Newsletters
- Account management
- 100% Satisfaction Guarantee

Signing up is easy:

1. Go to: oreilly.com/go/register
2. Create an O'Reilly login.
3. Provide your address.
4. Register your books.

Note: English-language books only

To order books online:
oreilly.com/store

For questions about products or an order:
orders@oreilly.com

To sign up to get topic-specific email announcements and/or news about upcoming books, conferences, special offers, and new technologies:
elists@oreilly.com

For technical questions about book content:
booktech@oreilly.com

To submit new book proposals to our editors:
proposals@oreilly.com

O'Reilly books are available in multiple DRM-free ebook formats. For more information:
oreilly.com/ebooks

©2014 O'Reilly Media, Inc. O'Reilly logo is a registered trademark of O'Reilly Media, Inc. 14373